ALL THE BEST, NEILL

also by Jonathan Croall

All the Best, Neill

LETTERS FROM SUMMERHILL

Foreword by Zoë Neill

Edited with an Introduction
by Jonathan Croall

Franklin Watts
New York
1984

Printed in Great Britain

First published in the United Kingdom in 1983 by André Deutsch Limited
First United States publication 1984 by Franklin Watts, Inc., 387 Park
Avenue South, New York, NY 10016

ISBN 0-531-09822-2

Contents

Foreword

Thinking of Neill and his writing leads me naturally to the everyday picture of him seated at his desk in the office. Writing was so much a part of his life that he spent many hours there. I think that anybody at all closely connected with him will remember the old office. It had a particular smell, a mixture of pencil peelings, pipe tobacco, paper and ink. We still have his desk and it smells exactly the same. Sometimes I was allowed to grub through the drawers. They were full of odds and ends – cigarette lighters, rubber bands, golf tees, pliers and the occasional old photograph. I remember my delight when small on finding a picture of Neill aged three with his mother. One drawer held masses of typewriter ribbons – a job lot bought cheaply I suspect! Also Neill's treasures, an old Parker 51 which he bought in America and his Dunhill briar pipe. The rest of the office was full of cupboards and drawers. A Roneo with locking top drawer where the pocket money was kept also had filing drawers underneath, though I don't remember anything actually being filed. Neill was frugal but not tidy and his office reflected this. Most of the cupboards were painted a revolting dusky pink, probably a few pots which needed using. There was a battered arm-chair by the gas fire and beside this two tins. One contained Yale locks, the other one keys. Also a plumber's bag full of bed springs. When anyone visited Neill for a chat he would sit and take the springs apart ready for bed mending sessions in the holidays, or try keys in the locks until he found one that fitted. The ceiling-high bookshelf by the door contained psychological and educational books. Serious stuff with long words and no pictures. On the shelf by the window was Neill's wine making equipment. If you were lucky, a glass of Elderberry might be in the offering. Quite strong, as I recall, and full of sediment but very nice. In the early days a box by the fire held a toy family made in the needlework class. They were mother, father, son and daughter, complete with penis, pubic hair and an unmentionable family name! I think we were supposed to act out our hidden inhibitions with them but seem to remember playing rude games instead!

As well as being a busy writer Neill also read a great deal. He liked 'good' books and crossword puzzles. He was always excited about his morning mail although in later years when it grew to 'fan mail' proportions he did grumble a little. It vexed him that people expected a reply

vii

without enclosing stamps. But just as he could never pass a hitch-hiker without offering a lift, so he religiously answered all his mail, even if it was only a few lines.

Reading through these letters which show Neill's warmth, wit and flair for writing, I feel it important that we remember not only himself, the man, but more importantly what he stood for in education and child-rearing. This was a man to whom the freedom, confidence and happiness of children was of foremost importance. He was deeply committed to his ideas for free children and spent his life working for those beliefs. In 1983 – one hundred years after he was born – his school Summerhill still leaves the rest of the world standing as far as education is concerned. Let us hope that it does not take a hundred years for the rest of the world to catch up!

Zoë Neill (Readhead)

Introduction

To most people, the name A. S. Neill means simply Summerhill – 'That Dreadful School', as he himself liked to call it. As it happens, virtually all his surviving letters were written during the Summerhill years. Yet he was already forty when he started his experimental school in England in 1924. Its creation was inextricably bound up with his earlier experiences, in particular those of his childhood in Scotland, which undoubtedly marked him for life.

It was a childhood characterised by fear and failure. The fourth of eight children, Neill was brought up in a small, inward-looking farming community in the Scottish lowlands, at the tail end of the Victorian era. His father was the village schoolmaster, or 'dominie', and a stern taskmaster both at home and school. His mother, struggling in conditions of genteel poverty, sought to give the family status and respectability. Both parents wanted their children to 'get on', and arranged for them to go on to the local Academy after their elementary schooling. The only one not to be sent there was Neill. A timid, slow, awkward and gullible child, adept with his hands and blessed with a fertile imagination, he could make little headway at school. His father, of whom he lived in constant fear, labelled him 'a good for nothing', and forced him to study while the other village children were free to play. Punishment was a frequent occurrence, reinforced by the all-pervasive Calvinism, whose doctrines concerning hellfire and damnation terrified the young Neill. At six he was beaten for showing an interest in his sister's naked body – a traumatic but by no means isolated incident in his childhood, and one that profoundly affected his later attitudes to sex, women, parents and authority.

Sent out to work at fourteen, Neill tasted failure again, first as an apprentice draper in Forfar, and then as a clerk in a firm of gas-meter manufacturers in Edinburgh. As a last resort, he became a pupil teacher in his father's school. Subsequently, with no other prospect in sight, he was appointed an assistant teacher in Fife, working with fear in his heart for three years under a particularly brutal head. Yet gradually he was able to make his mark as a teacher, bringing in some novel ways of working with the children, and breaking down many of the barriers traditionally erected between teacher and pupil. Nevertheless, he was determined to escape from the life of the schoolroom. Now thoroughly motivated, he studied in his spare time, and at the relatively advanced age of twenty-five gained a place at Edinburgh University. Here he discovered the works of Ibsen, Wells and Shaw, and had his first taste of the theatre, music-hall and concerts. He edited the student magazine, and used it as a forum for provocative and irreverent attacks on the academicism of the Scots education system. He was already showing a flair for communicating ideas and stirring people up with his iconoclastic opinions on a variety of subjects. Journalism, he now decided, seemed the best escape route from teaching. A brief spell in publishing and then Fleet Street was interrupted by the outbreak of the First World War, forcing Neill back into education, as Acting Head of the village school in Gretna Green in Scotland.

It was here that he was able to test out his increasingly libertarian ideas, soon turning a rigidly orthodox school into a 'play school'. He wrote up this experience in *A Dominie's Log*, the first of his twenty books, which immediately established him as an educational heretic as well as a writer with a fresh and lively talent. His experiment came to an end with his call-up, and a short and inglorious stint in the army. It was during this time that he met a man who was to point him firmly in the direction of Summerhill. Homer Lane was in charge of the Little Commonwealth in Dorset, a community for delinquent children, with whom he was achieving some astonishing results. His philosophy was to be 'on the child's side', and he used self-government as a means of encouraging his boy and girl 'citizens' to regain their self-respect. Neill came for a weekend, saw this novel community in action, and was conquered. A whole new world had been opened up to him, and he resolved to work with children 'the Little Commonwealth way'.

After the war, Neill taught at a 'progressive' school, King Alfred in London, where he tried unsuccessfully to introduce self-government. For a while he returned to journalism, and as co-editor of the *New Era* magazine he reported on educational experiments of the day, in England and on the continent. None matched up to his ideals, and he resolved to open a school of his own. Eventually he took over the International section of an existing school in Dresden in Germany, and then branched out on his own, moving to a mountain top near Vienna. Forced to move on by local and official harassment, as well as a financial crisis, he finally brought his small band of children to Lyme Regis in Dorset, to a house called Summer Hill.

For the next fifty years, first at Lyme and then at Leiston in Suffolk, Neill strove to prove that children could cope with freedom. Under the influence of Lane, Freud and the New Psychology, he based his early work with problem children on an understanding of their unconscious hopes and fears, and effected some remarkable 'cures'. In the belief that 'childhood should be playhood', he refused to make lessons compulsory, insisting that children learn best when motivation comes from within. He created a genuine self-governing community, in which children and adults collectively made and enforced the rules by which they were to live. Throughout his work Neill remained fiercely 'on the side of the child': there are, he argued, no problem children, only problem parents and problem teachers.

His experiment caused a tremendous stir both within and outside education, and Summerhill became a mecca for all those interested in working with children. Hundreds of teachers, parents and others were impressed by Neill's evident belief in the innate goodness of the child. Many tried to put his ideas into practice in homes and schools, with varying results. A great deal of Summerhill's success depended on Neill's rare ability to stand aside, to let children make their own decisions, and to learn by their own mistakes. Though this was a matter of conviction for Neill, it also stemmed from his temperament. Visitors accustomed to the trenchant and resolute tone of his books and lectures were surprised to meet a man of quiet humour and seeming reticence. In many respects a shy and uncommunicative man, he generally seemed more at home amongst children than in the adult world. As a result, the burden of running Summerhill on a shoestring fell to a great extent on his two wives. In different ways, Lilian Neustatter – who helped him to start and establish the school – and Ena Wood – the mother of his only child – provided the vital organisational skills that helped to keep Summerhill going, often in the face of formidable obstacles. Without them, Neill would certainly not have been able to concentrate on what he did best: practising and at the same time putting over his ideas about child freedom.

Neill was, by general consent, a brilliant publicist for his revolutionary ideas about children. In his books and lectures he persuaded his audience to consider the most subversive of notions, by presenting them in a thoroughly engaging and unassuming manner. He was read and listened to by thousands because, to a considerable degree, they accepted the portrait that he drew of himself, of a simple, kindly, down-to-earth, humorous Scot, with an unswerving belief in the goodness of children.

There was of course a good deal of truth in this picture, and this version of the Neill persona is consistently in evidence in the letters published here. Yet, taken as a whole, the letters reveal a much more complex character. Writing in an uninhibited manner to friends, fellow-educators, former pupils and staff, Neill communicates his doubts about his achievement and influence, the tribulations of being a pioneer having to plough his own furrow, and his forthright views on the failings of so many adults, including some of his own staff, to understand the needs of children. We see a man at once more fierce and more vulnerable than his public persona might have led us to expect, subject to a variety of moods, and struggling to maintain the image of the 'plain, ordinary guy'.

Neill frequently asserted that he was essentially 'a doer rather than a thinker'. Yet, as many of the letters make clear, he was by no means merely a skilful practioner with a genius for handling problem children. He was also a man who pondered on many of the questions that have agitated philosophers over the centuries, such as Freedom, Good and Evil, the Nature of Love, and similar issues. Because he was busy running Summerhill for fifty years, and because he invariably and swiftly brought any abstract discussion down to concrete examples or everyday experience, we tend not to think of Neill primarily as a philosopher. Yet, though his method of argument was often unscientific and sometimes quite illogical, his conclusions usually displayed a profound common sense. More than in most people, his 'doing' and his 'thinking' informed each other.

Before he founded Summerhill, Neill dreamed of having an 'out and out *doing* school'. He himself was never happier than when absorbed in some manual activity in his workshop or garden. 'My hobby has always been handwork,' he writes to Bertrand Russell, 'and where your child asks you about stars, my pupils ask me about steels and screw threads.' His anti-academic philosophy of education was partly a matter of his own temperament and inclinations, partly a matter of conscious revolt against the appallingly uncreative nature of the education system of his period. 'Books are the least important apparatus in a school,' he once wrote. Yet the longest section in the present volume is devoted to 'Authors, Books and Writing'. Aside from his own books, Neill had an abiding interest in literature, and at different stages of his life was an ardent reader of the works of Barrie, Wells, Shaw, Ibsen and many lesser writers. Several of these letters testify to his delight at being sent a copy of a book by its author, a gesture that he invariably described as 'casting pearls', before proceeding to put down some trenchant comments about the virtues and deficiencies of the book in question.

Neill was fond of quoting a sentiment from one of his favourite authors, Ibsen, that 'the strongest man is he who stands alone'. This was a position in which he often found himself, especially in the early years of Summerhill, even within the progressive schools movement. His letters to Bertrand Russell and Curry of Dartington Hall underline the comfort he gained from finding genuine allies among the pioneers of his time. 'How fine to talk to people you haven't to explain and defend with,' he tells Russell, shortly after he and his wife Dora had opened Beacon Hill School. To Curry he observes: 'We have the mutual effect of cheering each other up, even when the pubs are closed.' Secure in the knowledge of shared assumptions, Neill feels free to undertake some spirited sniping at all the other educators who fall short of his ideals, at the 'moulders' and the 'moralisers' who insist on bringing 'uplift' into the lives of children.

Despite his fierce individualism, and his view expressed in one of these letters that 'Life should be a gradual destruction of all crutches', Neill did find it necessary to lean on others, both in the intellectual and the personal sphere. During his life he was greatly influenced by certain 'mentors', men whose ideas or personality, or some combination of the two, swept him along in their wake, at least for a while. One of these was Homer Lane who, it seems, once called Neill 'a bloody sycophant'. Neill's uncharacteristically lengthy letters to Lane's biographer David Wills describe in candid detail the debt which Neill owed to Lane. Another mentor was Wilhelm Reich, Neill's therapist and close friend, many of whose controversial ideas struck a resonant chord with Neill. The correspondence between the two men has been published elsewhere in full. Here, writing to several of Reich's admirers and co-workers, Neill can be found in more dispassionate mood about his much-loved friend. He is able to see his faults as much as his virtues, while retaining his belief in the fundamental soundness of Reich's social analysis, and regretting the way in which, like so many eminent men after their death, Reich had 'become his admirers'.

This section of the book also includes a memorable exchange of letters with Paul Goodman, who accused Neill of letting Reich do his thinking for him. Though there is an element of truth in the charge, Goodman's letter is notable for its lack of humour, sense and, above all, clarity, and it draws a rousing reply from Neill. Here we see him at his best, defending his ideas with passion and precision, putting Goodman firmly and conclusively in his place, but doing so with restraint and grace, and with an absence of personal rancour. In similar vein, Neill has an exchange with one of his erstwhile literary heroes, H. G. Wells, and emerges with considerably more dignity than the peevish and dismissive Wells.

Humour, one of the most attractive qualities in Neill's character, is never far below the surface in these letters, and frequently well above it. 'I intruded. I apologise, and . . . being a Scot . . . refund your postage,' he tells Wells, after a disagreement about the value of Reich's scientific work. His humour is alternately bawdy, self-deprecatory, caustic and affectionate, of a kind familiar to those who read his books or heard him speak. What is more unexpected is his capacity to write imaginative nonsense of a deliciously awful kind, awash with puns, parody and utter zaniness. The letters written in this vein provide us with a glimpse of the fertility of his imagination, and of the verbal and narrative skills which made him such a spell-binding story-teller at Summerhill.

Neill was rightly admired for his striking ability to enter intuitively into the world of children, to understand their fears and fantasies, and to be able to respond to them with patience, sensitivity and approval. In many respects he remained a child at heart, and the letters in which he writes about individual children provide us with some clues as to how he was able to empathise so readily with the young. There was nothing sentimental about Neill's attitude to children: he had lived with them for too long for that.

As the letters touching on his daily life at Summerhill show, Neill had his share of problem adults as well as children, and could be quite blunt about what he saw as their shortcomings. His comments did not, however, always reflect the reality of the situation he was describing. There was in him a strong element of pessimism, a considerable need to find something to grumble about. In later years, as can be seen in many of the letters, this tendency becomes more marked, often resulting in periods of considerable depression. He writes with some gloom about the extent of his influence on teachers and parents, the value of the work he has done, the future of Summerhill.

One of his principal causes for complaint was the price he paid for the revival of interest in his ideas, occasioned by the publication of *Summerhill* in America at the beginning of the 1960s. The inspiration which his ideas provided for the radical school reformers, as well as for hundreds of parents interested in the newer ideas about child-rearing, was certainly a mixed blessing to him. The letters to leading figures in the Summerhill Society in America included here underscore the acute dilemma he faced, in trying to maintain some control over what was being done in his name at a distance of several thousands of miles.

Fame did indeed bring both compensations and drawbacks. Among the former, though he tried to pretend otherwise, were the three honorary degrees conferred on him by the educational Establishment he had spent so much of his life attacking. Neill makes a poor show in his efforts to conceal the child-like glee he experienced in being given this particular form of recognition: Am I out of date now? he inquires of his correspondents. He shows a similar ambivalence in his attitude to the enormous number of letters he received after *Summerhill* had been a success in several countries. Though he ritually complains of having become no more than an office boy, he nevertheless insists on continuing to answer each letter personally. More and more, as age and infirmity take over, his letters become a kind of lifeline, his principal means of keeping in touch with the world outside Summerhill.

In a letter to another of his heroes, Henry Miller, Neill writes: 'One of my boys defined masturbation as the pale shadow of sex, and I think we can call correspondence the pale shadow of friendship.' Though the observation may be apt, there is nothing pale or shadowy about the letters that Neill wrote during his long and full life. On the contrary, they stand as a testament to one of the most vigorous, determined, single-minded yet compassionate figures in the twentieth-century landscape.

CHRONOLOGY

1883	Born in Forfar, Angus, Scotland, 17 October.
1888	Began as a pupil in Kingsmuir Village School, Forfar, 29 June.
1897-8	Worked as clerk in gas meter manufacturer's, Edinburgh.
1898	Worked as apprentice draper in Forfar.
1899-1903	Pupil teacher at Kingsmuir Village School.
1903	Assistant teacher at Durham School, Bonnyrigg, near Edinburgh.
1903-6	Assistant teacher at Kingskettle School, Fife.
1906-8	Assistant teacher at Newport Public School, Fife.
1908-12	Student at Edinburgh University. Edited the *Student*.
1912-13	Assistant editor with publishers T. C. & E. Jacks, first in Edinburgh, then London.
1914	Art editor on *Piccadilly Magazine*.
1914-16	Acting Head, Gretna Public School, Dumfriesshire. Engaged to Jessie Irving.
1915	*A Dominie's Log* published.
1916-18	Army training with Royal Scots Fusiliers. Meets Homer Lane.
1917	*A Dominie Dismissed* published.
1918	Suffered nervous breakdown while waiting to fight in France. Invalided out of army.
1919-20	Teacher at King Alfred School, London. Became 'pupil' of Homer Lane. Met Lilian Neustatter.
1919	*The Booming of Bunkie* published.
1920	*Carroty Broon* published.
1920-21	Co-editor, with Beatrice Ensor, of *New Era*.
1921	*A Dominie in Doubt* published.
1921-4	With Lilian Neustatter founded the International School in Hellerau, a suburb of Dresden, moving subsequently to Sonntagsberg, Austria. Analysed by Wilhelm Stekel in Vienna.
1923	*A Dominie Abroad* published.
1924	*A Dominie's Five* published.
1924-7	Established Summerhill School in Lyme Regis, Dorset.
1925	Death of Homer Lane.
1926	*The Problem Child* published.
1927	Married Lilian Neustatter ('Mrs Lins').
1927	Moved Summerhill to Leiston, Suffolk.
1932	*The Problem Parent* published.
1936	Lectured in South Africa.
1936	*Is Scotland Educated?* published. Met Wilhelm Reich.

1937   *That Dreadful School* published. Started therapy with Reich. Refused visa to USSR.
1938   *The Last Man Alive* published.
1939   *The Problem Teacher* published.
1940–45 Summerhill evacuated to Ffestiniog, North Wales.
1944   Death of Mrs Lins, 30 April.
1945   Married Ena Wood.
1946   *Hearts not Heads in the School* published.
1946   Birth of daughter Zoë, 2 November.
1949   Summerhill inspected by His Majesty's Inspectors.
1947   Lectured in USA, stayed with Reich.
1948   Second lecture tour of USA.
1949   *The Problem Family* published.
1950   Refused visa for further visit to USA.
1953   *The Free Child* published.
1957   Death in prison of Wilhelm Reich.
1960   *Summerhill: A Radical Approach to Child Rearing* published in USA.
1962   *Summerhill* published.
1966   Received honorary degree from Newcastle University. *Freedom not License!* published in USA.
1967   *Talking of Summerhill* published.
1968   Defeated in election for Rectorship of Edinburgh University.
1973   *Neill! Neill! Orange Peel!*, his autobiography, published.
1973   Died in Aldeburgh Cottage Hospital, 22 September.

ACKNOWLEDGEMENTS

The letters in this volume have been selected from nearly a thousand which I collected during the five years I spent researching and writing *Neill of Summerhill*.* It is clear that this number is nowhere near the extent of Neill's total output, and that many hundreds more that he wrote during his long life have been lost, destroyed or simply thrown away. Neill himself never bothered to keep copies of his own letters, except in the case of his correspondence with Wilhelm Reich. The letters that passed between the two men have recently been published as *Record of a Friendship*.† I have included a few letters from this source in the early part of two sections of this book, on 'The Bomb' and 'Fatherhood', in order to fill two gaps in my own collection. Apart from a handful, all the other letters are, to the best of my knowledge, being published for the first time.

I am of course immensely grateful to all those individuals who were kind and trusting enough to grant me access to the letters they had from Neill. Of all those I approached, only two refused to release the letters in their possession for publication. Though I regret their decision, I must respect their reasons for making it. I don't believe anything of significance has been lost as a result.

For assistance in tracking down letters not in private hands, I am indebted to the following: to Ellen Dunlap, Humanities Research Center, University of Texas, for the letters to J. R. Ackerley, George Ives and Peter Owen; to Robin Johnson at the Elmhirst Centre, Dartington Hall, for the letters to W. B. Curry; to Taylor Stoehr for the correspondence between Neill and Paul Goodman; to Lady Cobbold for the letter to Homer Lane; to Robert Smart, St Andrew's University Library, Scotland, for the letters to Willa Muir; to Nikki Archer, King Alfred School, Hampstead, for the letter to B. H. Montgomery; to Sandy Stahl and the Department of Special Collections, University of California, for the letters to Henry Miller; to Diane Kerss, Bertrand Russell Archives, McMaster University, Ontario, for some of the letters to Bertrand Russell; to Louise Fitton, Library, University of Illinois at Urbana-Champaign, for the correspondence between Neill and H. G. Wells.

I would like to thank the New Education Fellowship for permission to reproduce the letter to Beatrice Ensor, first published in their journal the *New Era*, and the Freedom Press for permission to reproduce Neill's letter published in *Freedom*. For permission to publish letters written *to* Neill, I would like to thank the following: Betty Allsop for the letter from Kenneth Allsop; Sally Goodman for the letter from Paul Goodman; the executors of the estate of Henry Miller for the letters from Henry Miller; and the executors of the estate of H. G. Wells for the letters from H. G. Wells.

* Routledge, 1983. Pantheon, 1983.
† Edited by Beverley R. Placzeck. Farrar, Straus and Giroux, 1981. Gollancz, 1982.

NOTE ON THE TEXT

Where it has seemed helpful to do so, I have made certain cuts in a number of the letters that appear in this book, and substituted for the material omitted the mark (…). Some of the cuts were made in order to avoid unnecessary repetition, others merely to exclude material that would be of no interest to the general reader. In a very few instances, I have omitted a sentence or a paragraph which could, if included, have caused distress to someone still alive.

The large majority of the letters have been placed in one section only, either edited for one or more of the reasons given, or in full. A small number, in particular some of those written in the early years of Summerhill, have been divided into two parts, each part then appearing in the appropriate section.

I have only included footnotes where some kind of commentary or explanation has seemed necessary, or to give the full name of a person mentioned only by their Christian name in the text. Further information about all the people referred to by Neill, as well as about the principal schools mentioned in the letters, can be found in the Glossary of Names at the end of the book.

Since the overwhelming majority of these letters were written from Summerhill in Leiston, I have only included an address where Neill is writing from some other place.

The Letters

1

Pioneering

A. S. Neill, the Dominie, has brought his International School home, and has set up at Summerhill, Lyme Regis. He is specialising in problem children, and says that he wants boys and girls that other schools find troublesome, lazy, dull, anti-social. He steadfastly refuses to compromise ... 'Here is my school,' he says to parents, 'absolute freedom to work or to play. Take it or leave it.'

New Era, October 1924

To Bertrand Russell

Dear Russell   *18 December 1930*
    Have you any political influence? The Labour Ministry are refusing to let me employ a Frenchman to teach French. The chap I want is with me now, has been analysed, and is a tip-top man to deal with my bunch of problem kids. Other schools have natives to teach their languages ... and I naturally ask why the hell a damned department should dictate to me about my educational ways. I have given the dept a full account of the man and why he is necessary to me and the fools reply: 'But the Dept is not satisfied that a British subject could not be trained in the special methods of teaching in operation in your school.'
    Have you any political bigbug friend who would or could get behind the bloody idiots who control our departments? I am as wild as hell.
    Cheerio, help me if you can. I know George Lansbury, but hesitate to approach him as he will have enough to do in his own dept.
    Yours, A. S. Neill

1

To Bertrand Russell

Dear Russell   *22 December 1930*

Good man! That's the stuff to give the troops. Whatever the result, accept my thanks. I didn't mention psychoanalysis to them. I applied on the usual form, and they wrote asking me what precise steps I had taken 'to find a teacher of French who was British or an alien already resident in this country'. Then I told them that I wanted a Frenchman but that any blinking Frenchie wouldn't do ... that mine was a psychological school and any teacher had to be not only an expert in his subject but also in handling neurotic kids.

Apart from this display of what you call Bumbledom I guess that there will be some battle when Trevelyan's Committee on Private Schools issues its report. You and I will have to fight like hell against having a few stupid inspectors mucking about demanding why Tommy can't read. Any inspector coming to me now would certainly be greeted by Colin (aged 6) with the friendly words, 'Who the fucking hell are you?' So that we must fight to keep Whitehall out of our schools.

I'll let you know what happens.

Many thanks.

Yours, A. S. Neill

P. S. About time that you and I met again and compared notes.

To Bertrand Russell

Dear Russell   *31 December 1930*

You have done the deed.[1] The letter is a nasty one but I guess that the bloke as wrote it was in a nasty position. Sounds to me like a good prose Hymn of Hate.

I have agreed to his conditions ... feeling like slapping the blighter in the eye at the same time. It is my first experience with the bureaucracy and I am apt to forget that I am dealing with a machine.

Many thanks for your ready help. My next approach to you may be when the Committee on Private Schools gets busy. They will call in all the respectable old deadheads of education as expert witnesses (Badley and Co) and unless men of moment like you make a fight for it we (the out and outer Bolshies of education) will be ignored. Then we'll have to put up with the nice rules advocated by the diehards. Can't we get up a league of heretical dominies called the 'Anal'-ists?

Yours with much gratitude, A. S. Neill

[1] Russell had used his influence to persuade the Ministry to let Neill keep his teacher for just one year.

To Bertrand Russell

Dear Russell   *28 January 1931*

No, there is no point in replying to the people. Very likely the chief aim in govt offices is to save the face of the officials. If my man wants to stay on later I may wangle it by getting him to invest some cash in the school and teach on *as an employer* of labour. Anyway you accomplished a lot as it is. Many thanks. I think I'll vote Tory next time.

Today I have a letter from the widow of Norman MacMunn. She seems to be penniless and asks me for a job as matron. I can't give her one, and don't suppose you can either. I have advised her to apply to our millionaire friends in Dartington Hall. I am always sending on the needy to them ... hating them all the time for their affluence. When Elmhirst needs a new wing he writes out a cheque to Heals ... Heals! And here am I absolutely gravelled to raise cash for a pottery shed. Pioneering is a wash-out, man. I am getting weary of cleaning up the mess that parents make. At present I have a lad of six who shits his pants six times daily ... his dear mamma 'cured' him by making him eat the shit. I get no gratitude at all ... when after years of labour I cure this lad the mother will send him to a 'nice' school. It ain't good enough ... official indifference or potential enmity, parental jealousy ... the only joy is in the kids themselves. One day I'll chuck it all and start a nice hotel round about Salzburg.

You'll gather that I am rather fed up this morning. I'd like to meet you again and have a yarn. Today my *Stimmung* [mood] is partly due to news of another debt ... £150 this last year all told. All parents whose problems I bettered.

Yours, A. S. Neill

P. S. I wonder what Margaret Bondfield's views would be on my views on Onanie!

To Bertrand Russell

Dear Russell   *16 February 1931*

Many thanks for your recommending me to Dr Matthews in India. Boy sounds like a case of incipient epilepsy. I have said I can take him, but of course if the Dr is a moralist and reads my book[1] I won't get the lad. But medical men are less prone to morals than most professions.

He sent me a copy of your letter. I feel grieved at your possible giving up of the school, for then I'll stand alone against the four winds of respectability. So far I have felt a vague protection in the idea that B. Russell was there to point to as a defence ... 'He's a well-known bloke, philosopher and so on, you know; *he* believes in freedom and shit etc.' And now all I will have will be poor Elmhirst who couldn't shock an unmarried mother, and Faithfull, who shocks all and goes bankrupt. Besides I was relying on you to help me fight if the Private School Laws are to be impossible. A less honest chap would deplore your giving up on the grounds that The Children of England Need You (headline), but I don't give a damn for the children of England. Good old Ego. It must come first. Anyway tell me what you are going to do next. My real aim is to start a machine shop, but every penny I spend on buildings ties me eternally to running a school for the ungrateful.

    Yours, A. S. Neill

[1] *The Problem Child.*

To Bertrand Russell

Dear Russell   *14 April 1931*
    (...) Thanks so much for referring applicants to me. So far I have had a few applications for prospectuses ... then silence. I guess they read *The Problem Child* and then say that I am a dirty dog. Elmhirst is opening his Kindergarten in September and he will rope in all the bloody people with money and complexes. But we'll work off a few of our own complexes about people and kids when we meet again.

    Yours, Neill

To Ethel Mannin

Dear Ethel   *8 May 1931*
    Just sent back proofs to Jarrolds. It will be all right. Preface now rendered respectable.[1] By the way do you spell German nouns without caps deliberately? If not make em *Verbot, Schulgemeinde*, etc. And do try to take out the libel on Margaret Johnson! Also if possible take out reference to Russell's giving up. I don't think he will give up.
    It is a very good book, child, most sane and direct. God elp it to convert its thousands ... and to send a few of em on to us. You really are too good to me ... as if I were better than Freud and all of them! It's up to you now to procure a genuine Judas for Summerhill if the picture is to be complete.

I guess I can lay hands on the Two Thieves at almost any time, altho for two terms we have been thief free.

Cheerio and thanks and all that, Neill

¹ Neill had contributed a preface to her book *Common-Sense and the Child*.

To Bertrand Russell

Dear Russell   *9 May 1931*

On reading Ethel Mannin's proofs I drew her attention to her references to you, saying that I didn't agree with her description of your methods, saying also that she ought not to say that you are closing down, cos, if you aint, it will be a bad ad for you. Result is that I have a hasty note from her asking me to send you the proofs. She has written you to Cornwall. In case you want to send her an infernal machine by post or arsenic chocolates, her address for the next weeks is Rose Cottage, St Brelades Bay, Jersey, Channel Islands. The book is held up pending your verdict on the proofs.

I am not certain whether Ethel's recognition of me as a Plus Four Christ will ruin my school or make me a millionaire. Did Mary Magdalen's *Daily Mail* articles JESUS BEHIND THE SCENES make any converts for the saint? I think not.

Seems ages since we visited you. I hope it won't be long till you both visit us.

Best to both, Neill

To Bertrand Russell

Dear Russell   *13 May 1931*

Poor Ethel! I am very fond of her but she does make so many bloomers, and I really couldn't see her misrepresent you as she did. When challenged by me re you punishing by segregating she said it was in your book. I am glad you aren't closing down. I have signed the New Fellowship memorial to the Committee of Private Schools. Knowing that inspection is bound to come anyway I thought it as well to join the crowd for once. I am told that they had 'a most unsatisfactory interview with Chuter Ede the chairman'. Gawd elp us all.

What do you do about visitors? This week I have had three damn fool women each day, telling them the same old lies about the school. Result one pupil, but next week I have American teachers etc. Christ! I have no libido left to give the kids. Women get transferences to me from my books ... today an American one has told me her whole sex history from pre-natal days (four hours listening).

Limp as a rag.

Yours, A. S. Neill

P. S. Yes, we said the same about you two ... how fine to talk to people you haven't to explain and defend with.

To Bertrand Russell

Dear Russell   *15 January 1932*

Welcome back to this lovely land ... lovely since the heaven-sent Nat Gov brought the great revolution nearer. But I don't write to discuss politics. I want your interpretation of a letter from Norton. What does he mean by the medical parts?

I hear you spoke on the radio the other night. *Mein Gott* but I was told that the BBC would never allow such a sinner as you to pollute its microphones.

Yours ever, A. S. Neill

To Bertrand Russell

Dear Russell   *18 January 1932*

Righto. I'll cut them out ... with hate in my heart, for since a Nature Cure bloke took me in hand two years ago my feelings about doctors are really unprintable. Norton might have made the suggestion that you make.

I ain't afraid of being closed down by the govt. I chum up with the local authority and he lets me do what I like. Besides think of the warcry we would have ... NAT GOVT MAKES MORE UNEMPLOYMENT BY CASTING TEACHERS ON THE DOLE ... TEACH BRITISH. All the same I have a sneaking hope that they will shut us up, for this job is rather a life sentence.

My fees vary. I take kindergarten age at £21 a term, but the older ones run from £80 to £150 a year. I am filling up with infants these days and have had to build.

By the way my friend Dr Mary Adams on the BBC told me some time ago that she was threatening to resign if Reith wouldn't allow you to speak.

Just had a mother from Dartington Hall. If her story is true then Christ! Lovely manners, especially table ones, etc. How delightful it is to hear that D. Hall is wrong! Poor old Elmhirst has become the superfather-complex hate symbol ... vulgar wealth ... pah! Wish he'd divide out.

    Yours, A. S. Neill

To Bertrand Russell

Dear Russell   *22 January 1932*
    Thanks, but God knows where the MS is now. My agents took it to try other publishers. I think myself that Norton was rationalising, for if he had approved of the book in the main he would have suggested cutting the offending passages. Why they offend him I can't think, for I attack the law and the church just as much.

Brockway has asked me for an article on the school for the *New Leader*. I am giving him one.

After getting your letter I re-read your proofs. I found only two references to vaccines, so that Norton *was* rationalising ... I guess it was the masturbation that got his goat.

I am full up with kids now ... got a waiting list in fact, but how many problem parents will pay up I tremble to know. Queerly enough I am stoking up with infants now, and for months now I have had no problem adolescents. I don't think the Dept will interfere with you or me. I think our parents would let themselves be prosecuted in the courts anyway.

I am applying again for a foreign teacher ... Swedish girl this time. Some hopes!

(...) Wish we could have a yarn again ... you are one of the few people I like to talk to and hear talk. The other educational blokes and blokesses are simply not there. They have ideals, bless em.

    Yours, A. S. Neill

To W. B. Curry

Dear Curry   *17 October 1932*
    Re your suggestion that I should come down to Dartington for a weekend. You might discuss it with the Elmhirsts, for unless they're in with it I can't think of coming. I'd like to see it all the same, and find an

excuse to use my envy complexes. When a bloke like me has to think for six months before he can buy a radiogram for dancing, he... well, I needn't finish. Yet if I do come I'm sure I'll be more interested in the people than the things. I suppose I am unconsciously interested in people and only consciously in things, and that's why I don't make money.

Say, man, I rather regret joining that *Bund*,[1] I don't care much for the job of trying to make that bunch of sad faces laugh. By the way, I was told after the meeting that some of them have a grouse because the NEF shows favouritism in recommending schools. Why the 'ell didn't they get up and say so.

Cheerio, Neill

[1] A new Association 'of non-grant-aided schools' within the New Education Fellowship, 'pursuing new aims and methods'.

To W. B. Curry

Dear Curry   *25 November 1932*
I've told Mrs Ensor that I'm chucking those bloody meetings. You and Dora Russell and I talk a different language from them. We're the only ones who make child psychology the basis of our job. I can't waste my time going to town to hear a lot of bilge about self-government and Montessori, etc. Besides, Allen[1] is definitely against the left wingers, always tries to shelve me as a bloke who deals with abnormal kids. I will stay in the Association, but will come to meetings once every two years or so. The atmosphere of that room makes me sick, rouses all my old complexes about teachers and their 'damned education'. I get led on to say things I don't want to say. I could have kicked myself for arguing with Van der Leeuw about Montessori.

Well, well, count me out, sorry to leave you and Dora to educate the bunch of them, but I simply can't go on with it. And I've paid them £4.10s too.

Cheerio, see you about the 10th of January or so, Neill

[1] Clifford Allen had told Curry that he felt the way in which Neill presented his arguments put people's backs up, that they might be converted if he put things in a different way.

To the Editor, *Leiston Observer*

Dear Sir   *24 January 1934*
Prospective parents of Summerhill sometimes make casual enquiries about the school from Leiston and Aldeburgh citizens. Sometimes they get good reports, but sometimes they are told that Summerhill is a school for imbeciles. Hitherto I have paid no attention to these reports, but when an enquirer the other day was told the imbecile story in Aldeburgh, I decided to make the matter public. Summerhill brings a lot of money to Leiston and some to Aldeburgh, without taking any money from these towns. We live on good terms with most of our neighbours, but if some of the neighbours persist in continuing the imbecile libel I fancy that legal action could be taken.

I should not need to tell the local public that Summerhill does not deal with imbeciles. A school that is visited by enthusiasts from all parts of the world, a school that has produced a famous golfer, a famous cinema star, and a rising authoress, a school that is known to be in the van of modern education should not require to be explained to people living at its very doors.

Summerhill does of course sometimes get 'problems', but only problems that can be made good citizens by proper treatment. But because we can cure children who have been ruined by ignorant treatment, we do not deserve to be libelled by ignorant busybodies.
Yours sincerely, A. S. Neill

To Paulus Geheeb

Dear Geheeb   *7 April 1937*
Sorry to be late in answering your letter, but I have been away for some days, glad to be free from children for a time.

Alas, I can't help you to get a teacher. I find it so difficult when I need one myself, and too often the type who wants to teach in an advanced school is the introverted man who is really wanting to come as a child. Have you tried the New Education Fellowship for a teacher? They have a list I understand.

I like your School of Mankind idea, but I doubt if it can be carried out well under Capitalism. Socialism would be the natural environment for it, but so long as 'education' is only a branch of profit-making civilisation, you and I are working heavily handicapped.

(...) If you are ever in England do come and see me. You are one of the few educationalists I have wanted to talk with.
Yours sincerely, A. S. Neill

To W. B. Curry

Dear Curry   *12 June 1937*

Don't know what to say. Filled and fed up with visitors, and if the kid really thinks she ought to see our zoo, it will be £2.10s a week. The ten shillings goes for a room outside the school. If she's half-hearted about coming, tell her the bloody school ain't worth seeing. Rogers and his wife stayed weekend: non-intrusive, but asked many questions in rather a cloudy way. They were agreeable visitors anyway. Tired out psychically, partly living on the edge of the volcano Hitler seems about to set alight, partly visitors and talking about the school, partly that I want to live with adults nowadays, haven't the old patience and interest in kids.

Yours, Neill

To W. B. Curry

Dear Curry   *13 June 1940*

Forgive my delay. I've been busy, sent all kids home for summer holidays. Am off tomorrow looking for a school in the west.[1] Parents don't seem to want me to go Devon way now. Yes, I also wish I could talk to you. The only thing certain is that we must keep freedom for kids going until they shoot us at the dusk of civilisation. I'd like to live long enough to see what the common people make of this world after all this hellish work of uncommon people. Pity about Devon, would have been nice to have been near enough to drop in for a smoke and a chat. A sort of real Federal Union, or Headeral Union.[2]

All the best and keep the flag flying, Neill

[1] With invasion threatened, Summerhill's position on the East Coast was a vulnerable one. The following month Neill found a house in the village of Ffestiniog in North Wales, where the school remained for the duration.
[2] Curry was a leading member of Federal Union, a movement for world government.

To Lilian Morgans

                                                  Ffestiniog, North Wales
Dear Lilian   *22 June 1942*

(...) Why should I become an RC? Tut, tut! Can you think of my accepting dogma from any kirk? I have no use for any religion and don't think I ever will have. Religion means leaning, but 'the strongest man is he who stands alone' (Ibsen). Life should be a gradual destruction of all crutches. Your philosophy is good ... not regretting what you've done, only what you've neglected to do. What you must miss is what everyone should have – a personal life and a community one together. I am lucky there ...

Yours sincerely, A. S. Neill

To W. B. Curry

Ffestiniog, North Wales
Dear Curry   *17 July 1944*

(...) Most pleasant seeing you again, in spite of the pain of seeing your lovely house, and all the kitchen gadgets in the school, not to mention an actual bar on the premises. However, such little envies pass away, and the big thing was seeing you again. Queer fancy kept coming to me that fundamentally you aren't a schoolmaster at all, that you are out of place in Dartington Hall. Christ alone knows where you should be in place, although the devil probably knows. Feel you should be swaying crowds of adults or leading an army to victory. All vague, only feel that it must be an effort for you to regress to the child mind all the time. Your almost indifference to the dangers of the Education Bill made me suspicious. Methought perhaps the bloke would welcome the closing down of schools, so that he might get a start to doing something better. Maybe all projection on my part.

My thanks to your wife for letting me feel at home. If you meet Heath Robinson give him my admirations for his design of your sawdust monstrosity. If the Welsh wet gets me down I may invite myself down for a few days to watch your crowd working, or rather study their methods of evading same.

Neill

To Ishbel McWhirter

My dear Tish   *11 January 1946*

(...) More than most Summerhillians you seem to grasp the awful gulf between school and outside. It is true, I feel it often ... other day met new head of secondary school here, usual type, head not heart, hostile to me obviously. You can't make contact with them. Here it is easy; we don't need to make contacts; once you leave you have got to live. All old S's feel it more or less, hence the London ones try to meet each other. (...)

    Love, old bean, Neill

To the Editor, *New Statesman*

Sir   *19 January 1946*
    Even if Mr T. C. Worsley dislikes my book and its method of presentation, he should not write of the 'provoking title' without trying to figure out what the words *Hearts not Heads* mean.[1] I tried to make clear the point that, if the emotions are free, the intellect will look after itself, thus giving Hearts priority, just as the average school prospectus, state or private, gives Heads priority. One doesn't expect Harry Pollitt to write a book entitled Communism plus Capitalism. I question whether the truth is reached by the man who claims to see both sides, better when each enthusiast sticks to his own case, leaving it to the other fellow to take the other side.
    Mr Worsley seems to think I am out to shock. He flatters me, for I have the apparently silly belief that nowadays only diehards who never read my books are shockable. I am sure that Mr Worsley isn't in that class, although I wonder what class he belongs to when he is doubtful of my 'negative attitude to authority'. Or, alarming thought, have I failed completely to show that a self-governing school is full of authority, an authority that sincerely tries to balance the rights of individuals and community? If so, I do hope that my good critic will come down and spend a weekend with the only authority that should matter – the community.
    Yours sincerely, A. S. Neill

[1] *Hearts not Heads in the School* had been reviewed the week before in the *New Statesman*.

To David Wills

Dear Wills   *24 April 1948*
    Sorry to hear you have got the sack (I wonder why) and think it dreadful that you have to seek a job like the Maidenhead one. Surprising indeed, for with your name for tackling problems I'd have thought there would be competition to get you. You are up agnst ... the social view that a delinquent must not be treated with love; the blighter must first

repent, get punished, and live happily ever afterwards, a philosophy that fits in with recent church approval of the atomic bomb. (...)

Yours, A. S. Neill

To Bill MacKinnon

Dear Bill   *19 May 1952*

I got a poor account of the conference[1] from Mark; yr letter told me much more. (...)

Yes, maybe I should return to the fold. I was put off mainly by the fact that we were all invited to come to a programme already made up by Jack[2] and Co. Religion in Schools e.g. what the hell! Also I have to soft-pedal myself there. Have to keep up the pretence that we are *all* advance guys, for the alternative, *S'hill is right and you are all wrong*, would not be politic nor mannerly. True, I got a few arrows in on the religion target, and certainly on the sex one. Your suggestion to Paul Roberts is, I think, not so good, for it would make me an 'outsider' worthy of the reply: 'Who the hell does this Neill think he is. We don't want anyone to come here with an I'm Telling You attitude.' No, Bill, if I come back it will be as an ordinary member. But I'd like some say in the agenda all the same. Paul would agree, but the Jack-Swain-Barnes-Quaker lot might not.

Love to both, Neill

[1] The Co-Educational Schools Conference, held every two years.
[2] H.B. Jacks.

To Summerhill ex-pupils, staff, parents and friends[1]

(*October 1953*)

(...) It was all overwhelming, embarrassing to a humble Scot; I use the word humble because your generosity and love just knocked me over, made me feel as I used to do at the age of seven when an aunt brought me a present. I fancy that then I was so bad a boy that any kindness surprised me. And today I have some of that old surprise, conditioned, no doubt, by my memory of being rather an inferior article ... unable to learn lessons, a dud at football (they chose me last when tossing for sides), a poor fighter, but too cowardly to back out of a fight. So that when they showed me the de luxe radiogram I felt like the rustic who exclaimed, when he first saw a giraffe: 'Hell, I don't believe it!'

Then came a sudden comforting thought … 'They aren't giving me all this because I am an educationalist; they are giving presents and telegrams and letters because they love me.' I know that presents are often given as a substitute for love, but that does not apply to you folks at all.

Mind you I am not patting myself on the back because you show this love. I am trying to avoid saying: 'What a good boy am I.' You love me because I love you. Not sentimentally. When there is a Summerhill atmosphere love comes automatically, for there is nothing to inhibit it; there is no authority, no fear, no moral or aesthetic demand for behaviour. Possibly the greatest thing about Summerhill is the fact that we all accept people for what they are. We do not try to make a silk purse out of a sow's ear, nor vice versa as many a school does. It gives me much pleasure to state that the school staff has always been splendid in refusing to mould (i.e. change) any child's character.

A woman at the London party (I can't remember who she was, for she spoke to me after the Black and White bottle had been opened) said to me: 'There is something different about those old pupils of Summerhill. They are so grown up, so calm, so natural. How do you do it?' I replied: 'I don't do it. Freedom does it.'

Freedom. I don't mean freedom for Poland or India or China; I mean inner freedom. I think it is this inner freedom that showed itself in the joy the old pupils had in meeting again at the birthday party. Summerhillians do feel a difference between their old pals and pals from schools which have had no freedom, outer or inner. It was this difference that made old pupils travel from the Midlands to the reunion; it is this difference that brings so many down for our end of term celebrations. Our freedom is deeper than any political freedom. But, as I said at the party, it is only a small beginning. The world is not ready for freedom, not yet. I have been a pioneer, but you also are pioneers, for your influence will grow as you get older. The young are too busy living to bother about pioneering consciously.

Well, you made me proud, just as Summerhill makes you proud.

Neill

[1] Sent as a printed circular 'To all who helped to make my 70th birthday a delight'.

To Bill MacKinnon

Dear Bill　　　　　　　　　　　　　　　　　　　　*19 April 1954*

(…) God, I came home feeling depressed and hopeless. Two yrs ago you wrote me saying I shd come back cos the conference was in the hands of the religionists. So I came back. Yr diagnosis was right. But I was disappointed at the lack of support from the younger brigade. John Aitkenhead hardly spoke at all, and although what Ernst Wangermann said was always good and to the point, he didn't say enough. Arthur might have said more. As it was it was a battle between me and the Bedales, Barnes, Lyward brigade, with men of woolly words in no-man's land, saying damn all at great length. No names no pack drill. But, *mein Gott*, what sort of schools Morton and Wood etc think they are running I dunno. Bedales and Wennington at least know what they are doing and stick to their guns (small range ones I think).

(...) Don't feel like attending the next one in two years ... You get nowhere. Just words; if the buggers could only laugh a bit more, but they are so earnest.

Love to Käte. It was good to see you both again. Neill

To Constance Butler

Dear Constance   *28 April 1954*

Dear, dear, what a pity. But I told you it might happen.[1] No good giving Aitkenhead's name; he also isn't recognised. Shaw and Wills run homes for delinquent boys. Some so-called progressive schools are recognised ... Wennington Hall, Wetherby, Yorks (moral, religious, opposite of S'hill); St Christopher's, Letchworth, veg diet, advertises 'ordered freedom', but I hear not bad. (...)

I dunno why the LCC pays for our girl. Father has three here, and she is the oldest, eleven. He just applied apparently. They haven't ever sent an inspector to see what she is doing ... damn all it would be in his eyes.

I can't advise you, but myself I'd demand all or nothing, no *Ersatz* half and half freedom school. I've just come from a conference of such school heads and was odd man out all the time, asking what the hell's the use of a so-called progressive school when in essentials it stands for what Leiston Grammar School stands for.

I wish I could help you. Some educ. directors write me as friends, but, alas, not yr Derby one. Have you no local medical man who knows of S'hill, who will demand that it is the only place for the child psychologically?

Yours, Neill

[1] The local authority had refused to pay for her daughter to attend Summerhill.

To John Aitkenhead

Dear John   *5 March 1958*
   (...) I think it was you that proposed that I shd be guest of honour
at the conference. I can't do a thing myself but I think you should write
to Paul protesting that my name does not appear on the programme,
whereas Lyward and Simpson were starred as authorities. My first reaction was not to go, but then I thought it childish and a little cheap. I grant
that I have no desire to sit at the feet of Rose Hacker, who had two brats
with me in Wales, and O'Malley, whom I met years ago and thought a
sitter on the fence. Also, after my *Hearts not Heads* I feel it a bit of an insult
to have an unknown guy March lead on that topic. But I dare not say
a thing to Paul myself. Dunno who engineers the programme anyway,
possibly chaps like Jacks and Kenneth Barnes who might not approve of
my being a star turn. (...)
   Be seein' yuh in Totnes, Neill

To J— B—[1]

Dear B—   *21 January 1961*
   So kindly of you to write me. Yes, I knew old J. H. Simpson, a fine
chap. He was religious, I wasn't, but that difference never obtruded.
   There are so few guys like you in state schools, why I dunno. Most
accept the Establishment.
   Good luck; carry on and fight the diehards.
   Yours, A. S. Neill

1 A state school teacher.

To Nina Kai Nielson

Dear Nina   *16 May 1961*
   (...) You know, Nina, people like you make me feel such a swindler
when you speak and write about the good I have done. I really don't feel
I have done so very much. My chief asset may be that I never fuss and
bother, and so give the impression of being wise and good. Tut, tut!
   I can't write more with this pile of letters facing me ... damn em. I hate
writing strangers even when they are Neill fans.
   Love and blessings, Neill

To Hubert Child

Dear Child (Autumn) 1961

Maurice Richardson did a profile of me for the *Queen* mag. I didn't get a proof, and was shocked to find that he'd quoted me as criticising Dartington.[1] Whether I used the words or not I'm not clear, only that I may have done. For I am not a big enough man to be past making digs at other schools. We all say things we don't want published, and MR ought not to have done it. Anyway, I'm sorry. Moral: Beware of interviewers, even if they are friends, as in this case MR is.

Regards to both, Neill

[1] The offending passage, in the 27 September 1961 issue of *Queen*, reads: 'He is distinctly scornful of some of the progressive schools such as Dartington, which have moved slightly to the right. "I hear," he says, "they've stopped mixed bathing without bathing dresses. They'll be starting compulsory chapel in a few years." '

To Bill MacKinnon

Dear Bill 14 March 1962

Yes, the programme is as dull as hell, so I'm just going to try to fight that deadness the conf always has. Gardiner is Bedales, and the programme is typically Bedales ... and the new Dartington . . . compromise, respectability, religion... I hope to say something when McKay talks on this topic. Looks as if the holy ones ... Jacks, Kenneth Barnes etc, are to run the conference. So come along, John and all, and let's try to bring a little life into the dead horse. We can relieve the tedium by a visit or two to the local.

Love to all, Neill

To B. H. Montgomery

Dear Montgomery 1 October 1964

I think I was in King Alfred School abt two years. Yes, right, clash of views. I wanted more self-govt; J.R.[1] and staff didn't. J.R. said to me: 'Neill, either you or I must resign.' I said: 'Me, J.R., you've been here longer than I have.'

I think both experimental and demonstration are words that can be dropped. Possibly KAS and S'hill began as experiments and went on to be demonstrations.

I hope you do old J. R. credit in your book. His name has disappeared from books on education, but in his day he was a pioneer. We differed. He was a moralist. At one call-over he said that something dreadful had happened in the school ... Patrick, aged 10, had kissed Clare, aged nine. But I was very fond of him, and in spite of my rebellion, I think he liked me. I never liked the adoration he and Earle got from old pupils, girls mainly, who sat at their feet and worshipped. (...)

Yours, Neill

[1] John Russell.

To the Editor, the *Guardian*

Sir   *2 February 1965*

You describe Michael Duane as my disciple. I do not consider he is. He has been a frequent visitor to Summerhill for some years. He came because he believed in what we believe in – freedom for children. That he learned something from my school is true, but that does not make him a disciple. (...)

No man does something entirely original. He culls from others what he can accept and rejects what he cannot accept. So that no man who has any basic honesty will claim to be a master, and where there is no master there is no disciple.

Duane has done a great job and the Risinghill incident shows that treating children with love and not with the cane is dangerous in this so-called Christian country. The story brings memories of Ibsen's *An Enemy of the People*, and it isn't much consolation to recall Ibsen's words: 'The majority never has right on its side.' But Ibsen's other dictum comforts: 'The strongest man is he who stands alone.' (...)

Yours sincerely, A. S. Neill

To Ben Morris

Dear Ben   *7 February 1965*

(...) I had a visit from Duane last night. Bloody hero he is. He has got more publicity for freedom for kids than all my books got. He is a good fellow. I advised him to clear out of the LCC if closed down, for they must have too many black marks against him.

Nice to hear your family is flourishing, but are they all mad? Anyone entering education is dotty.

Love to Margaret and self, Neill

To Seishi Shimoda

My dear old friend Shimoda   *17 December 1965*
(...) I only regret that our message for freedom, yours and mine, goes out to a world that has no freedom, only nationalism, hate and bloodshed. (...) There are not enough free children growing up to make the world one of peace and love. The majority has the power and as Ibsen said the majority never has right on its side. Sorry at this time of the year to be such a pessimist, but who can be optimistic today? America's motto is better dead than red and it looks as if it would rather destroy the world than see Communism spreading. I am no communist, neither am I a capitalist. I am just unhappy about this sick world that could be so pleasant. (...)
It is a great joy to me to know that Japan has its Shimoda, but, alas, I guess that you have as little influence on conventional schools in Japan as I have in England. But we must carry on fighting for youth and freedom.
Long may you be able to carry on the good work.
Yours, old friend, Neill

To Gordon Leff

Dear Bunny   *24 January 1966*
(...) My definition of a heretic: A guy who doesn't need to be clever or learned, just a guy who must challenge or die. 99.9 never challenge. You are one of the other .1 crowd. (...)
All the best, Neill

To Kenneth Barnes

5 May 1966
Thanks, Kenneth, for your kindly words in the *Guardian*. I missed you at the conference, not only because of our friendly sparring, but also for your grasp of essentials. I found the conf. just deadly dull. The new heads talked mainly about O's and A levels. Apart from a brilliant talk by Duane I didn't once hear co-education, freedom, sex mentioned in three days. It might have been a gathering of prep school heads. (...)
All the best, Neill

To R. F. Mackenzie

Dear Mackenzie   *22 August 1966*

(...) You and I should meet one day. We could compare notes about Germany. My period was before yours – 1921 to 23 in der Internationaleschule, Hellerau, Dresden, then nine months in Austrian Tyrol. Later I heard Hitler speak in the Tempelhof and his voice scared me. I wonder if you found what I found, a woeful lack of humour in German kids. On a hot July day I put a notice on the board ... *Skilaufen Ausflug Morgen um acht Uhr*. Neill. [Skiing expedition at 8 a.m. Neill.] The whole bloody lot came to me ...*Es gibt keinen Schnee!* [There is no snow!] (...)

What future has a marked man like you? Duane was banned from every advertised LCC headship and now is lecturing in training colleges, a bit of a waste of a good guy. (...)

Yours, Neill

To R. F. Mackenzie

Dear Mackenzie   *1 September 1966*

Yes, we must meet. (...) Duane called the other day and said he had enjoyed meeting you. We three plus John Aitkenhead seem to be the only rebels in the great scholastic Establishment. (...)

I wish I could be optimistic about schools. So few ever challenge a bloody thing, training college students as well. I don't think I have had much influence really, and this isn't false modesty. (...) No, guys like you are the heroes who work inside the system with all the handicaps that never touch me.

Weel, here's to a meeting one day as soon as possible.

Yours, Neill

To R. F. Mackenzie

Dear Bob   *6 October 1967*

Every Friday I open the *TES*, vainly looking for something I can read. I never find it, but today yr article delighted me. Alas, you will have as much effect on teachers as I have ... bugger all. I'll be surprised if there is a single letter in reply to you. Try an experiment: write a letter to *TES* on the teaching of arithmetic and you no doubt will have any amount of replies. You and I can't contact the Establishment cos it runs away from all things emotional ... hence M. Duane's inability to get a headship.

What are you going to do? Have you damned yourself for ever by attacking the Bumbles of Scottish education? Like Duane you may have to go lecturing in training colls. Mike wd prefer a school, but I dunno, maybe you guys can have more influence by getting at the young teachers. (...)

Yours, Neill

To R. F. Mackenzie

Dear Bob   *24 December 1966*

Damn the buggers with their 1500 kids. I want to see schools with less than 100. But, laddie, if you are a pioneer you have a lifetime of fighting all the dead people who are in authority. You have made your name and remember that the devils are scared of any guy who writes books. Keep on fighting them. (...)

Yours, Neill

To R. F. Mackenzie

Dear Bob   *25 January 1968*

Unglaublich aber merkwurdig! [Incredible but strange!] Good old Aberdeen. Man this is most encouraging news, that the Establishment in Fife kicks you out and one in Aberdeen rescues you.[1] They must of course know all about you thro yr books and the press. London still outlaws Duane though ... does it mean that Scotland, that fell behind England in pioneering, sticking to its Leavings[2] and MAs, is now ahead in eddication? (...)

Man, it isna false modesty that makes me feel I haven't done very much in education, simply the logical aftermath of Freud's Unconscious ... let the emotions take precedence over the head in schools. (...)

I foresee a difficulty for you. If the Aberdeen lot are on your side you canna write any more books of challenge, but much better, you can write entirely about the creative side of your S'hill.

Go on working and writing, Neill

[1] When Braehead School was closed down as a result of reorganisation, Mackenzie was appointed head of Summerhill Academy in Aberdeen. The name was a coincidence.
[2] Leaving Certificate.

To R. F. Mackenzie

Dear Bob   *5 February 1968*

   Man, I dinna ken. Sure *die Eltern* [the parents] will be the main problem. New primary school here with go-ahead Head; chattering kids all
doing different things. Some parents wanted to protest to headquarters
at first but I hear that they now accept the system. Parents to me in Gretna
Green 50 years ago ... I send ma laddie to the skale to lairn, no to play.
In yr place I'd ca canny to begin with, not so much compromising as
being (...) a conscious hypocrite. I don't know what the set-up will be,
maybe the traditional chalk and desks and tawse and silence. The worst
snag is the parental belief in Leavings or today maybe O Levels. Dunno
how you can evade that snag unless very gradually. Shown round a new
school in Dundee some years ago I said to the Head ... I'd like to see the
workshop. Workshop? What has a workshop got to do with education?
I fancy Aberdeen parents have still that attitude. I think you are to have
many a headache, but what the hell! I have scores of them, not usually
parents or kids, often staff and HMIs. I am too far off state schools to
give you advice of any value. You'll wrastle through, but as I say ca canny
[play safe] until you discover what you can do and what you won't be
allowed to do.
   I'd like it if you could one day visit us. Mike Duane often comes of
a weekend.
      Carry on, Neill

To R. F. Mackenzie

Dear Bob   *8 October 1968*
   (...) Yr two news items sound hopeful, specially the fourth-year
kids. Snag is that of Bedales or Dartington Hall with 300 pupils. My lot
meet in a big room, every one of the 60 kids and 14 staff. All can speak
and vote. With numbers that can't take place, and so you have to have
MPs, and everyone loses interest in that kind of democracy. You'd have
to make your democracy a series of groups, each appointing one or two
delegates for a general meeting. I have no experience of self-govt in a day
school and wonder how it wd work, for here things like lessons are never
mentioned, only social misbehaviour or social laws in general. True in
a day school you have anti-social acts, but again you don't want self-govt
to become a court with a judge and jury. We tried that and gave it up
for a 'trial' by the whole lot of us. I can see you will have a grand time
trying different methods. But ca canny till you get to know the parental
set-up in Aberdeen. (...)
   Auf baldiges ... hoffentlich. [See you soon, I hope.] Neill

To Ben Morris

Dear Ben   *11 February 1969*
(...) Sudden phobia that Dartington Hall conference won't have a
bar. Last time it was held there we had to trek to locals. I do hope you
will be there. Last conf. I vowed that I'd never go to another, for it was
all O and A level talk, but with Lambert and fresh young uns it might
be alive. For years it has been a bloody funeral of men who died years
ago but were not yet buried. A solemn lot indeed, but teachers are in general. (...)
Love to you both, Neill

To Terry Philpot

Dear Terry   *6 March 1969*
Ta for a very pleasing article. I have a vague idea that the *Humanist*
doesn't do enough about kids and indoctrination and sex repression. So
many humanists seem head ones rather than guts ones. I wonder how
many of the readers would approve of S'hill. (...)
Oh, re-reading yr letter ... remember that my correspondence with
Russell[1] dates back to 1923 or 4. We always differed about head v heart.
I wonder if he ever believed in true freedom for kids. Long time since
I read his *On Education*, and can't recall what he said of cuddling, where
he is all haywire. Walking with him on a starry night in 24 I said: 'Russell,
the difference between us is that if we had a kid with us you would want
to give him a lesson about the stars, while I would leave him to his own
thoughts.' I fancy that sums up the difference between us ... he is a thinker
and I am only a doer. (...)
All the best, Neill

[1] Bertrand Russell

To Nicholas King Harris

Dear Nicholas   *22 May 1969*
(...) Missed you at Dartington Hall. Same old conf largely abt O and
A levels. But good to meet again Ben Morris and the bright Irish

brigade.[1] Royston Lambert seems to be interested in organising more than in kids. I didn't find him inspiring in any way. (…)

All the best, Neill

[1] Ruarc Gahan and others from Sutton Park School.

To R. F. Mackenzie

Dear Bob   *24 December 1969*

Yr letter made me sad for it told me that the Scots education is where I left it over 60 years ago. You are in a hole, laddie. Got to support yr family, so that you can't tell em all to go to hell, so that it means that a pioneer, years before his time, has to compromise with all the bloody anti-life buggers in Aberdeen. It sounds worse than Braehead in a way. I was surprised that you ever got that job, seeing that Mike can't get a headship in London. I was silly enough to think that Aberdeen was advanced enough to appoint a rebel like you.

What you say about kids accepting belting is so sad. Poor devils are indoctrinated from cradle days. On TV a group of 18s were asked abt the cane. 60% were for it. (…)

Sorry we are so far apart. I thought you a great guy when we met … and that isn't a compliment, just a bare truth. (…)

All the best and go on fechting, Neill

To Seishi Shimoda

My dear Shimoda   *21 October 1970*

(…) TV pictures of Tokyo make me sad. It has become all Americanised with all its vulgar neon lights and silly theatre shows. Technology is killing natural life. A workman does not create now; he stands at a travelling belt in a factory and has no pride in his work. There isn't a worker in Suffolk who could make a pair of shoes or a teapot. As children we made our own kites and wooden guns, but today children buy them in shops. I make the guess that for every one who goes to your art exhibition twenty will go to a pop song gathering … or a football match. Art is in danger in this mechanical, money-making world. You and I, by seeking to go deep into human nature, are lonely men fighting a great hateful machine called progress. But we shall go on fighting till we die.

I shall look forward to that book you have sent me.

All my warm respects to you, dear old friend, Neill

To Roger Tilbury

Dear Roger   *23 June 1971*
    Good to get yr report on the conf. Rumour says that it was better than before, more young uns taking part ... I always was disappointed that so few ever spoke. The Irish brigade seems to have been as keen as usual. Alas, my conf days are over. (...)
    Carry on, you young uns. Really good for you that the old horses – Paul Roberts, Kenneth Barnes, myself – have all gone out to grass. Snag is that you'll have as nasty a fight as we had with the Establishment. But life wd be dull without the fight.
    All the best, Neill

To Tony Hill

Dear Tony   *2 September 1971*
    I can't say a bloody word to help you. You are in the wrong place but the snag is to find the right place, since the bosses of such schools are naturally selected by the Establishment cos they carry on the tradition of suppression. Was in a similar position in 1919 in King Alfred School, Hampstead, and had to clear out. The only man I know who has your attitude to kids is Howard Case, Epping House School, Hertford, Herts. His kids were at S'hill all the way. He deals with junior maladjusted kids. Why not ask him if he needs staff, telling him yr attitude?
    If you stay in that place you will either go crazy or accept the anti-life system and live unhappily ever after.
    You might also try Otto Shaw, Red Hill School, Sutton Valence, Kent. He is outwith the state system, but won't take kids unless with a high IQ.
    Let me know if you get a more agreeable job.
    Neill

To R. F. Mackenzie

Dear Bob   *16 December 1971*
    (...) Man, I pity you in yr fight for the tawse abolition. Teachers and lawyers are the most reactionary bastards I know. All this talk about violence in schools but none about the cane strap violence of generations. I fear your voice won't get a hearing until you retire and get free from bureaucracy and a dead system of learning rot. Wd like to have a census

at a Cup Final to find how many cd do a square root or tell what Crom-
well did. But it ain't only the teachers; battle axe Thatcher wd subscribe
to all the profession's anti-lifeness.[1] (...)

I still wonder why they ever gave a rebel like you such a job. Poor Mike
keeps applying for headships in vain.

All the best, Neill

[1] Margaret Thatcher was Minister of Education.

To Keith Horsfield

Dear Keith   *31 May 1972*

Were I a conventional head I'd have a roll of honour on the wall with
names of guys like you and Barton, Bunny[1] etc. The kids wd tear it down
anyway. (...) Query: How long can the Summerhill freedom to skip lessons go on in the rat race where, soon, you'll need four O levels to sweep
the streets? My lot, many from USA and Germany now, seem unconscious of the rat race and go on having a fine time loafing, but, to be fair,
as they leave they seem able to tackle life because freedom does give guts
to most of em. You and Clive[2] are damn good ads and answers to the
anti-lifers who say that freedom can't work. (...)

I hope you have a long and great career down south.

The best, Neill

[1] Gordon Leff.
[2] Clive Horsfield, Keith's brother.

To Dora Russell

My dear Dora   *6 December 1972*

I sat through the two hours of that TV thing, furious at its stupidity.
Did you notice that they quoted John Holt from USA, and not you or
me? So the Tuesday *Guardian* Educn pages unreadable. We are still fifty
yrs ahead of all the other buggers and bitches. (...)

Love, Neill

To R. F. Mackenzie

20 December 1972

Man, that's a hell of a picter you paint of Scots dominies. But English ones are similar; same proportion for the cane. Makes it difficult to be an optimist abt education. In essence the Scots are where I was when I wrote my *Log* in 1915. (...)

Rumour said you had been ill. I do hope it is wrong, for the world needs bonny fechters like you; there are so few about now ... Duane, Aitkenhead, Holt and others in USA. The so-called progressive schools are half dead. St Christopher's advertises itself as having 'ordered freedom'. You must feel very lonely amongst the local teachers who are so anti-life. I admire your sticking to the state system ... I ran awa from it.

Aweel, as guid a Noo Year as this lovely world of Mrs Whitehouse, Nixon, Heath etc will allow. Neill

To R. F. Mackenzie

Dear Bob   *12 February 1973*

(...) You poor devil but I expected it. Guys who are a generation ahead of their time can't expect anything else than hatred from the stupid anti-life buggers named the teaching profession.

Snag abt a book is how will you live. You aren't pensionable age, I fancy, and, as you know, authorship isn't a living unless you are a best seller. But that book must be written and writ in words of blazing fire. Scotland seems to be behind. In the last 46 years I have been in Leiston I have not heard of one caning in the local schools. Bob, Scotland needs your biting pen, but, alas, the teachers won't be the least affected. I hate the bloody profession. (...)

Alles gut, Neill

P. S. A Scots teacher married a whore and it took her three years to sink to his level.

To R. F. Mackenzie

Dear Bob   *27 April 1973*

(...) I despair more and more of teachers. The *Teacher* is the paper of the National Union of Teachers and the editor tells me that my recent article was disapproved of by the head gins. In it I said that at a meeting of 100 teachers 96 were in favour of the belt, but where I got that item I dunno. Can't have been from you if you have them over primary age, for these sods wanted to tawse primary kids. (…)

Mike Duane looks in to see me every second weekend. A joy to hae a crack wi' a body that goes all the way.

I canna see you write a book on yr S'hill as long as you are in it. That wd mean the sack, yet Mike, to whom they won't give a headship, draws his full salary for doing bugger all. So get sacked and write that book. (…)

Bloody hero you are; a colonel with his regiment agin him. In USA they wd be carrying gats.

All the best Bob. You are a real fechter, but, like me, you won't get credit till you are deid.

Yrs, Neill

2

Education

Mr Neill seems to be collecting more and more
evidence in support of the theory that children,
given freedom from restrictions, threats,
punishments, sexual misinformation, and other
manifestations of adult neurosis, develop spon-
taneously a strong social and community sense.
Self-government, which means that children
run the school and each member of the staff has
only one vote, seems to work with extraordi-
nary smoothness.

Observer, April 1937

To Beatrice Ensor, the *New Era*[1]

Hellerau, Dresden

Dear Mrs Ensor   *5 September 1921*

I know that you picture me spending my time running round visiting the schools of Germany. The truth is that I spend the day lying in
the sun, clad in a pair of bathing drawers that would not satisfy the critical
eye of Councillor Clark. Of course the dishonest explanation is that the
schools are all closed for the summer vacation, but the real truth is that
at the present moment I am much more interested in sunbaths, beer and
baccy, than in all the new educational experiments under the sun.

Still, two mornings ago, I donned my trousers and went up to visit
the school here – the *Volkschule*. I liked it at once. No punishment, no
rewards, any amount of outside rambles for Geography and Nature
Study. In school quite a lot of creation ... child of six draws a pig, and
then writes PIG underneath. The staff seems to be composed of young
people who are out to find and give freedom. But I am told that in neigh-
bouring villages one may find the old type of teacher who believes in
stern discipline.

I suppose you know that Hellerau is a famous name. It was here that
Dalcroze came in 1910. (...) I have spent a few delightful evenings over
at the Dalcroze School ... and I warn you solemnly that I am not coming

29

back to London until I have taken a full course here. I have seen Dalcroze's own demonstrations in Queen's Hall, but I learned more here. Frau Baer's methods were simpler. She took a class of village children who had never heard of rhythm.

'Now, just do anything you like while I play the piano,' she said, 'but when I call *hopp* run back to your original places in the ring.' The audience roared at some of the antics, and the children enjoyed themselves hugely. The wonderful thing to me was that after ten minutes these children had grasped the idea of moving to rhythm. Incidentally, I noted that the girls learned more quickly than the boys. (...)

I am certain that the school here has a great future before it. One thing pleases me: among Dalcrozians there does not appear to be that unfortunate Montessorian habit of waiting for guidance from the fountainhead. I see Montessorianism becoming a dead apparatus-ridden system, but I see Rhythm extending its influence in all branches of education. Thank heaven, there is no apparatus required for Eurhythmics!

I like Germany. Everyone I meet is kind. The only Hun I have discovered is the language.

　　　Sincerely, A. S. Neill

[1] In the October 1921 issue of the *New Era*, in which this 'letter' was published, Beatrice Ensor wrote: 'All that I have been able to extract from the Co-Editor.'

To Bertrand Russell

Lyme Regis, Dorset
Dear Russell　　　　　　　　　　　　　　*23 March 1926*
　　　I marvel that two men, working from different angles, should arrive at essentially the same conclusions. Your book and mine are complementary.[1] It may be that the only difference between us comes from our different complexes. I observe that you say little or nothing about handwork in education. My hobby has always been handwork, and where your child asks you about stars my pupils ask me about steels and screw threads. Possibly also I attach more importance to emotion in education than you do.

(...) I do not share your enthusiasm for Montessori. I cannot agree with a system set up by a strong churchwoman with a strict moral aim. Her orderliness to me is a counterblast against original sin. Besides I see no virtue in orderliness at all. My workshop is always in a mess but my handwork isn't. My pupils have no interest in orderliness until they come to puberty or thereabouts. You may find that at the age of five your children will have no use for Montessori apparatus. Why *not* use the apparatus to make a train with? I argued this out with Madame Macaroni,[2]

Montessori's chief lieutenant, a few years ago. Is it not our awful attitude to learning that warps our outlook? After all a train is a reality, while an inset frame is purely artificial. I never use artificial apparatus. My apparatus in the school is books, tools, test tubes, compasses. Montessori wants to direct a child. I don't.

(...) To me the most interesting thing about your book is that it is scholarly (nasty word) in the sense that it is written by a man who knows history and science. I am ignorant of both and I think that my own conclusions come partly from a blind intuition. I say again that it is marvellous that we should reach very much the same philosophy of education. It is the only possible philosophy today, but we cannot hope to do much in the attack against schools from Eton to the London County Council. Our only hope is in the individual parent.

My chief difficulty is the parent, for my pupils are products of ignorant and savage parents. I have much fear that one or two of them, shocked by my book, may withdraw their children. That would be a tragedy.

Well, thank you ever so much for the book. It is the only book on education that I have read that does not make me swear. All the others are morals disguised as education. (...)

Yours very truly, A. S. Neill

[1] Russell's *On Education* and Neill's *The Problem Child* were published this year.
[2] Anna Maccheroni.

To Bertrand Russell

Lyme Regis, Dorset
Dear Mr Russell   *28 March 1926*

(...) The bigger question of direction we must leave for a talk when we meet. As you say, we cause a child to speak English rather than Chinese. We don't really; environment does, and that part of direction cannot be got over. I find myself supplying environment according to my own interests. I buy clay for modelling, wood, brass, chemical apparatus. Another man might buy Latin books or gardening tools. But if I were rich I should make an environment that would give a sort of universal direction. My ideal staff would then be made up of Communists, Tories, Christians, Muhammadans, etc ... but there again would I introduce Sadists, Burglars? No. Then I do direct!

Where I do not direct is in the individual case. I never try to teach a child to read. My lot all begin to read mainly because the adults refuse to read the sub-titles in the cinema for them. So with everything. I have a specialist and a Chemistry Lab, but half my school never goes to Chemistry. So with music and art. Certainly the system should make children find their level, for nothing is done unless the inner urge prompts it. Think of the million bad pianists we have because of parental direction when there was no inner interest. But do not take this as argument. A discussion by letter gets nowhere.

I enclose a review that your press–cutting agency may miss. The writer is, I think, Director of Studies in Dundee. He once came to one of my lectures and abused me.

Sincerely, A. S. Neill

To Seishi Shimoda

My dear Shimoda   *2 October 1950*
(…) I can give you an answer to the critics who say that under freedom to stay away from all lessons children will never compete with other disciplined children. This summer we sent 6 pupils of 16 in to take the Oxford School Certificate Examination. In all they took 39 subjects. The marks given are Failure, Pass (over 35½), Credit (over 50½), Very Good (over 70½). Our results were 24 Very Good, 12 Credits, 2 Passes, 1 Failure. Wonderful really. (…)

A. S. Neill

To the Editor, the *Observer*

Sir   *23 February 1956*
Says Mr Mortimer Standing, 'If anything distinguishes Montessori from the Froebelians, and the promoters of many of the "Activity" schools, it is the fact that she stands definitely for work and not for play.'

Childhood is playhood and Montessori made it workhood, imposing her own ideas on the young. But when a child is free to be its natural self it plays all the time, even up to the age of fifteen or sixteen. Give children freedom in a workshop and they will not make pen–trays and tables and dovetail joints; they will always make something to which they can attach a play fantasy – an aeroplane, a ship, a sword, a wooden gun.

The teacher can of course say that children must be moulded and trained, but they have been for centuries and society is quite sick. It seems to me that Montessori adopted the old theory of the teacher's being akin to the gardener: the gardener prunes the bushes in order to get good fruit. The gardener knows what kind of fruit he wants, but who is wise enough, bold enough to claim that he knows what a child should grow into?

Many years ago I saw Montessori's lieutenant, Signorina Macaroni [sic], snatch the Long Stair from a child who was playing trains with it. The child was furious. So was I. From that moment I disliked the rigidity, discipline, moral suasion of the system. I am all for Froebel and Caldwell Cook's play way.

Yours sincerely, A. S. Neill

To Seishi Shimoda

My dear Shimoda   *15 July 1957*
(...) This year every private school has to be inspected by the Ministry of Education and if the teaching is not good enough the school can be closed. My trouble is that I cannot get teachers. I cannot afford to pay the salaries the state pays and for the past years I have had to work with teachers who were not in the main good enough. I have only 45 pupils and need seven teachers if they are to get the chance of passing examinations. The fees never are enough. (...) Friend, I am afraid that pioneering in education does not pay. To lose Summerhill would break my heart and bring misery to the happy pupils. Life would be so empty without it. (...)

It is difficult to analyse the reason why teachers will not come to me since the war. The original enthusiasm for the new psychology has died down, and many schools have given more freedom than before. Also the state now pays for the training of all teachers and naturally expects them to work in state schools. And where I can pay only about £12 a month with food etc they can get four times this sum in government schools. (...)

Best wishes to you, old friend.

Yours, A. S. Neill

To Colin Ward

Dear Colin   *29 October 1966*
Caldwell Cook died young. I never met him again after my visit to the Perse School in ... oh, 1920 or so. Rumour said he was a queer, but what the hell anyway? My criticism of his book is that he uses the play way with an end in view ... learning; but to me play has no ulterior motive barring fun. (...)

The best, Neill

To the Editor, the *Daily Telegraph*

Sir   *23 November 1967*
    I have had teachers, qualified and unqualified. Some were good,
some were bad in both categories. I fancy that training will not make a
heavy, unimaginative teacher a good person, and possibly our standard
of O and A levels does not necessarily lead to brightness and vim and,
yes, humour, without which a teacher is a menace to children. But I may
be biased; after a four years' apprenticeship as a pupil teacher I sat a com-
petitive exam for entry to a Normal School ... we called it that around
1904. A hundred and four candidates sat. I was no. 103 on the list and
didn't get in.
    One of my old pupils trained under Bernard Leach, the world-known
potter. My pupil could not get a job in a state school, but a teacher who
had made a few pots and had a certificate could be appointed to teach
ceramics. A Picasso could not become an art master under the Ministry.
    I am not saying that all training is bunk. I don't want my appendix cut
out by the man who wheels me into the theatre. Training can make a sur-
geon, but it does not invariably seem to show results with budding
teachers. It is tactful to take illustrations from abroad. I have had scores
of letters from American schoolchildren. The pattern is always the same.
'I hate my school. We are pressurised all the time. The teachers make
every lesson dull, and if they don't stick to the book they jump on you.'
I assume that these teachers have all been trained.
    Really teachers should not be blamed. Which of them could be bright
and enthusiastic when preparing children for the dreary, dead questions
in the usual O level English Language paper? Dull subjects must produce
dull teachers.
    Yours faithfully, A. S. Neill

To J— B—[1]

Dear J— B—   *24 November 1967*
    Yes, I was a bit naughty. I grant that the essay selection has improved
a lot, but I don't like the comprehension and worst of all the précis, which
I think is on the way out. Also the grammar. A year ago a girl who had
sat O level asked me to tell her where she had gone wrong in a grammar
analysis of sentence question. I couldn't do the question ... I got only a
2nd Hons English in Edinburgh long ago. When I taught English here
my pupils complained ... 'But this won't see us through O level.' Because
I dwelt on the creative side all the time, not the analytical. I wrote in my
last book that I'd give a kid a sheet of paper and say: 'You have two hours

to write any damned thing you like.' But I added that some teachers would rehearse and make their kids write papers from A to Z, so that there would have to be a stipulation … write about any subject beginning with K or S. But some teachers would, as I say, do the whole alphabet.

Kenneth Barnes. We have known each other for many years, often differing deeply but always admiring each other. So with J.H.S.[2] I used to lecture to his students in London. (…)

Just been inspected. Inspectors see unpainted walls, untidy rooms, but they never seem to see kids.

Yours, A. S. Neill

P. S. What silly bugger would tell a kid to masturbate? I never saw a kid who had to be guided in that line.

[1] A state school teacher.
[2] J. H. Simpson.

To Seishi Shimoda

My dear Shimoda   *4 March 1968*
(…) The National Union of Teachers are demanding that all private schools be abolished. The future for all private schools is a dark one. I don't think they will allow Summerhill to continue when I die. Their standard is learning and exams and science, all head things. To a Ministry emotion does not exist. Their cure for a sick world seems to be more exams and more university graduates, but then the state does not want free children; it wants obedient ones, moulded and indoctrinated to be sheep, to think alike, dress alike, live alike. (…)

Best wishes, my dear old friend, Neill

To the Editor, the *Guardian*

Sir   *11 June 1968*
Leila Berg's kind and generous article could give to some folks the suggestion that I am having a cold war with the Inspectorate. A difference in attitude does not constitute a war, cold or hot. There is a difference. The Ministry is primarily interested in efficiency, and I fear that this efficiency applies to learning rather than to living, to tidy rooms rather than to happy children, to the number of water closets rather than to the absence of illness. An inspector can inspect learning; he can tell whether the

history teacher is doing his job well, but he cannot inspect tolerance or happiness or balance. His job almost makes him take a short view – Willie can't read at 13 – but two of our Willies who couldn't read at 15 are now successful engineers. Inspectors, like cops, do not make the law; they carry it out and unfortunately have to act as sanitary inspectors, a job that they must hate.

No, I have no quarrel with the Inspectors, but I wish that someone high up would change the name, for the word 'inspect' suggests that someone is doing wrong – like the bus inspector whose job is to see if the conductor is fiddling. But I do have a quarrel with the policy behind the Inspectorate, one that 'recognises' any private school that canes the boys but has a plethora of O and A levels, while Summerhill that has no cane is only 'registered'. True, I know that a school must apply for 'recognition', but to me recognition is something bestowed: one does not apply for a title or for an honorary degree.

I gladly admit that Summerhill has had two full inspections with full reports that were at once critical and generous. But, as long as education is geared to O and A level exams, schools that do not accept that standard will be odd men out, and Inspectors with conventional views of education will be the wrong men or women to evaluate them.

Summerhill must obey the Inspectors when they condemn premises. At the moment we are spending a lot on repairing and rebuilding, thanks to many generous friends – but Summerhill will not compromise in its educational philosophy, and I am optimistic enough to hope that the Ministry will not ask it to compromise. Britain, I think, is still the freest country in the world; I know of no country that would have allowed Summerhill to carry on unmolested for 44 years, but I realise that I am protected by the dear old class system that keeps its Etons and Harrows, and therefore its many feeding private schools.

Sincerely, A. S. Neill

To John Blackie

Dear Blackie   *1 October 1968*

About the only time I get to read is in vacation. So I came kinda late to your Primary School book.[1] First impression was your ability to write clearly and plainly. So many who write about education are dull or long-winded or both. I find Dewey such a writer, plus 90% of the guys who write for the *TES*. I'd like to say that you are all wrong, but, dammit, I found myself agreeing with you all the way, especially about the necessity of play and creation. I've told my staff to read at least their subject section of the book.

I visited one of Leicester's show primaries.[2] Kids busy and happy, chattering away, all doing something, but that something had a pedagogical aim ... to learn something. I had a kindergarten woman whose classroom was filled by kids painting, constructing, clay modelling. She left and I got a Montessori man from USA. Apparatus everywhere but half the attendance. Montessori, her son told me, thought that a child should not phantasy.

I said to the Leicester head: 'How do you feel when these kids leave you and sit at O level desks, immobile?' He sighed and said he felt bloody awful. So, friend, yr next job should be to write for the sec mod and grammar bods who are away behind the primaries you advocate. But can they escape so long as O and A stand as barriers to true education?

As you know I am not primarily interested in the learning process, only the living one, and I wonder if all the new school ways will change a civilisation whose *Weltanschauung* is football and bingo and the *News of the World*. Today I fancy a million workmen think and talk football the whole time. I have had some lousy teachers in my time, self included. I taught maths (not my subject) to Barton, now prof of maths in London. The history man wasn't much good, but Gordon Leff, reader in York (he had refused five offers of a profship) got there. True they were bright lads, yet I doubt if I'd had two brilliant teachers the other pupils would have made much of it all. (...)

Go on writing. You have something vital to say. Maybe you are too gentle, too mild. I'd have liked to see you slash out at fear and caning in the schools, at the stupid dignity of the teachers. In my 60 weekly USA mail a woman teacher writes: 'I nearly got the sack because the head heard a kid call me Mary. I was told that I must keep my distance.'

Makes me wonder if you are handicapped by your having been an HMI, that is a guy who was muzzled by officialdom. Now that you are free I hope to see you take sides.

Good luck and bumper royalties.

Yours, Neill

[1] *Inside the Primary School.*
[2] Ravenhurst Primary School, whose headteacher was Bill Hazell.

To Christine Meek

Dear Christine   *12 April 1969*

Yr letter saddens me; I get so many like it. What can you do in a mad system? (...) The misery is that you are in a small minority; the majority accept the idiotic system. To think that at one time Scottish education was thought to be in advance of England.

I wish I could give you some sensible advice. Maybe try to get a village school of your own; but then you'd be like me in Gretna Green long ago, when the parents cried: 'I send my laddie to schule to learn, not to play.' And you'd have the HMIs, with their criterion of learning, not living.

Yours sympathetically, A. S. Neill

To the Editor, the *Times Educational Supplement*

Sir   *13 June 1969*

One argument for the retention of the cane or tawse is clear and logical. Take the situation of the teacher in, say, a slum part of any big city. He has a large class and in that class are almost certainly bound to be a few tough guys who upset the class and the teaching. What can the teacher do?

Michael Duane solved the matter when he refused to use the cane, but he was no ordinary teacher. The average teacher sees no way out but the way of violence, and caning is violence and must breed violence. And, indeed, the poor man is in a hole.

There is a solution. In Sweden, apparently, the young tough is taken out of the school and sent to one run on psychological lines which attempts to help the child to overcome his anti-social ways. It could be done here; it should be done here. (...)

Not having seen them I cannot fairly judge borstals and approved schools. A few may be very good, but from what I read, I take it that the methods used are those that made the inmates crooks ... discipline from above, strenuous work, obedience without question, shortage of free time. Punishment cannot cure what is individual and social sickness. (...)

The chief difficulty, as we all know, is the environment that makes young delinquents, the bad homes, the ignorant parents, so that such schools would have to be boarding ones well away from slumland. But one snag would be the question of staff. (...)

I would suggest that such schools should be run by psychologists if I did not have the disturbing fear that many trained psychologists are taught more about rats and pigeons than about child psychology, meaning that if a man is a BA (Psychology) it does not follow that he can understand children. (...)

Yours, A. S. Neill

To the Editor, the *Guardian*

Sir   *20 October 1969*
    I find the Black Paper dull as ditchwater.[1] The authors show no con-
cern with the child, with the emotions, the happiness of a child. They
postulate that education is for the part above the neck; they think of education as learning and not living. They fail to see that exam knowledge
is mostly knowledge that will soon be forgotten.
    I got a high mark in history at the university, but today I couldn't tell
what the Long Parliament did, and am uncertain about who won the
Wars of the Roses. I once studied Latin and Greek and today I doubt if
I could say the Greek alphabet, and am sure that I couldn't read the Latin
inscription on a gravestone.
    How many copies of Shakespeare or Tennyson would one find in the
homes of a Cup Final crowd? The criterion is all wrong. As Michael
Duane said recently, the problem is largely a social one, a question of class
education, the social assumption being that a grammar school boy with
five A levels is better educated than a potter or a skilled toolmaker.
    'Education' does not consider the motives of children, their desire to
play, their longing to be free, to escape moulding by adults who do not
know how to live themselves. The Black Paper ignores the fear in many
schools, the barbarous use of the cane and tawse, the character moulding,
the inculcation of obedience, the worst of the seven deadly virtues.
    Why all this concentration on high academic qualifications for
teachers? I have had teachers with the best degrees who couldn't teach
for nuts. I have had unqualified teachers who were excellent. Teaching
is an art, not a science. People have aptitudes – Laver, Henry Cotton,
Chaplin. All the training in the world would not make me a Tony Jacklin.
    If academics are so important why do we have anyone in our Cabinet
who hasn't taken an honours degree? A BA can be a hopeless neurotic.
I am an MA myself.
    Yours, etc., A. S. Neill

[1] *Fight for Education: a Black Paper*, eds. C. B. Cox and A. E. Dyson, the first of
a series of attacks on 'progressive' methods and ideas.

To the Editor, the *Daily Telegraph*

Sir   *18 December 1969*
    A schoolboy is sent home because his trousers are the wrong colour.
Another because his hair is too long. Why? Policemen and postmen wear

uniform so that they can be identified, but who wants to identify a schoolboy? (...)

School uniform means uniformity. Dress alike, behave alike, think alike, be members of a select crowd. A teacher back from Russia saw in a kindergarten a child reading in a corner. The teacher hastily dragged her into the crowd. 'She is being an individualist.' It could happen in our own schools.

Everything points to an increase of crowd compulsion. The psychology of Pavlov, Watson and now Skinner thinks of the masses and how they can be conditioned by wise (sic) men. The freedom of the individual is being curbed all round. The Parliamentary Whip is similar to the headmaster who demands that individuality must give way to mass psychology.

And it is all so petty, so stupid, so narrow. Who cares what Picasso or Auden wears? Who is impressed by the brigade of City men with their bowler hats and striped breeks?

Education should deal primarily with the emotions, for if they are free the intellect will look after itself. Coloured trousers have an emotional content that O and A levels have not. Alas, so many teachers are scared of emotion ... hence their tinpot dignity, their 'Sir', their fear of being thought human by their pupils.

Yours, A. S. Neill

To the Editor, *The Times*

Sir   *26 June 1970*

I hope that the new Education Secretary[1] will take a new look at the term 'recognised as efficient'. (...)

Recognition means nothing to me personally, but if I had it poor parents could send their children to Summerhill. A poor widow wanted to send her boy, saying that her county council had offered to pay half the fees. Then the council discovered that we were not recognised and therefore they could not pay the fees. So I have to continue being ashamed that I have to take middle-class pupils only.

I am not trying to sell my school when I say that it is 'recognised' in a dozen countries. (...) What pains me is this: if I had a private school with ideal premises and teaching plus fear and the cane I would be recognised. It would be great if Mrs Thatcher would begin her reign[2] by abolishing the barbarity and cowardliness of corporal punishment in all schools, but, if she tried to, she would have many teachers against her.

I appeal to her to drop the Ministry yardstick that makes all schools fit into its criterion of education, or should I say learning? The new freedom in many primary schools should encourage her to put school subject education in its uncreative place.

Yours, A. S. Neill

[1] Margaret Thatcher.
[2] The Conservative Government had come to power the month before.

To Gwen Horsfield

Dear Gwen   *14 July 1970*

I understand yr anger with *The Times*, but they always do that. I know of two others who replied and weren't published. Tell Keith I gave yr address, not knowing his, to a guy asking to meet old pupils. I know that K would speak almost as well as his mamma abt S'hill. Send me the letters he and Clive have after their names to flourish at the silly buggers who ask how free kids can compete with Establishment school kids. (...)

Bugger the press. I suffer from it too; as you say, it prints tripe all the time. Politics don't concern me; both sides are of the Establishment. I hear that Mrs Thatcher voted to keep hanging so I doubt if she is a Neill fan. Still S'hill is safe under the Tories, for as long as they keep Eton and Harrow I am safe. Good old private enterprise.

Love to the family, the most Summerhillian one I have had. Neill

To the Editor, the *Sunday Telegraph*

Sir   *21 January 1971*

Nicholas Bagnall's penetrating and disturbing article, in a recent issue about teacher training, prompts me to suggest that we put the clock back and return to the old pupil-teacher system. Seventy-two years ago, at the age of 15, I became a pupil teacher in my father's village school in Scotland.

My father was a born teacher and naturally I copied his methods, teaching all the subjects. But the teaching was a minor matter; it was the living with children that was important. At the age I was then, I could be one of them in games and fun. I got to know child psychology by living practice, and not by books and lectures. (...)

Teaching practice must mean taking a class of kids one knows nothing about, making teaching a matter of imparting mostly useless and soon-forgotten information, instead of making education a living rather than a teaching process. Anyway, one can never teach the important things;

one can teach maths but not how to love, or how to be charitable and tolerant.

By making education a matter of knowing instead of feeling, of discipline and placidity ... children sitting at desks all day when childhood is movement, we are turning out robots and emotional misfits. Students should be studying the causes of train-smashing, gangsterdom, crime, all the result of an education that leaves the emotions out, leaving them to the cheap TV stories, the sensational press, the commercials.

Some training colleges may be doing this, but, according to the many student teachers who visit Summerhill, I get the impressin that they find much of their studies futile and dull. And this goes for some universities also. I asked a man who had just taken his BA in Psychology what they taught him to do with a kid who is stealing. 'Good God, they never tell us things like that, they only tell us what happens to rats when you condition them.'

Of course, I know that my pupil-teacher plan is a dream. No one will take it up. Pity, for apprenticeship should be doing, not theorising, not poring over books on education.

Yours, A. S. Neill

To John Blackie

My dear Blackie   *12 January 1972*

I want to ask pardon for using yr name without yr permission. The Min sent me a stiff reminder that unless we pull our socks up re lessons and teaching ... well, they give us a year and then will consider whether we go on being registered. I seldom get annoyed but I wrote a letter in which I said that 'S'hill has never been inspected by HMIs who seemed to have any understanding of what the system stands for – living first; learning second. I make one exception, John Blackie (1949).' I went on to say that I rejected the HMI making a criterion of mere book learning. Said how puzzled I was that thousands all over the world thought S'hill of great importance while the Min, if not hostile, was at least indifferent. Dunno what happens to such a letter in the Min.

(...) Query: how did you escape being made into a bureaucrat in the official atmosphere? I guess I have a complex abt inspectors, and when one, guy called Downes, said: 'Mr Neill, we are not interested in your system of education,' I was too shocked to answer him. Maybe the mere name inspector dehumanises; it suggests the bus inspector looking for fiddling conductors. I know they say that is no longer so, but everything they said was a criticism, and they seemed to find nothing good in S'hill whatever. (...)

I wish I could meet you again. Pemberton and you were the only human HMIs I have had here. Poor old Pemberton was so delighted when I gave him a fat bunch of illegal petrol coupons.

All the best and no need to answer.

Yours, Neill

To John Blackie

My dear Blackie   23 *January 1972*

I read yr little book[1] at a sitting. I think it tells as much abt you as it does the Inspectorate. In a letter a few years ago you called yourself a middle of the road man, but I wonder if you are. Can a Brother go ahead of the other Brothers? Maybe not easy. Yr book tells a hell of a lot in its short space. It brought back the days of payment by results, when my poor father had a splitting headache on Inspection Day, knowing that his salary depended on the number of passes of Standard V, which always seemed to consist of morons. My HMI complex dates from then. In my father's Logbook 1902 is an entry abt me in the HMI report ... 'This candidate is warned that his work all round is weak.' My last year as a pupil teacher. No, laddie, I still think the Inspectorate too academic, too Establishmental. When Lady H grumbled abt our bad teaching[2] ... I grant I had a few teaching duds ... I said to her: 'I take a long view. My old pupils have made good; I can think of only one who can't hold down a job.' 'Yes, Mr Neill, but I can't see them, can I?' You would not have said that.

I still think that most HMIs go by the book. I am sure that if a team came to inspect – four profs of education ... Ben Morris, Robin Pedley, Harry Rée and Brian Stanley, they would not show any interest in lessons. (...) I still think that the teachers should not be inspected. The doctors and lawyers would reject it totally. Yr analogy of armies being inspected like schools isn't good. Death merchants v life merchants.

My local man Keeney is a historian and he, I am sure, will not like it when I tell him I have abolished history and geography and appointed an ecology teacher ... maybe the first school to have one. For years I have failed to get a teacher of both subjects who could get kids interested. (...) Damn it, if it weren't for the O and A level barrier I'd abolish the whole bloody lot of subjects, barring maths and science for those who wanted them. I got over 90% in my degree exam in history and I am not sure who won the Wars of the Roses. My plan would of course abolish the Inspectorate ... or maybe expand it, for if O levels had to go on I'd have them in tennis, chess, football, stamp collecting, etc. In the last crowd of visitors, 170 or so, a woman teacher said: 'I don't agree about freedom to stay away from lessons. If I hadn't had to go to maths I'd never have learned any.' 'Can you solve a quadratic equation?' She said no. I asked for a show of hands ... three went up, maths teachers. (...)

My experience has been that few HMIs seemed to know a thing about psychology or to be interested in kids as kids, not as Top of the Form walking encyclopedias. I made you an exception and I think I was right. Maybe the Brother in you is academic, but the deeper guy is wider in outlook than the other members of the Brotherhood. (...)

Thanks for the book. In spite of my complexes I enjoyed it a lot.

Yours, Neill

[1] *Inspecting and the Inspectorate*.
[2] Lady Helen Asquith.

To David Hume

Dear David   *13 February 1973*

Yr letter cheered me up because it came with one from a Scots head whose large staff is rebelling because he wants to abolish corporal punishment. Most of them want the belt for primary school kids. It is so depressing to know that the majority of teachers either hate kids or don't want to see their point of view. I fear you will meet it when you are qualified unless you seek a job in one of the new primary schools. The bitter truth is that you cannot pioneer in a state school ... Duane, Mackenzie.

Pardon brevity. At 89 I find even writing letters a bit of an effort.

Carry on with the work when I have gone.

Yours, Neill

3

Daily Life

You sit in his study and he is invaded all the time. A boy wants a key, a girl smoking a cigarette wants a piece of chain, two little chaps want tennis rackets. Another knock. 'I'm busy. Go away,' shouts Mr Neill. 'Oh damn,' says the voice.

News Chronicle, July 1934

To Bertrand Russell

Lyme Regis, Dorset
Dear Mr Russell   *30 March 1927*
    Your letter has cheered me up considerably. I have heard nothing more from the correspondent and hope to hear no more.
    I shall refuse the offer of the Teachers' Labour League. The situation is awkward because the secretary Duncan is an old pupil of mine. I must, however, keep clear of all politics.
    I am very glad to know that you will visit us in May.[1] I trust that you will stay a few days at least. (...)
    Meanwhile my school is acting three plays (by me) next week for the local hospital. I am acting most of the evening. At the moment life is very, very full of rehearsals and costumes.
    Many thanks for letter.
    Sincerely, A. S. Neill

P. S. You will tell me all about your school when you come.

[1] Russell was visiting a number of schools before setting up his own, Beacon Hill.

To Bertrand Russell

Lyme Regis, Dorset
Dear Russell   *26 May 1927*
    (...) We have taken the Suffolk house, and unexpected friends are offering to lend us money. I'm afraid that I may not sell you the car after

all. Lord Sandwich comes next week to see the school; he brings Bertram Hawker with him.

I have it on my conscience that I docked you of that maths lesson. Especially so when I learnt that Mrs Barton was annoyed at me for not bringing you in. It transpires that she had a specially brilliant lesson that day. I think therefore that you'll have to come back again ... bringing your wife this time. (...)

Yours, Neill

To Seishi Shimoda

My dear Shimoda   *15 July 1930*

Many thanks indeed for the volume of your translation of *The Problem Child*. Unfortunately I shall never be able to read it! The only things in it I understand are the photos, which take me back to days that seem so long ago. We are as you saw us, only a bigger family, too big now. My wife and I are overworked all the time. There are 44 pupils now and the house is full in every corner. (...)

The man you mention, Hadano, wrote me wanting to translate *The Problem Child*, and I told him that you had the matter in hand. It is very gratifying to me to feel that you have translated my book. You have my full permission to translate any other books of mine. (...)

With all best wishes.

Yours, Neill

P. S. Mrs Neill sends her best regards.

To Agnes Parker

29 September 1931

Sorry, Agnes, but we have enough on the women staff side at the moment. But can you help me find someone who will take on the crafts? Jewellery, repoussé, woodwork, but especially metal work and also pottery. I suppose you can tell me of someone ... but just you wait ere ye hear the rest ... times are hard and cash weak and all we can offer is board and lodging and maybe enough to buy the daily dose of Woodbine. Try like a guid sowl. (...)

You won't get abroad, Gord pity you, so come and see us on your travels. We had a month at Mentone and it was rare.

Love to you both, Neill

To W. B. Curry

Dear Curry   *29 December 1932*
    Miss Buckworth? Blowed if I remember her. Fact is that crowds of
people come round asking for jobs, and to get rid of them I say sweetly,
Now there is Dartington Hall. What about applying there? Sometimes
I send them on to Beacon Hill; most of them I send to hell, but not audi-
bly. All the same I suppose Miss B was one of those I felt sorry for, for
there are a few genuine cases who want the new ideas and hate the school
in which they teach.
    I'm not quite sure yet about coming to see you. My wife is feeling done
up and in need of bracing air. She's at the moment suggesting that I motor
her to the Yorkshire moors if the weather permits. But if I can persuade
her that Devon might be as bracing, though it ain't, I'll manage to work
in at least a short visit.
    All the best, Neill

To W. B. Curry

Dear old Curry   *17 June 1933*
    Information wanted. Can you find out what the electric washing-up
affairs in the kitchen cost, and who sells them? I may be able to rise to
them with the help of God and the Devil. And about Leach the potter.
Is your offer to lend him to me for a week or two still open, or has he
gone back to Cornwall?
    All well here, full to the brim. Let me know when N— begins to have
a grouse: nice kid, but always wants to have a grouse.
    All the best, and kind remembrances to your nice wife, Neill

To W. B. Curry

Dear Curry   *23 June 1933*
    Thanks muchly, I'll have a look at the machines when I go to town.
Though I am willing to be shot at dawn for you, don't ask me to come
to that meeting. As for Leach, I quite understand the difficulty, and will
wait until he is less busy.
    Am full to the neck with visitors daily and am a dry sponge now.
    My thanks to Miss Nicholls for her valuable information, I only wish
I didn't have to spend sleepless nights counting up how I can buy the

blamed things. Being poor may form a character, but I have come to the age when being poor begins to make my character worse.

    All the best, Neill

To W. B. Curry

Dear Curry   *26 July 1933*
    Dorothy Hall came two days ago as a paying guest. Never saw her before; seems capable and nice, and is possibly worth a trial. (...)
    I haven't risen to the washing machines yet. Why the hell should Dartington Hall have more than it needs, and Summerhill has to go on living on wish fulfilments? In heaven I'll have a golden harp, while you and Dorothy[1] will be in hell playing mouth organs.

    All the best, Neill

[1] Dorothy Elmhirst.

To W. B. Curry

Dear Curry   *18 March 1934*
    (...) I think I may go to Berlin at Easter. In any case, it isn't good for my soul to visit Dartington Hall, it makes me too hatefully envious of material things that I need so badly here. My present prevailing fantasy is that I find a thousand pounds to build a sanatorium – we have chicken pox now. With the dollar down the Elmhirsts will possibly have to draw their horns in too. However, if I don't go abroad, I may come down in my Hillman Straight 8, 1932 model, £75. If you ever want a new second-hand car come here to my man Watson in Aldeburgh.

    All the best to you both, Neill

P.S. Do you love me? If so, for Christ's sake persuade the Elmhirsts to keep on P—in any capacity. M—owes me about £150; if P—leaves Dartington Hall I'm in the soup. But I don't expect you can do anything.

To W. B. Curry

Dear Curry   *19 January 1935*
    Goodman[1] was, without punning, a good man. Kids liked his teaching, and I liked his energetic part in community life. Very Left in politics,

but that toned down after a time. I mean he ceased to show it in school life. He would bring energy and push with him if you do try him out. (...)

Afraid little chance of my coming south; the kids have just come back. Do you know the P—'s address? I seem to be one of half England that wants it badly. My share £219.

Yours, Neill

[1] Richard Goodman.

To W. B. Curry

Dear Curry   *5 November 1938*

If you got as many life histories as I do, you'd want to charge pounds. Lady last week came: Mr Neill, I'm sure that the story of my life would interest you as a psychologist. Can even a Scot listen to fools like that for nix? Sad thing is that when I chip in about the fee they change their minds about telling me their stories. I've made two guineas in a year on this sideline.

The O'Malleys have been here for ten days or so. They say so very little. But Curry, is it you who has condemned the wretches to go visiting schools? That's a hell of a life. If you give your staff leave of absence, make it conditional on their giving you a vow that they will forget all about schools for a year. To their eternal damnation, the O'Malleys seem to like visiting schools.

Know of any houses to let? If war comes i.e. when it comes, I'll have to move from here. Unfortunately no one will ever buy this house, else I'd sell it now. Dora Russell offered us space during the crisis, but when Mr Chamberlain does his next double-cross I want to get away just before it. What a bloody world! I feel depressed, for with a castrated Labour Party, I see nothing ahead of us but some sort of Fascism.

Thine, Neill

To Claude Ferrière

Dear Claude   *9 October 1939*

Sorry to be so long in writing. I spent a nasty three weeks in Ipswich having my piles cut out, and then came home and fell off a chair and broke a bone in my foot. Now we are all back to work. (...) We have a works plan and the kids are doing the garden nobly. Bunny[1] has a gang that works four hours a day. The *Stimmung* [atmosphere] of the school is better than it has been for years. I used to fear the days when we should black out, thinking that problem children would show lights. They use their black-out so well that the authorities of the town say that the school is the best black-out in the town.

We miss all our continental students, especially our Scandinavian girls. Nina[2] writes long letters to us, difficult to answer, for in war time no one knows what the censor thinks dangerous or not. (...) P— continues with her Private Lessons, but somehow psychology does not interest me as much as it did; the larger issues make dealing with individual problems seem insignificant. (...)

What a pity the war interfered with your plans to return to us. Later – but who knows what will come? A new world for all of us, for things are moving at a stupendous pace now.

I expect Pat Avery gives you the news of the school. I am a bad news giver.

All the best.

Yours, Neill

[1] Gordon Leff.   [2] Nina Kai Nielson.

To W. B. Curry

Dear Curry   *15 May 1940*

I've no intention of leaving here, but there may come a time when the authorities evacuate all kids from the area of the East Coast. I wonder if you know of any vacant place round about Devon where we might retire to at a pinch? As I say, I don't want to leave here, especially after spending about £400 on steel dugouts, and after slaving to make the large garden productive. We are within two hundred yards of a munitions factory, but that doesn't worry us much so far.

I wonder how the war has affected you? I find it most difficult to carry on analysis, and am happiest in the garden or workshop or teaching maths, which I now do owing to shortage of staff. But I love maths anyway. (...)

What of the future? Rather blackish for progressive teachers at the moment. Almost sorry now I refused to start in Johannesburg, when some rich boys offered to finance a school. Almost.

All the best, Neill

To W. B. Curry

Ffestiniog, North Wales

Dear Curry   *July 1940*

Your letter reached me after many days' delay, owing to my coming here suddenly. Alas, I can't go on with the overseas idea now.[1] I have saddled myself with a hell of a house, but a grand scenery. Only house I could get, being too late in seeking, needs about £400 spent on it to make it water-tight. I'm getting it on a nominal rent on six years' lease, rather three with renewable option. Kids returning next week, though we are far from ready for them. But it feels safe here after sleepless nights in Leiston. Never see a plane, food very dear and scarce, coal a ransom. God knows how I shall weather it financially. And the Welsh sabbath is to be hell. The pubs close at nine, no Sunday openings, Sunday golf and tennis barred by local opinion. But we'll flout it I fear. No tradesman wants to do a job, always next week or a month hence. (...)

So, laddie, I'll have to stay here and risk that concentration camp if Right triumphs over Left. Thanks for your proferred help. Let me know how you stand now that overseas evacuation is stopped.

All the best, Neill

[1] Neill had been contemplating evacuation to the USA.

To W. B. Curry

Ffestiniog, North Wales

Dear Curry   *9 November 1940*

(...) So you didn't go to USA. Lucky to remain in Dartington Hall. Here I feel miserable. House smaller than in Leiston, and I have to refuse kids daily. Rain always. Welsh sabbath, Welsh tradesmen, will never come to do a job. House needing many repairs, central heating not working, hot-water boiler a dud, and no one will come to mend them. We had two months without electric light. Fruit almost unobtainable, coal and coke only rumours.

Curry, I'll give you Wales freely and willingly. It stifles me altogether, and Summerhill is now a military house. (...) I'm afraid I live from day to day now, thinking not of the morrow. Even my psychological work is almost in abeyance, for I have to mend doors, stoke fires, teach maths, cater, and worst of all interview all the damned officials who still think in peace terms. Medical Officer of Health, an old man, objects because I'm overcrowded, and evaded my query what he was to do about the thousands of kids who have bad air in shelters and tubes. My secretary[1] remained behind to do his work as Communist Party councillor, and I have to do it all for myself. When the village bobby came lately to lodge a complaint by mourners that my kids had watched a funeral without apparently looking funereal, the camel's back nearly broke.

Sorry to be so miserable a correspondent, but it has rained daily since I came here a thousand years ago, I'm out of fags, and, oh well, what really gets me sore tonight is our kitchen man we've had for ten years was called up today and I hate to get a local into the house. (...)

All the best, Neill

[1] Paxton Chadwick.

To Lilian Morgans

Ffestiniog, North Wales
Dear Lilian   *23 October 1942*

'Why the hell don't I write?' I'll tell you. Life has gone all wrong lately. A wife who has had a stroke and is nearly mental and very sad and difficult to live with. I am trying to get her away to a Home. A staff that is new and largely non-Summerhillian ... mostly pacifists whose main interest is not S'hill. With no woman in authority now all the women on the staff trying to get their own way. Lack of good teachers makes the kids discontented, added to the awful rains we have all the time so that they can't get out. Result was I had to go to Edinburgh summer hols to do a 'cure' for my kidneys.[1] My book stopped short[2] and I can't restart it, just worn out with worries and work and hating the wet of Wales. So, if I had written, it would have been a dirge like this one. I long to get away for a bit among other folks, stimulating folks. I long for ugly Leiston daily, but see a long war with revolutions at the end, and fear often that I'll never get back.

Sorry to be so doleful. I've just been called in by the cook to row the maids, and it ain't my job and I hate it and to hell with them all. But the kids are grand and my only happiness is with them. (...)

Don't know when I'll be back east. Perhaps New Year if I can get Mrs Lins[3] fixed up somewhere. Sorry to be so uninspiring and dull. Write and cheer me up. Mostly my life has been spent writing to people who wanted cheering up. Queer to have it the other way round now.

All the best, Neill

[1] At the Kingston Clinic, founded by J. C. Thomson, which Neill visited regularly from 1929 onwards.
[2] *Hearts not Heads in the School*.
[3] Neill's first wife.

To Lilian Morgans

Ffestiniog, North Wales
11 December 1942

Dear Lilian

My last letter wasn't cheerful, and, having just had three weeks of flu, I may not make this one any better. You won't find me cheerful till the day when I once more live in Leiston, I fear. (...)

It is end of term, and kids rehearse their own written plays, a little sadly, for here we have no audience barring a few dull Welsh locals. In Leiston we never had locals; lots of parents etc came from town. Also our plays have a little too much irreverence and obscenity for locals.

My next visit to Suffolk shd be Easter. (...) I can't say I enjoy visiting the old place and seeing its misery and forlornhood. Like seeing it in a dream, for it now has all the intangibility of the dream world ... a never-never land, I sometimes think. How long O Lord? Months of death to thousands ... makes one feel that worries about houses and places are so small and petty. And one idealises a bit. To me the thought of Saxmundham Street is warm and inviting, but I know I have been there often without having any feeling of comfort or joy. What annoys me is that we might have been safe at Leiston all these years.

A selfish letter. I don't even ask how you are or what you are thinking. That's as should be. But I feel that when I come east a chat at a cosy fire (without Watson,[1] who talks too much) would say more than a year's letters. I must have a complex about letters. In the past three days I have written about 50, most of them unwittingly, for they did not interest me. Secretary and office-boy work. Oh, to live only creatively, writing plays, novels, books, painting, making things of wood and metal. Here we are so out of things, seldom see a film, for it means queueing for buses, usually in heavy rain. Visitors can't come. One gets tired of the faces of the staff; one exhausts one's and their conversation. And it doesn't help to know that millions are suffering *real* hardships and pain and misery. I'd die I think if I hadn't the hope of a rebirth of civilisation in my time.

But first we have to face the class war that will follow this one (a hint of it in the Darlan affair[2] ... set up pink Fascists in case Europe goes red). Still, the future is potentially grand, and I wish I were 19 instead of 59 (but then they'd make me a sodjer).

Not much of a letter, but at least a sincere one. Reply with as egocentric a letter as you like.

Yours sincerely, Neill

[1] A second-hand car dealer with whom Neill played golf.
[2] Britain and America's alliance with Admiral Darlan, a French Fascist, created an uproar in England.

To Lilian Morgans

Ffestiniog, North Wales
Dear Lilian   *30 March 1943*

(...) I have been away a lot looking at bigger houses in England, but in vain. If you hear of anything a bit inland from Leiston do tell me. I have had much trouble too about my wife, and at last have got her in a Home about 34 miles off, where she is unhappy, but what can I do? She was too ill to live with 75 kids. (...)

I have too many dull letters waiting to be written (this week I have had to tell ten parents I had no room) ... Leiston and Saxmundham sound paradise to me now, but I know that if I come back for good they will once more become wee dull places, with windy station platforms and meagre shops. Paradise is only the creation of misery, a mirage.

Yours, Neill

To W. B. Curry

Ffestiniog, North Wales
Dear Curry   *May 1943*

Enclosed is the only thing I've had lately. Like you I found the staff business hopeless. I've had a run of pacifists who are no good at all, all negative, in the clouds, castrated and wanting to tell me how to run the school on Jesus lines. I miss the contacts of old. The isolation here is bloody, the sardinity of the house awful. I have a hundred on the waiting list now, but can't find a bigger house. Sometimes despair of returning to Leiston, seeing the peace as a signal for global class wars, with the fascism rising here.

Bad signs now, anti-semitism, Winston's 'Hold what we have', new attacks on the *Daily Worker*, Polish hitch, can't feel optimistic about our little private schools in a looming super-bureaucracy. Got a book in the press on this topic,[1] fighting the Communist Party, Trades Union Congress, National Union of Techers, planning in externals only.

Wish we could meet again: we have the mutual effect of cheering each other up even when the pubs are closed. (...)

Sorry old man to be so unhelpful about staff, but if anything comes in I'll send it to you at once.

Yours, Neill

[1] *Hearts not Heads in the School.*

To W. B. Curry

Ffestiniog, North Wales
12 July 1943

Dear Curry

If you need an art teacher, I have two, and must economise. Piggy Pilling, 21 or so, has been here a term. Pleasant girl, with subsidiary subject voice production and dramatics. At a guess she is virginal. Kids like her and she works well. Can't honestly say she would set Dartington on fire. She succeeded a girl here who was a sculptor and saw in bulk, and the kids say that Piggy sees in line. She's sad at leaving, but I must reduce staff. Thirteen for 75 kids in wartime, including a few refugees who can't hammer in a nail. I think of having an ad: 'History master wanted, must be expert bogs clearer, stoker, plumber etc.' And how to get out of this bloody Wales. Don't you know of any houses to accommodate my waiting list of a hundred or more?

All the best, Neill

P.S. Woman visitor lately: Mr Neill, your school is modelled on Dartington Hall, I hear! I sometimes get fan mail: You are a follower of Ethel Mannin. I think they mean the wrong type of follower. My latest visitor, a man, said: Do you think Freud is a good psychologist? By the way, Dent of the *Times Ed* is a good man, trying his best to wake up blimps. I never thought I'd appear on the *Supp*'s pages, but it's hopeless, no replies. I think of writing a letter alleging that Froebel ate raw artichokes for breakfast. Quite sure there would be a hell of a lot of replies.

To James Stern

Ffestiniog, North Wales
14 July 1944

Dear Jimmy

It was fine of you to send me so wonderful a letter. Yes, although Mrs Lins has been an invalid since we evacuated here in 1940, her passing was a cruel cut of fate even if it was a relief to see her out of her misery, for her arms and speech were paralysed and her mind gradually went. S'hill can never be the same, yet it must carry on and will as long as I can keep it going. I can never replace her with any woman who had her *Weltkentniss* [knowledge of the world], her broad culture that could entertain a dustman or a genius. (...)

I seldom see Ethel now.[1] Once in a blue moon ... or should I say in a blue funk these days in town? She is chairing for me at a lecture in town in Sept. I'll give her your message. She is still the same old dear Ethel. We have agreed to differ about her pacifism.

I long to get back to Leiston to a dry climate and a county where the pubs don't close at nine as here. *Aber* [but] when?

Well, Jimmy, your letter touched me a hell of a lot, its sincerity and kindness. Bless you for it. And when I come to USA after the war on a lecture tour I hope to meet you.

All the best.

Yours, Neill

[1] Ethel Mannin.

To Eva and Solomon Leff

Dear Leffs　　　　　　　　　　　　　　　　*12 December 1945*

Thank you a lot for your letters. It is very sweet to have appreciation from parents; they overbalance the father of A—, who attributed her improvement in S'hill to her keeping rabbits.

Yes, 25 years is a long innings, but I hope for a longer one. The celebrations have their sad side, for here am I taking the credit and good wishes alone for all the magnificent work Mrs Lins did. That is the sad part. (...)

Your three brats had the luck to have a free home. Others in S'hill never had. I don't know any family that would be entertained by Herr Louis's dinner-table yarns anyway.[1]

Now I must sit down and write a play for Saturday night. So, just a short thank you for being kind and generous and loyal.

Yours, Neill

[1] Louis Leff, the youngest of the three Leff children.

To W. B. Curry

Dear Curry　　　　　　　　　　　　　　　　*6 October 1946*

If you at any time need a piano teacher let me know. I have a Viennese lady of 45 or so, had her seven years, but as only a few pupils take music lessons now, I can't afford to keep her on, but would dread to tell her to move, seeing I brought her myself from Norway in 1939.[1] She's a brilliant player and has some special method of teaching that strikes oil. I hear our kids playing Chopin with more or less success. She seems to cut out all finger exercises. Just thought I would approach you first, as she is Summerhillised, and would hate to go to any ordinary progressive school with morals and uplift. (...)

Yours, Neill

[1] Erna Gal.

Daily Life 57

To Angus Murray

Lieber Angus   *14 January 1949*
    Vielen Dank für Deinen Brief [many thanks for your letter] and for
the good wishes for 49. I was lecturing in USA and was away from beginning of August till mid November and had a wonderful reception, lecturing. They haven't anything so free as S'hill there. I found publishers for
my books and the new one[1] is to appear in New York this month. (...)
    Sorry I couldn't do a thing for your Austrian friend. Fact is that the
school is now losing money every day, thanks to high prices and moder-
ate fees, and I can never afford even one visitor who hasn't *das Geld* to
pay. Other schools are similar, and in any case I never recommend anyone to go to another school, for I don't believe in schools, see? (...)
    All the best for 49.
    Yours as ever, Neill

[1] *The Problem Family.*

To Antoine Obert

Dear Toni   *9 October 1949*
    Gott, I see your letter is dated July. Tut, tut.
    You ask if I could do with you here. *Mein Gott ja.* We haven't had any-
one in the workshop since Parsons left in 1938 or 9. The big upstairs shop
is empty save for the old lathe, and I have to let kids work in mine. Luckily I've gone off workshops, but it pains me to go in to mend a lock and
find the tools all gone and broken. (...)
    We hope to come out again in August next summer, but all depends
on my getting lectures enough to pay my exs. I found USA behind on
kid nature, and my message seemed to stagger a lot of people, which it
often doesn't here and in Scandinavia. (...)
    My best to Eve and yourself.
    Yours, Neill

To James and Tania Stern

Dear Both   *22 March 1950*
    Mein Gott, you do sound depressed about USA ... just as Ena[1] and
I have been talking of coming over for good if S'hill finances don't start
to make ends meet. We realise that we saw the country through rose-
coloured glasses ... feted, welcomed, delighted to see shops where we

could buy what we wanted. I recall my first trip abroad, to Holland. I thought to myself: 'In this landscape, with its coloured barges and cheap cigars and plethora of butter and cheese, every native must be happy.'[2] So to a lesser extent did I feel in USA; why even the Babbitts I picked up, or rather who picked me up in pullmans, had a touch of that glamour that tints the unknown. Damon Runyan and his romantic train of crooks and pimps on the one side; Damon Runyan dying wretchedly of cancer of the throat on the other. Every promised country has a touch of the promised land, of Arcadia. When the other night I heard *echt* Viennese spoken in the film *The Third Man*, I felt a nostalgic thrill.

I take it you both have got over all this nonsense and are seeing USA without glasses of any kind. I can understand the difficulty of making a living in writing there. As Wilde put it: England and America have everything in common except language.[3] We do talk a different language, a fact I soon discovered when lecturing … damn em, they seldom twigged my jokes. (…)

Why not teach? Set up a school for teaching prospective film stars to speak English, but of course don't call it English. Get Auden to be a partner and his name will maybe bring in scholars.[4] We've just got two American kids of 6 and 10 and the air is full of beths and cendies. I recall the shock I got in New York when I recommended seeing the film *The Day of Wrath* (Danish). 'Oh,' said the young lady, 'The Day of Wreth!' (…)

The school has been losing about £800 p.a. for the last umpteen years and the outlook ain't so good. Part of me, and of Ena, wants it to fail so that we can accept the offer to start a self-regulation school for infants in USA. Same offer comes from Australia, which would be hell I fancy.

Alles gutes, Neill

[1] Ena Wood, Neill's second wife whom he had married in 1945.
[2] On 10 November 1920 Neill sent a postcard from Rotterdam to his fiancée Jessie Irving: 'Glorious place, Holland. Cigars a penny each. I love the place, so peaceful. ASN.'
[3] It was in fact Shaw who said 'England and America are two countries separated by the same language.'
[4] Neill had met Auden over lunch in James Stern's apartment in New York.

To W. B. Curry

Dear Curry   *30 June 1952*
Low-down required. E. Martin applies for an advertised job here. Seems to have had a varied teaching career, ship's purser etc. Does not

give his age, but best to enclose his letter. Be a good pal and tell me if the guy is any b.g. as a teacher and a person.

Hear about you sometimes from the women teacher students who make my weekends a bore. They all ask the same questions. Means me giving them a £25 lecture each weekend for nought. And if you think I'm overvaluing my services damn you, I got £30 for one hour's lecture in Sweden last summer. My usual question when one says she's been to Dartington is, Did you see Curry? Usual answer is, No, he was away at the time. Just give me the dope on how to do this.

Rumour you have been ill; hope it isn't true.

All the best, Neill

To Seishi Shimoda

My dear friend Shimoda   *9 November 1956*

(...) I wonder how you got on at the Psychoanalytic Society meeting, for in this country no Freudian approves of me or my work, and at any conference my name would not be mentioned. They really do not believe in freedom for children.

It has been a regret to me that I could not come to Japan to lecture. I have much difficulty in getting staff and did not like leaving the school even for a few months because I simply did not like the idea of others, new teachers, who did not know enough of our methods to carry on the work. Also, to be honest, I did fear the long journey and the meeting many new people. I was invited to lecture in Israel last month but had to refuse because if I went no one in the school could teach mathematics. In any case, the war situation would have made a visit impossible. (...)

I have a bad conscience about having many letters from Japan that I have not answered. If I asked you to put an advertisement in a Japanese paper or educational journal, thanking my many correspondents and apologising for not being able to answer them all, could I pay for it out of my frozen money[1] in the Tokyo and Shanghai Banking Corporation? (...)

I hope your health is better than it was. All good wishes.

Yours sincerely, A. S. Neill

[1] Royalties from the translations of his books into Japanese.

To Constance Butler

Dear Constance   *10 June 1957*
(...) Tell you about the HMIs when you come. In a nutshell they say
our teachers aren't good enough. True, and can't be when we can't pay
em nearly enough; only duds and neurotics seem to want to come for a
small salary these days. HMI standard of education is neat exercise books
etc. Happiness of kids escapes them. (...)
     Be seein' yuh, Neill

To Richard Tolson

                                                  30 August 1957
Dear Richard ... Dick ... or whatever the kids will call you here.
     Fine. Term begins Thursday 26 September, but you shd come a day
or two before to settle in. Can I say to the Inspectors, 'I know we are short
of staff, but I'm having a Geography expert next term?' Just tell me again
what you can teach, I think you said history and Englais ... Of course
it is all trial and error, but as long as both sides know this it is okay. S'hill
is an easy place to live in ... in many ways, difficult in one or two...
     Yours, Neill

To Constance Butler

Dear Constance   *13 September 1957*
(...) The dull dog has played some golf lately and has worked like
hell answering letters that shd have been answered years ago. Usually I
begin: 'Dear Mr X, I had your letter the other year ...' (...) I may be dull
but not nearly so dull as most of my correspondents ... one lady from
Australia has written me 18 pages, mostly about her life story. Usual style
... Dear Mr Neill, I have read your last book with much pleasure. I am
sure you will be interested in my life, for we seem to think the same way.
I was born in —.
     Yours not so dully, Neill

To John Aitkenhead

Dear John   *5 March 1958*
(...) Dunno if you saw a smear letter in the *Observer*. Chap unqual-

ified I took for science, the only applicant after an advt. Turned out to be unbalanced, cuffed kids' ears and hardly one wd go to his lessons. I sacked him. He has come down the last two weekends and eaten our food gratis. Dunno what to do about him, dangerous I think, kids say he nearly strangled a boy of 12 with a rope ... he said in fun, but I am in a hole. If I ban him from the place he may murder one of the kids or me or anyone, he is just that sick mentally. I am not replying to his letter; why the *Observer* published it beats me, for it belongs to the gutter Sunday press region.

Keep your pecker up. In a way I look forward to inspection myself, but I am in a bad patch at the moment, many new boys from 14 to 17 living out complexes and doing no lessons all day, only destruction. I am so tired of watching the crooks and gangsters living out their hates, but to make it pay I have to take any damn kid offered me. (...)

Love to the family and Bill and Käte.[1]

Neill

[1] Bill and Käte MacKinnon.

To Richard Tolson

Dear Richard   *16 October 1968*

No, no staff yet. My ads brout me abt 20 replies, but only five were possible (rest included two priests, three disciplinarians etc). I wrote the five last week telling the screw [wages]. Only one has replied, and he isn't the best for he is a mod language chap. I have been taking Eng myself with III and the new IV (Jenny etc), finding it difficult after so long a period of rust. I've dodged the set books as much as I could decently do, for I have no appreciation of 12th Night ... when today I criticised the dullness of Shakie's clowns Amarilla said: 'You seem to be trying to make us hate the play.' And Mr Hardy's poems I cannot rhapsodise about. Haven't tackled Mr Davies yet, only to compare a long paragraph of, to me, ordinary prose with a par from the Van Goghish word painting of *The House with the Green Shutters.*[1] Teaching every period plus an hour or more with Mervyn's maths at night, I feel what I'll be in a day's time, 75 and some. (...)

Got a golden labrador puppy and feel I ought to follow Dan Leno's example; he told of his dog Carpenter, and a stooge in the theatre asked why the name. 'Cos he does odd jobs about the house.'

All news when I see you.

Neill

P. S. Our love to you both ... but qualified, cos I haven't really forgiven you for leaving.

[1] George Douglas Brown's novel, published in 1901, remained Neill's favourite book.

To Evelyn Williams

Evie, me dear   *29 October 1958*
   I couldn't get to your opening day but looked in a week ago. The ground floor was just beyond me. Chappie in charge pointed out with some rhapsody the merits of The Kiss, but, alas, I still couldn't see the bloody kiss anywhere. You're beyond me, cheeild, but upstairs I got on much better, The Moving Crowd especially appealed to me. I think I missed colour.
   Dunno if our Evelyn is a genius or just dotty. Time will show, meaning that if someone bids half a million for a picture in 2058 we'll know for certain.
   I rashly told the gallery guy that I had taught you. He became most embarrassingly delighted and, so that all the gallery could hear, introduced me to a coloured lady as 'the greatest schoolmaster on earth'. I think he had some idea that your show was the result of yr having been to S'hill ... poor school, what it has to suffer!
   I looked in vain for some notice in the Sunday press and the *New Statesman*.
   Oh, my doctor brother, now 78, has had five paintings accepted by galleries. He sent me a catalogue of the Walker Gallery list with one picture in it. His is abstract placings of rectangles etc which also are beyond my grasp.
   I do hope you managed to sell a few, old thing.
   Love and blessings (non–religious ones), Neill

To Constance Butler

Dear Constance   *4 December 1958*
   Ta for *Big Sur*.[1] I go to Cheltenham Tuesday and it shd last the journey there and back. I'll return it safely along with the Perlès book.[2] (...)
   Cold, damp, depressing. Loads of worries to carry ... gardener who loafs all day one of them. I wish I were a real he-man tough guy who

cd boss people, but if I were I guess it wdn't be S'hill.
   Cheerio, Neill

[1] *Big Sur and the Oranges of Hieronymous Bosch*, by Henry Miller.
[2] *My Friend Henry Miller*, by Alfred Perlès.

To John Aitkenhead

Dear John   *29 January 1959*
   (...) S'hill Socy has raised about £800 and I'm not optimistic about
its getting much more. Lots of old women leave their cash to be given
to charitable and educational purposes, and my Socy has a list and is applying, so far without result; my fear is that such sums will be given only
to schools with religion, and if I were controlling one I'd be inclined to
say: Why the hell shd we help middle-class parents pay their boarding
school fees?
   I'd like to hear more about the Min of Ed demands, for on 17th March
we are to be inspected by Lady Helen Asquith, HMI, who did Burgess
Hill and, altho the Min call her The Dragon, I hear she was quite reason-
able there. I've put in the smokescreen doors they wanted and I think my
duffies [toilets] are good enough. But you and I are feeneshed so far as
freedom is concerned; we'll never be free again. The whole world is moving away from freedom and the bleak future looks like Orwellism. (...)
   Love to you all, including Morag, and the Jaguar owners to be, curse
the plutocrats. Neill

To Richard and Rosalind Tolson

Dear Both   *5 September 1959*
   (...) Thirteen kids left and only so far four coming in and a hell of
a red figure in the bank. I'm giving up the car and must do without a gardener all winter ... Felix gets over £400 p.a. and we have to buy loads
of greens in addition. Reducing staff also. Not taking on a science man.
I guess we shd cease preparing for GCE. Eight teachers for less than 30
kids is just lunacy. I fear we'll have to take maladjusted to keep the place
alive. If our bad payers paid we'd almost balance. (...)
   Love to both, Neill

To John Aitkenhead

Dear John   7 *November 1960*
    (...) We are down to 24 kids now. They now leave and go to you
or New Sherwood ... three going there next term. I began in England
in 1924 with five kids, and it looks as if I'll end with five. The causes?
Mixed I fancy. Some hesitate cos of my age ... what if I die when the kid
has been here only for two years? Some say that. Also, more important,
parents write me and say if I make lessons compulsory for the mornings
they will send their brats. I can't compromise abt that; it wd wreck the
whole basis. (...)
    Love to you all, Neill

To Constance Butler

Dear Constance   *3 September 1961*
    (...) I cd meet Henry[1] in town but I think he'll want to see S'hill,
even if empty. (...)
    In my downish moods I wonder if there will be a school to open on
the 28th, but I carry on mending beds and blacking blackboards ... the
black paint not being the best for raising optimism.
    It will be good to meet Henry.
    The best, Neill

[1] Henry Miller.

To Constance Butler

Dear Constance   *28 June 1962*
    (...) How are you? How the pains and privations? I dunno if my pal
Bill Curry of Dartington Hall didn't take the best way; he had diabetes,
and last time I met him he got tight on whisky, some weeks ago. Now
he is dead, run down by a van, possibly in his cups. I liked him a lot. But
my fissures aren't at the stage when I want to eat all the constipating grub
on the market and die a blissful full-abdomened death. (...)
    Love and blessings and to Bill, Neill

P.S. Hell, a car just driven up. More bloody visitors. I'm to hide in my
office but some kid will say: Neill? I saw him go into the office.

To Josie Caryll

Dear Josie   *20 October 1963*
    I have a nasty confession to make. When I spoke in the hall I completely forgot about the cheque, the car, the subscriptions, the people who had organised it all.[1] Not entirely the whisky; deeper, I think it was a way of hiding my emotions meeting so many dear and warm old friends. And my ill-timed jokes must have been another cover-up for my fear of getting sentimental. (...) So, my dear, what should have been for ever a memorable evening for me has become one in which I failed to meet the situation. Yet it was grand to see so many old *kent* [familiar] faces, but bad to have only a minute or two to talk to each one. (...)
    Ay, I forgot to mention the money and car because all the faces meant more to me, I suppose.
    Thank you and David for everything. And the brat too.
    Love, Neill

[1] The occasion was Neill's eightieth birthday party, held in London.

To John Aitkenhead

Dear John   *6 June 1966*
    M— is a damned good teacher, but I have the feeling that she is at the root of the anti-social behaviour of all the small kids. They obey no laws. I think I told you that when P— was chucked out of a meeting for being a nuisance he ran to her and she wouldn't put him out. She is anarchical and the kids must feel it. She never says no to a kid, lets em do anything they like, e.g. take out school blankets to make tents when Ena says that this must not be done. (...)
    Love to you both, Neill

To John Aitkenhead

Dear John   *9 November 1966*
    P— is a good teacher. Socially a mystery. In his cups he is reported to have said: 'I don't believe in freedom for kids and only came here cos I want to go to USA and S'hill is an Open Sesame.' He began by resenting Ena ... 'I refuse to be under petticoat government.' Kids seem to like his lessons, but he, alas, isn't the sort of guy who will see a blocked drain and do anything about it. The kids say he is a homo. I hate the idea that

he is here for his own bloody ends and not to support us all the way. Sexually the big girls see him as part of the furniture.

I may have misjudged him but he never talks to me, only about getting books, chalk etc. We'll see how he develops. (...)

Love to Morag and self and Bill and Käte, Neill

To Lucy Francis

Lucy dear   *16 November 1966*

I've told this woman we are full up, which we are, and suggested she apply to you.

L— has made a lovely shop but apart from that he is a difficult chap to live with, an old wife, fussy, over tidy, looking for slights all the time. Reminds me of P—'s inferiority complex, always on the defensive. Kids like his lessons but don't find any emotional contact with him. Touchy if Ena or anyone asks him to do a job ... mend a door etc. His philosophy seems to be ... I came here to teach, not to be an odd job man. Worrying. I guess you found him much the same. He seems to resent being asked to do anything by a woman. He is so far okay with me, but I dunno for how long. Oh hell, what I have suffered from staff in my day ... you also I guess.

Love, Neill

To Ben Morris

Dear Ben   *16 November 1966*

(...) Yes, we shd meet again, but at 83 Bristol is a hell of a step away. I hardly ever go lecturing now, and almost regret that I go to Manchester to a training college next week ... I'm not telling them that I took it on to get my fare paid to see an old pupil there who is sick.[1] I can't get over thinking that I am still poor, but I have forced myself to travel first every time now. (...)

You are a real old friend ... I have very few Scottish ones left since Edwin Muir died. I visit his widow Willa when I go to town, a poor cripple with arthritis. She is doing a life of him.

Aweel, back to the bloody visitors and fan mail.

As ever, Neill

[1] Margaret Ritchie.

To John Aitkenhead

Dear John   *19 November 1966*
(…) Just had a dust up with the staff. A section including friend P—
is up agin us, but when asked why they shut up. They seem to want more
control. One woman said to Ena: 'Why did you buy a Bendix washer
without consulting the staff?' But ye ken what it is like. I dunno P—'s
attitude, but in his cups he spouts a theory of psychology which seems
to have the basis that women are no good. Why do our schools attract
so many unbalanced neurotics? It makes it a *sehr fecht* [tough fight].
    All the best. Sorry you are having trouble with new kids and new staff.
Myself I think I'd welcome a completely new staff.
    Neill

To Lucy Francis

Lucy my dear   *22 February 1967*
(…) L— leaves this weekend. Bitter. He wanted to run a disciplined
shop … Stop talking and get on with your work … and gradually his shop
has got empty. Odd thing is that since he gave me notice he has become
human, joking, laughing. He must be glad to be free of us. On my side
also. I couldn't ask him to mend a door panel for he said he wouldn't be
an odd job man. A poor unhappy difficult chap with a big chip on his
shoulder. (…)
    Love to self and Sally, Neill

To John Aitkenhead

Dear John   *5 June 1967*
(…) I'll have to get rid of P—. He gets tight nearly every day and
when so storms agst S'hill. He is a very sick guy … thinks that he will
get me to sack Peter Wood … Ena's son. I told him he didn't fit in, hoping
he wd resign, but he apparently isn't going to. At my age I can't take
worry as I used to.
    Love to Morag, Neill

To John Aitkenhead

Dear John   *20 June 1967*
   After days of tiresome wrangling and mutual recriminations, P—handed in his resignation. M— calling me unjust etc. I feel limp. I hate playing God; I see the other guy's viewpoint and feel sorry for him. He is a sick man, Wilde's man who must kill what he loves. (...)
   Love to you both, bless you ... I'm under the influence of Billy Graham. That anti-life face of his, power, not a spark of love in it. Neill

To Carlos Kruytbosch

Dear Carlos   *20 July 1967*
   I am needing a teacher of maths and chemistry and it is almost impossible to get one here; they get double salary in business firms. I often get applications from USA, but the snag is that I can't see them before they come. Now if you would shove up on the notice board an advert saying apply to you, I would trust your judgement of any guy applying. I want if possible a guy not a guyess, for we must keep the sex staff balance straight. I couldn't afford to pay a fare over and to an American the screw is nothing ... £35 gross a month with board and laundry. One snag is that I guess all universities are by this time closed down. Anyway if you can do anything I'll bless you.
   S'hill kids in revolt agst visitors ... 40 last weekend. I dunno what to do about it. They bugger up our meetings cos no one will bring up anything that cd give visitors the idea that we are a school of crooks etc. (...)
   All the best, Neill

To Carlos Kruytbosch

Dear Carlos   *21 September 1967*
   The kids return next week and, getting no applications, I took on a London chap with a B.Sc. He hasn't taught before and may be no good. In that case it will be good to have your chap in mind. I feel I have let you down in a way, but I have a few lads keen on maths and chemistry, and I couldn't face em with a 'Sorry, no teacher.' Getting staff is a sod; home teachers can't be got even in Grammar Schools ... they get more dough in business with science and maths.
   But thanks a hell of a lot for helping even if I couldn't accept the help.
   Thine, Neill

To James and Tania Stern

Dear Jimmy and Tania   *25 November 1967*
We had two inspectors, typical dead officials. Everything wrong, not one word of praise. Wanted me to retire and close the school. Our premises won't pass the Ministry standards, and it wd take a few thousands to put em right. We haven't got em, and it looks as if S'hill after 40 years is to have it. Now we get a full inspection from headquarters and it will also condemn the set-up and ignore the fact that this is a Mecca for hundreds of educationalists every year. One said: Mr Neill, we are not interested in yr philosophy of education. I wish I could send that to This England in the *New Statesman*, but one can't ever quote an official who is not allowed to reply in print.
We all feel as depressed as hell, also very angry and disgusted. Two Establishment formal dead men my judges. To paraphrase Shaw ... He who can does, he who cannot inspects. Alas, never having had any interest in politics I have no pals in the govt who might take my side. (...)
Love to ye both, Neill

To Ben Morris

Dear Ben   *29 November 1967*
Mein Gott, your carrier pigeon service must be wonderful. It is only a week since we had two HMIs. (...) 'Even if you get your premises up to standard I doubt if your teaching would allow you to continue. Yr pupils at most take five O levels, but grammar schools take ten.' The wrong men, little officials with small minds. I think the whole set-up of freedom shocked their little souls. (...)
Thanks, Ben, for your offer to help. I think no steps should be taken until we get that full report in summer or spring. We can't attack two dull officials doing what they considered their job.
Man, it is grand to feel that loons like you are ready to fecht for me. But how you heard the news I can't guess.
I dunno if the two inspectors were acting on authority from higher up. Could be. My often remarks about the Min and its Recognition may have annoyed some of them.
Aweel, again my warm thanks and my love to you both. Neill

To Carlos Kruytbosch

Dear Carlos   *20 December 1967*
(...) The chances of the school's being allowed to carry on by the

Ministry are feeble ... so an inspector said. He said S'hill shd die with me.
I don't want it to, but I can see snags which you and I both know. (...)
Then the current demands of the Min that all private schools must come
up to its standards in five years or be shut up ... meaning for S'hill much
expenditure replacing Carriages, teaching huts, and then having no
guarantee that we'd be allowed to carry on. Stumbling block lessons. Inspector: Why do your pupils take only five O Levels when Leiston Grammar School has ten for each pupil? My reply, also a question, did not re-
gister ... Why do hundreds come to see S'hill and not the local grammar
school? You can't talk to a guy who speaks a different language.

   We are promised a full inspection next year which may decide our fate.
Meanwhile we are trying to make the place shipshape ... Joan Baez gave
a concert in the Albert Hall last week for S'hill, and sent a cheque for over
£1400. Lovely of Joan. (...)
      Alles gute, Neill

To Harold Hart

Dear Harold   *16 March 1968*
   (...) Worried as hell. Inspectors coming this summer and I need an
infant teacher and no one applies. If I were younger I'd transfer the whole
school to some part of the USA or some island where we would be
wanted. Sixty kids and 44 of them from USA. England doesn't want us
and certainly the Ministry of Education doesn't. (...)
      Yours not too cheerfully, Neill

To Constance and Bill Butler

My dear Constance and Bill   *1 May 1968*
   I hate taking *geld* from friends, but since it is only paper money I'll
accept it with glee and thanks.

   But they aren't trying to close us, only saying that we have to make
a hell of a lot of improvements to pass their muster. Had the local HMI
again last week. I am sure he hasn't the faintest idea what S'hill is, a typical
bureaucrat, stiff, formal ... I called him Keeney; he replied Mister Neill.
But the big inspection will be by bigger HMIs from Whitehall. I hope
they come this summer when we look our best and all the kids are drown-
ing in the pool ... with luck an HMI might fall in.

   A parent wants to send a letter to *The Times* and asked for names. I
gave him a few, Henry Miller, Bertrand Russell, Lord Longford, Joan
Baez, Robert Morley, Derek Hart, etc.

Oh, but I wish I were much younger, for I fear for S'hill when I pop off. Even if I get another eight years I'll be 92 and senile.

Sweet of Di to send her fiver. I must reread the papers to see if any of the name Butler are doing 30 yrs for train robbing.

Love to you both, Neill

To Ben Morris

Dear Ben   *28 May 1968*

(...) In three weeks we get our big Inspection, maybe to decree whether we are to be 'recognised'. I'm quite satisfied to be recognised by lads like you and Brian Stanley and Harry Rée. But to have a Minister who thinks that handicapped kids can be caned if the teacher thinks they ought is a bit alarming to guys who don't accept the Min standard of education.

Love to the family, Neill

To Seishi Shimoda

My dear old friend   *13 September 1968*

I thank you warmly for your kind gift, feeling at the same time rather guilty at taking the money because you have done so much for me and Summerhill already. Friends have helped us a lot; we have had about 15,000 dollars and we shall use it all, for the Ministry of Education ordered us to rebuild and replace houses that seem to me as good as they were when I bought the house 41 years ago. Luckily the Ministry does not ask me to rebuild my theories of education. My sadness is that I shall have to leave all the new buildings soon, for at 85 I cannot expect to live long. I hope my family will be able to carry it on when I am dead, but, without my name, I do not know if it will continue to attract pupils. But even if it has to die with me it has been an honest bit of work for 47 years. (...)

Thanks again for your wonderful gift, you true friend of freedom and Summerhill. Neill

To Ben Morris

Dear Ben   *23 January 1969*
    (...) Nay, laddie, no more mixed up staff if I can help it. I have a
school full of em ... most of them roundly slated in the HMI report I had
recently. (...) No, lad, I seek teachers who know how to teach and I can't
get em. Had a lassie MA St Andrews fresh from training college with an
Hons Eng degree. Her teaching was lousy. Now got a BA Eng lass and
the kids are complaining that she can't make the subject interesting. So
your Christine wouldn't stand an earthly even if I had a vacancy. (...)
Sorry I can't suggest anything. Her lack of confidence would be fatal in
a school like this. She might come out under the father morality of a Kenneth Barnes. I dunno. One nice feature ... she was the means of yr writing
me. (...)
    Neill

To R. F. Mackenzie

Dear Bob   *17 January 1970*
    (...) Snag about USA teachers is that you can't see em first. I have
a Canadian maths and science man I took *ohne* [without] interview. Dull
teacher; he'll have to go. I get scores of applications from USA.
    Letter recently from USA addressed Neill School for Problem Chil-
dren, England. It was stamped all over ... try Borstal, Approved School,
etc, but it didna say try the other daft school in Aberdeen. (...)
    Ta for the *Good Housekeeping* cutting. As usual I get no reaction; sel-
dom got any from the *Times Educational Supplement* when the editor was
a pal of mine. The new man I dinna ken but am having lunch with him
soon. I think he may be too academic to want explosive bombs from guys
like you and me.[1] (...)
    Bugger distance. I wish we could have chats over a pint.
    Yours, Neill

[1] Neill's pals were H. C. Dent, and subsequently Walter James. The new editor
was Stuart Maclure.

To John Aitkenhead

Dear John   *12 May 1970*
    How are things? We have just reopened and look forward to a quiet

term, with the kids outside mostly. My headache is staff. Advertised for a junior teacher and one for maths and science. Not a reply of any good. Science man an RC, another with three kids, another 65. We get on average 60 visitors a week yet none want to come and teach. We now pay £800 with board etc. (...)

Love to Morag too, Neill

To Gordon Leff

Dear Bunny   *4 December 1971*
    Yes, I may be too pessimistic. Arose from a conversation with two journalists in the educn line; they said the Lab Govt had S'hill on its list for closure if it didn't come up to their scratch. With battleaxe Thatcher I may be safer, since all private schools are protected by Eton and Harrow. The journalists were sure that the Ministry hates our guts ... guess it does to judge by the HMIs who have plagued us. The Establishment wins always. (...)
    You'd abolish educn at 12. Make it 12 days. I think it was one of the Sitwells[1] in *Who's Who* says 'educated during holidays from Eton'.
    I'll look forward to yr visit.
    Love and pagan blessings, Neill

[1] Osbert Sitwell.

To Michael Lynch

Dear Mike   *23 October 1972*
    (...) The new maths man seems popular and had more young uns come to him than C— had. And the new kindergarten lass seems capable, so we are lucky again. Christine has a lot of Germans. I asked her if they were learning English. 'No, but the English kids are learning German.' (...) Dunno if the new Patrick is as keen on plays as you were, but they staged three sketches for my birthday, one in French was kinda lost on me. I guess that you are finding 90% of the other guys Establishmental, with the mental underlined. (...)
    Fed up at having to give up driving. Insurance kept mounting my premium cos of my age. I liked driving.
    Nuff said. I am so tired now and leave my mail to Ena.[1] (...)
    Love, Neill

[1] Ena Neill.

4

Children, Parents and Psychology

A little girl came up and reached for his hand, said 'Hi, Neill,' held his hand for a few moments, and then said, 'Goodbye Neill,' and wandered away smiling. 'When she first came here,' Neill explained, 'she used to poke her head round my study door about twenty times a day. You see, her father left her and she wants to make sure that I don't suddenly disappear, too.'

Woman's Mirror, July 1964

To the Editor, the *New Age*

Sir   *27 April 1916*

Your reviewer complains because I am not developing the child by careful encouragement of its own processes.[1] I fancy that he means that I am not encouraging the child to learn by doing. Modern education discovers a boy making mud pies; it gently takes him by the hand and leads him to the cleaner plasticine ... and the infant Rodin is discovered. I am quite in sympathy with the learn by doing business, but my book really begins where the doing leaves off. When Johnny asks his teachers why crows are black, the doing theory breaks down. In spite of your reviewer, I hold that the child is a little adult; he has to reason in the same way; he has to think about things that his father thinks about. Moreover, he is very much in the company of adults; the biggest part of his education is what he learns from the conversation of his parents. If Peter Brown, labourer, votes Liberal, young Peter shies divots at the Tory candidate; if Mrs Brown thinks that woman's place is in the home, young Lizzie puts out her tongue at the local Christabel Pankhurst.

Your reviewer asks what I want to teach. I think my book shows that my chief aim is to counteract the influence of the home. Controversial subjects are eschewed by the average teacher; I take a side. I see my children nourished in an atmosphere of Bottomley and the daily press, and I make a modest attempt to fight agin this environment, for I cannot see that all the child processes in the world will stand against the home influence. Your reviewer describes Shaw and Wells as mere revolters, and warns me against a too excessive admiration for them. But I hold that revolt is urgently needed. Every advance in ideas is a revolt against something, and when your reviewer says there is no real reason why my views should be offensive to parents, I marvel ... I set out to tell my scholars the truth that our teachers ignore ... I offend the reactionary parties. (...)

Yours sincerely, A. S. Neill

[1] A review of Neill's first book, *A Dominie's Log*, had appeared the week before in the *New Age*.

To Bertrand Russell

Lyme Regis, Dorset

23 March 1926

Dear Russell

(...) I read your book[1] with great interest and with very little disagreement. Your method of overcoming your boy's fear of the sea I disagreed with heartily! An introverted boy might react with the thought: 'Daddy wants to drown me.' My complex again ... arising from my dealing with neurotics mostly.

I have no first-hand knowledge of early childhood, for I am so far unmarried, but your advice about early childhood seems to me excellent. Your attitude to sex instruction and masturbation is splendid, and you put it in a way that will not shock or offend. (I have not that art!)

(...) By the way, to go back to the sea fear, I have two boys who never enter the water. My nephew aged nine (the watch-breaker of the book) and an introverted boy of eleven who is full of fears. I have advised the other children to make no mention of the sea, never to sneer at the two, never to try and persuade them to bathe. If they do not come to bathing from their own inner *Drang* [urge] ... well, it does not much matter. One of my best friends, old Dauvit in my native village, is 89 and he never had a bath in his life. (...)

Yours, Neill

[1] *On Education.*

To Bertrand Russell

Dear Russell   *26 May 1927*
   (...) Christine is improving a bit. Most interesting material I am on
to now. She has the fantasy that she is a princess stolen from a palace and
made ugly by a gypsy. Her sleepy sickness may be a waiting till the prince
comes along to wake her with a kiss. I took up the Sleeping Beauty tale
with her yesterday and today she has been asking all the boys to kiss her.
Even John ... much to his alarm and indignation. (...)
   Yours, Neill

To Bertrand Russell

Dear Russell   *16 February 1931*
   (...) Interesting bit of psychology today. Boy of 15, very bad writer,
almost illegible. *Der Grund* [the reason] ... every letter home shouts:
'Dear Parents, please to note that my hand is so useless that I can't mastur-
bate any more.' But his handwriting is on the mend now.
   Yours, Neill

To Bertrand Russell

Dear Russell   *22 January 1932*
   (...) Just got a girl of 16 from Crichton Miller's clinic to teach dancing. The doctors there write her letters telling her to be good and sociable.
Mein Gott, what the hell do they think psychology is? They believe in the
almightiness of the Conscious ... the bloody fools. I am at present encouraging her to be bad and anti-social. (...)
   Yours, Neill

To W. B. Curry

Dear Curry   *18 February 1933*
   Thanks for your fiver. Your prospectus is well-written and clear,
but when you ask me what I think of it I simply can't say. For my own
mind is radically different. I found on psychology, Dartington Hall on
education. It's certainly unfortunate that a poor bloke should found on

smash-and-grab foundations while DH, which could afford a helluva lot of smashing, founds on an orderly life. Tonight at our meeting I hear there is to be a helluva row about food chucking in the dining room. Some of the staff say the staff should join in, others say no. Kids also divided. Wish you were here to take part. We are more alive here. DH has no common centre point, too big. If you had a weekly self-government meeting you'd find a helluva difference in social spirit. Your life would bring you grey hairs soon.

Last weekend I couldn't take it all in, and the fact that I was a guest kept me from criticising, even to myself. Now I can see you all in a better perspective. My one important criticism is that you're not making psychology nearly important enough. What is happening to your kids' anal eroticism, hate, destruction, parental complexes, masturbation guilts? My dear lad, I fear me they're repressing them. You have few problems of discipline, but damn it all you ought to have fifty a day. The past three days a gang of twelve-year-olds has rebelled against the government. They put up a notice for volunteers to join the gang, and I at once put my name down. The result: I've got the cook and maids on my neck, and it aint pleasant. It is a life. The quiet lads of 17 and 18 here all went through this gangster stage, and I've had to live through a score of rebellions in my time. Why should you get a quiet life when I don't?

By the way, I learned something important last weekend, that the fault of DH doesn't lie in its wealth, as supposed. The fault lies in its poverty of ways and means for living out primitive instincts. Your gangster age ought to be in dirty hovels, moving up gradually to the swagger rooms all pupils now have. Tomorrow night we have a debate on 'What's wrong with Summerhill'. I expect to hear many worse things about it than I could think of Dartington Hall. Anyway, our schools may differ, but you and I have much the same standpoint.

    All the best, Neill

To W. B. Curry

Dear Curry   *18 March 1934*
    (...) G— had his boy and girl here for a year or two. Taken away because his father had no money and had doubts about freedom. Boy P—, a nice kid, did a hell of a lot of sly hating and damage here, and was getting a decent chap when taken away. You'd find him quite a nice kid by now if his neurotic mother hasn't mucked him up again. And how G— can even afford to think of Dartington Hall now I don't know. (...)
    All the best, Neill

To W. B. Curry

Dear Curry   *31 July 1934*

Yours today. D— came yesterday, and is to send his boy next term. Seemed quite sensible for a major. He had a grown-up son with him, a dentist bloke I rather jib at. It's no bloody good to get a kid when the father's dead against the system, for you can't make headway if he has to see his father and realises the father is against us. Father comes next weekend, I fear I'll be straight with him, and tell him our conditions, that he gives me a free hand. O'Malley wrote me an exhaustive account of the kid.

Do come along next week if you can. I'm lying to all the visitors who write asking to see me. I write a letter and sign it with the name of an imaginary secretary, saying Mr Neill is in Scotland. But you are no visitor, and I'll be glad if you come.

Yours aye, Neill

To W. B. Curry

Dear Curry   *3 October 1934*

D— stole a three shilling packet of cigs from a shop. An old pupil took them off him and gave them to me. I sought the bold D— and said: 'Here's a present to you,' and gave him the packet. He keeps telling folks he was surprised. You blighter, you didn't tell me you were sending me another crook. I'm analysing him, and like him. (…)

I'm going to build a special outhouse for my analysis work, with all sorts of symbols in it. I need it badly for the younger kids, but can't afford it yet. Why don't you get the Elmhirsts to build one for you, and show the world what can be done in kid analysis. But keep the Melanie Kleins and the anal-ists out of it.

All the best, Neill

To W. B. Curry

Dear Curry   *19 January 1935*

(…) D—: difficult to give a report on him. He's not liked by the other kids, too feminine, smokes a lot, and does no work. Comes regularly to his analysis with me, and seems to like me. Has no interest in any bloody thing. Pinched from a shop when he first came, but have heard nothing more about further thefts. I think his main complex is jealousy of the woman his father lives with. He wants to be his father's wife, an inverted Oedipus situation. Nice agreeable lad, but will take a hell of a lot of analysis. (…)

    Yours, Neill

To W. B. Curry

Dear Curry   *12 February 1935*

    (…) We've got a new economic plan here now. Kids must earn their cash by manual work, building a sanatorium and a swimming pool. Parents and I pay the wage bill equally, and I pay the material, although only God knows where I am to get the dough for it. Interesting thing is that the atmosphere of the school is much better under it. Kids feel important, and better still lose the conscience that not going to lessons gives the diehards. So that when you and I take our respective flocks to that South Sea island, I may see your lot standing watching my navvies work, if they have a shop nearby to spend their wages in.

    Off tomorrow to speak to sex reformers on Love, with no confidence on such a subject.

    Yours ever, Neill

To W. B. Curry

Dear Curry   *24 January 1936*

    I've decided no.[1] It took me some time. The situation is this. Have a few women in training college here, teachers all wanting analysis. I took on three, and have regretted it ever since. The others are jealous etc. But the deciding point is that, owing to taking on adults, I've been neglecting the kids. I have enough of them needing attention as it is. On the other hand, I feel guilty at not helping the poor girl. So if you cannot manage to get her to an analyst in London (I know of none in Sheffield) I'll be compelled to reconsider my decision. You dirty dog, for shoving a new responsibility on to me.

    You see what I mean, I am falling between the two schools of kids and adults, and it worries me. For example, I had to drop D— from my timetable last term, much to his disgust.

    I've begun a play analysis room for the smaller kids, but am handicapped by a lack of proper, or rather improper material. You should have seen the salesman in Abbott's Toy Shop when I asked him where I could get a doll with an unscrewable penis. Finally, he suggested Paris.

All the best, Neill

[1] Curry has asked if he would take on a problem student.

To the Editor, *New Statesman*

Sir   *15 May 1937*

May I answer briefly Joad's review of *That Dreadful School*? It is a good review, a fair review, a flattering review ... surprisingly enough, for friend Joad believes in square holes, while I live in a round one. His is an intellectual approach, while mine is an emotional one. Thus he cannot grasp the difference between freedom and licence because he is presumably occupied with philosophical ideas of both. He thinks about children; I live with them. And his thoughts lead him astray.

He says that 'to "allow children to be themselves" is to allow them to pull the wings off flies and to inflict pain upon one another for the sheer satisfaction of inflicting pain'. In the years that Summerhill has been running, I cannot remember one case of a child picking off flies' wings, although there have been cases of bullying (in general due to lack of love in the home).

Joad's ideas of child nature would seem to agree with those who believe that the bombers of babies in Spain are expressing 'human nature'. We daren't dogmatise about human nature; all we dare do is attempt to discover what it is. When Joad says that 'children are intellectually lazy and averse from effort', he is dogmatising without sufficient observation. All or nearly all children are lazy when faced with the Old Men's tasks of learning Latin and Maths, but adults are lazy when faced with things that do not interest them. I spend hours at my lathe, but I am a lazy devil in tidying up afterwards. Life itself compels 'free' children to do a thousand things that they don't want to do.

Joad mentions the multiplication table, which he says won't be learned without outside compulsion. Well, what about it? When I went on the staff of King Alfred School around 1918, I was appalled by the ignorance of the pupils. If I asked ' What are seven nines?' a girl or boy of 15 would have to count up painfully almost on the fingers. Yet today some of these boys and girls are successful doctors and engineers and lawyers.

But I like Joad's story of the girl who just lay about in the woods and *developed*. I don't think, however, that she belonged to Summerhill. We have no woods, and of course the word develop would be beyond her vocabulary. Here she would probably say in answer to the question: 'What would you do all day?' 'Oh, we do every inquiring visitor that strolls along.'

Yours, A. S. Neill

To Elsworth Baker

Dear Baker   *1 June 1951*

(...) I am much perturbed about the two R— children. The mother's promise to have them over this vacation became a promise to come over herself to see them. Both are furious at the change. Both resent strongly being kept from America. J— is always grumbling and hates England and the school laws ... 'I thought I was coming to a free school but you can't do a damn thing here,' this his reaction to bedtime rules made by the community. S—, if in any trouble, weeps and hates England. 'Why are we not like the other kids? We never go home, and I don't think I'd know my mother if I saw her; I've forgotten what she looks like,' says S—.

Mrs R— keeps telling me that there isn't a hope of having them with her in USA. That's her business, but I only see mine and the kids. I can't see either making a success here, and I'm fed up with the scenes every vacation when they see the others go home. I want her to take them home for good. We like both of them when they aren't together. Then J— is a sadist and S— a hysterical tease. They are in the position of being orphans, knowing that they really aren't.

I suppose they have made some headway here. S— is more loving, but J— is a sly destroyer with a very hypocritical moral attitude when another sins against the school laws. He always wants to scrap with the boys here, and when they refuse he scorns them ... 'English boys are sissies; I like tough guys.' (...)

I've never had experience of nationalism in kids before. If an American comes to visit, or even a man wearing blue jeans, J— almost cries with home emotion. I expect exiles have lived like that down the ages. Nothing seems to act as a compensation. (...)

If you can think of ways and means to have the two R—s back home, I'll bless you. I funk the departure of the mother this summer, for the kids will go off the deep end then.

Yours sincerely, Neill

To Constance Butler

Dear Constance   *9 February 1954*
    (...) Kids of 4 and 5 never seem to miss mothers here, partly cos they
play so much with others and only need mothering if ill or at bedtime.
What they get from housemothers seems to satisfy them.
    Stealing, yes, it is home stealing, not from shops etc. We don't worry.
    Accent. Difficult matter. As a boy I spoke two languages, dialect in
school, English at home, for my dad was the village schoolmaster and
we had to be Politely Brought Up. We changed tongues automatically
as we crossed thresholds, but the situation was better than yours, for a
Scots accent is an asset anywhere, while a Midland one is a handicap.
Dunno what you can do about it in your case, simply trust that self-
interest will one day make him speak correctly, though here again, if a
boy speaks Cockney as a kid, he never quite gets over saying that it is
a 'fine dye'. If you try to guide him in this he will become defiant of
course. Ragging him won't do any good. Only a good English spoken
at home will have any chance of counteracting the dialect. (...)
    Yours, Neill

To Bill MacKinnon

Dear Bill   *29 May 1956*
    (...) As for your shitty problem, the prognosis doesn't seem too
good. John advertises 'no problem children',[1] but I guess he has got a bad
one who might be better in some home where he could get special or
group analysis. For my part I'd give him up as too abnormal for ordinary
kids to live with ... and ordinary staff too. We had one such years ago
whose ma took him away cos he was learning to swear. He came to see
me when he was 22 or so, a neurotic dud unable to do a job. (...) Now
that your one associates Killy with women who made him help with the
clean-ups, it may be difficult to treat him there. Sounds to me one of the
rare cases that need analysis, plus analysis of the parents.
    Our love to you both, Neill

[1] John Aitkenhead, head of Kilquhanity House – 'Killy' – where Bill MacKinnon
worked as a teacher.

To Elna Lucas

Dear Elna   *22 February 1958*
   (...) E—, who seemed to improve last term, is a social pest to all the smaller kids, bosses em all day and is hateful nearly all the time. Just shows that the moment you begin to crow about a kid it lets your optimism down with a plonk. She is so hard and defiant that no community law touches her. Wot a life ... and I thought I was *fertig mit Problemkinder* [skilful with problem children].
   Love, Neill

To Willa Muir

                                          Kingston Clinic, Edinburgh
Dear Willa   *24 December 1959*
   (...) I am £1500 in the red and that amount lying out unpaid fees. I gave my car up and my gardener too and worst of all have had to revert to problems to try to make ends meet, and how I hate them! Nothing in them for me; I just know that my Etonian thief of 15 will raid the larder, go unwashed, pinch from shops, and, oh, how sick I am of all that. (...)
   Love, Allie

To Bryn Purdy

Dear Bryn   *16 November 1961*
   (...) Glad to say that when I retook over the classes there was no protest, mainly due to their all being half dead for lack of sleep. And to add to the normal daily problems, F— and J— went round today opening every tuckbox, not to steal, just for fun. We are failing to get at them at all.
   Neill

To John Aitkenhead

Dear John   *17 March 1963*
   I've got a problem. F— came at 8 and was 15 last month. Lousy home, stepmother who hates him; all living in a caravan till new house is ready in July. Father pleads with me not to send him home. But we

have filled his bed and he should move on from here. Frankly he is a bully or can be, not very intelligent but marvellous with his hands. (…) Alas all our big boys at the moment are Yanks and too busy living out their own complexes to trouble about helping with lads lilke him.

I can hear you crying a loud No when I ask if you'd have him for the summer term. I doubt if he'd be a nuisance to you, for, as you know, kids don't show themselves till the second term. I think Bill[1] wd be able to do a lot with him in the games line. (…)

Love to the family. Neill

[1] Bill MacKinnon.

To Carlos Kruytbosch

Dear Carlos   *28 December 1963*

Oddly enough the post that brought yr letter brought one asking me if I'd have a discussion with William Golding, to be published in the USA magazine Redwood … no, *Redbook*. I shd be meeting him next week. You are right, S'hill kids would have had charity, kindness. I hear that Golding believes kids are born bad and must be disciplined to be civilised. Note he had no girls on the island.[1] Note his boys were, barring Piggy, middle class and much indoctrinated. I have never seen S'hill follow a leader. For a time in small gangs maybe, but the adolescents never followed. Our talk shd be breezy.[2] (…)

Love from us all, Neill

[1] In his novel *Lord of the Flies*.
[2] Golding refused the magazine's invitation to meet Neill.

To John and Morag Aitkenhead

Dear John and Morag   *28 January 1964*

S— is a nice kid but he can't keep his finger out of other pies, hence a nuisance to younger ones, not so much bullying them by hitting but annoying them till they get desperate. Sadly enough the others don't like him so that he spent a lot of time in the café in the town, where he was a bit of a nuisance the owner said. (…)

Last term he tried to get into bed with bigger girls and they all told him to go to hell. Then the story goes that he made a hysterical girl of 10 take down her knickers, also assaulted two other little ones, all from America. Holidays, and hell let loose. The first girl, M—, a clever hysterical butchy kid, went home and told the parents. Result cables, phone calls to me. She was kept at home. Other parent, a psychiatrist, sent insulting cables abt seduction. S— denied all. The other two girls tell me he never touched them, and there he was speaking the truth to me. Dunno abt M—. He swears nothing happened, but there must have been something. Over the phone the hysterical mother screamed: My daughter was raped. Oh, those bloody American parents. I've told the psychiatrist to take his damn daughter home if he thinks she is going to be raped.

Poor S— wept bitterly when I told him he was going. (…) I am really touched by your helping in this case. Maybe you can succeed where we failed; maybe with his homelessness, his being indoctrinated as an RC, the going will be hard, but he has a nice side to him which you'll discover. I parted with him with real sorrow. (…)

Love, Neill

To Carlos Kruytbosch

Dear Carlos   *18 December 1964*
(…) A parent recently at a Summerhill meeting, answering a guy who asked why old pupils didn't send their kids to Summerhill, said: 'Lack of money isn't the main answer. We sent our kids because we felt we had failed with them, because we were inadequate. Now they are parents they don't feel that way; they feel they can bring up their kids freely even if they have to attend the local establishment village school.' Some truth there.

Your quote from Margaret Mead is balls. Self-government isn't any tyranny, and even if it were it eliminates the chief danger of adult authority – the Oedipus complex. Hence never any resentment when a kid is fined for bullying. (…)

What the hell about ex-pupils? Isn't Summerhill justified if only on the grounds that it gives kids happiness and tolerance when they are here? My motto is: when a pupil becomes a success the school has done it. When he or she turns out badly it is of course the fault of the home. (…)

Best for New Year, also to that guy Monk who, I suspect, still has a screwdriver of mine.

Neill

To Eva Leff

My dear Eva   *21 December 1964*
    Again my thanks. True it's only money, but I ain't thanking you for
that, only the warmth behind the dough.
    I am trying to recall when we first met. Doesn't matter, only that you
were ideal parents from my point of view, never troubling about minor
things like tidy or rather untidy rooms. Or swearing. Still I can't grumble, for most of my present parents are pretty good. (...)
    Love to both, Neill

To John Aitkenhead

Dear John   *7 May 1965*
    I don't take em over 12 now. Can you take this loon? They bring
him over here in three weeks to see me, altho I told em I cd not have him.
He doesn't sound a bad problem if you let him play his guitar the whole
bloody day. (...)
    The best to all at Killy, Neill

To Elsworth Baker

Dear Baker   *24 May 1965*
    (...) An American girl who was here for a term and is now 17 or so
implores me to give her the address of an abortionist in USA. Neill the
know all. Even if it were England I couldn't help the poor kid, for no
doctor is insane enough to do an abortion. If she were here I'd ask her
parents to take her to Denmark or better Israel, where they have more
sense about things like that. (...)
    All the best, Neill

To the Editor, the *Observer*

Sir   *31 October 1965*
    In discussions about abortion the plight of the mother is always em-
phasised, never the plight of the unwanted child. Every child psychologist knows that the most difficult case is that of the child who has had
no love as a baby – a want, I fear, that no system of education, no therapy

can overcome completely. No one knows anything about pre-natal influence, but it is possible that a pregnant woman, frightened, hopeless, tense in her body, conveys her state to the unborn child, the result being a baby made anti-life from the moment of birth.

During 45 years of Summerhill I have had quite a few adopted children. Some of them were problems. I doubt very much whether they were rebelling against their foster-parents; I strongly suspect that their hate attitude to life sprang from an unconscious feeling that they had been deprived of a mother's warmth and love – indeed, several kept demanding to see their mothers. They had, quite properly, all been told that they were adopted.

So, thinking primarily of the child, I want to see abortion made legal. I want to see a system in which any woman, married or single, can claim the right to have an abortion.

Yours, A. S. Neill

To Willa Muir

My dear Willa   *23 October 1966*
Das bottle has arrived and will be well looked after, bless ye. Black Label is the super whisky; if you guessed you guessed well.

Had a great party on Friday, meeting tons of old pupils, and was kissed by all the lassies. Wonderful feeling to be loved, and I get a hell of a lot of it. In train coming back a very bonny lassie came up to me. Six years ago she was sent by the London County Council as a problem, had tried suicide three times, face hard and voice harder, a model of hate all over. Anti-social for a year, then a slow change, and after another year left a changed girl. Now at twenty she is soft and gentle and kind. Cases like that make my life well spent. (...)

Love, my old, oldest now friend, Allie

To Christopher Exley

Dear C. D. E.   *8 January 1967*
I have to be brief for on my desk are about 35 letters to be answered.

What you say about caning is appalling. Can't someone ask the Christian teachers if Jesus said: 'Suffer the little children to come unto me ... and get a damn good hiding'?

We have only a wall newspaper. My dog is Biscuit.

Buck up; your school days won't last for ever.

Yours, Neill

To Carlos Kruytbosch

Dear Carlos   *9 August 1967*

(...) Every now and then some guy writes from USA asking if he can make a study of old pupils. I always say no. I still keep wondering why hardly any old pupils send their own brats to the school. (...) And every time I lecture I get ... Mr Neill, why have you never inspired any of your old pupils to start a S'hill? From all accounts they never seem to challenge anything, never march in protests, never take up social work like local govt etc. Then, *sotto voce* ... you produce a lot of selfish buggers. I get a mild satisfaction in replying that we haven't produced an LBJ or a Reagan.

Neill

To Daphne and Robert Byng

Dear Daphne and Robert   *29 December 1967*

Good, the natural way out of S'hill, the ideal way: 'I have had my freedom and now I want to face the world outside.' Doesn't matter at this stage if Hannah has no idea what she wants to do. That will come. I'll have a few talks with her when she returns.

A big thanks for the bottle ... I shd really try to persuade H to stay on for the next ten years so that I'll be sure of the annual binge.

As happy a new year as this sick world will allow. Neill

To Bertrand Russell

Dear Russell   *2 December 1968*

Someone asked me what I thought of your description of the Telegraph House bunch of hooligans you wrote of in vol.2.[1] I said your mistake was that you didn't wait to get a few adolescents who would take to self-govt. I think I am proving that I was right. I took on 15 new brats from seven to eleven this term, mostly Americans. Most of my older ones are new and have not grasped what freedom means. Result one hell of a time of hate and destruction from the new batch. I think that most are problem kids and the parents didn't tell us lest we refused them. Some from broken homes. What made them into little devils I only guess. We are gravelled to know what to do with them. Law doesn't mean a bloody thing to them; they laugh at fines and clearing the grounds. They prove that the conscious mind doesn't matter a damn when unconscious things have to be *ausgelebt* [unlearned], prove that the Freudian fallacy of curing by making a complex conscious was bunk. Individually each is charming; as a crowd they are at the same level as the football louts who destroy railway carriages. But I still can't believe that this aggression is natural. I have a few kids from homes where they were self-regulated and they don't seem to go through this hate stage. (...)

Time will make em social, *aber Mein Gott*, we'll have a few years of anti-social brats. (...)

All the best, Neill

---

[1] Of Russell's *Autobiography* in which he wrote: 'To let the children go free was to establish a reign of terror, in which the strong kept the weak trembling and miserable.'

To John Aitkenhead

Dear John   7 *May 1969*

(...) Margaret Duane looks like fitting in, and my Gord, she has to, for we have the nastiest bunch of little haters in our history, mostly USA kids whose parents didna tell us they were sending them in despair. The HMIs condemned our railway carriage bungalow and we had to rebuild. Kids came back Friday night and same night wrecked it, beginning with the windows. I feel bloody wild, for I wanted it as a bike shed and a pet shop. Self-government without a seasoning of big ones fails ... S'hill today is not Summerhill, just a kindergarten of hateful kids in the majority. I deserve more peace at my age.

Love to you all. It was grand to see you and Morag again. Neill

To the Editor, the *Observer*

Sir   11 *May 1969*

(...) What can the conditioning of pigeons and rats do to help a sick world become healthy? What can Skinnerism do for a lad with a guilt about masturbation or a guilt about the gulf between him and his parents? What can it do to help the problem child who had no love as a baby and who goes through life with a chip on his shoulder? What can it do to counteract the making of children anti-life from cradle days, especially about sex? Has it any cure for the authority that disciplines children in school, making them potential Fascists if and when circumstances make Fascism a possibility?

When I had my school in Dresden, I saw a nation conditioned by heavy book-learning, strict discipline, its emotional life killed in the bud. It was no surprise when later a whole nation raised its *Heil* Hitler arms in unison ... pigeons in a very big dovecote.

The answer does not lie in psychoanalysis. (...) Analysis deals with words and memories, but the damage is done before a child can speak or remember. And, although Freud rightly saw the conflict between a child's natural instincts and its cultural environment, the analysts did little to deal with the latter. They kept analysis for the paying patients, and only a few, such as Anna Freud and Susan Isaacs, tried to get at the roots – the ignorant moulding of children by parents and teachers.

The only hope for humanity is prophylaxis, the prevention of neurosis by self-regulation from cradle days onward. I should like to ask Skinner if he knows of anyone wise enough, good enough, to mould anyone's character. Alas, the mechanistic psychology seems to be catching on, especially in the United States.

Yours, A. S. Neill

To Nicholas King Harris

Dear Nicholas   *22 May 1969*
(...) S— reacted to S'hill as they all do ... let off his four-letter words, broke laws etc. Clever kid with angel face. I guess you'll find him normal. Dunno abt his background. I fancy our set-up wasn't posh enough for his Jaguar-type father. (...)
All the best, Neill

To Lydia Hollowell

Dear Lydia   *14 October 1970*
You ask for advice but you don't need it. You are lucky at your age to challenge the stupid thing called schooling, and if you keep it up for life you will find your own freedom. Cheer up; schooldays don't last for ever. Living is a million times more important than book learning. So live, and don't let the anti-lifers get you down.
Yours, A. S. Neill

To Howard Case

Dear Howard   *10 December 1971*

You will see my replies in *Telegraph* and *Guardian*[1] tomorrow, I hope. I am in a dilemma. To resign hands a gift to the Thatcherites; to stay on without any control over what the young editors publish is bad. I must think abt it.

I admire Duane and his analysis of class education, but I think as an ex RC his views on sex are not mine ... community masturbation to me is as mad as community fucking. But the dilemma is great. Headline ... Neill doesn't want child rights. The trouble is that so many advocates of freedom are sick, especially abt sex ... *Oz*[2] etc. *The Little Red Book*[3] has some good ideas about challenging teachers but, as I said in a review in *New Society*, how can a kid challenge a bad teacher when he has been moulded to obey and fear? I don't want to play into the hands of the compact teacher majority that is anti-freedom and anti-life by announcing publicly that I sit on the fence re children's rights. A true dilemma. (...)

Yours, Neill

[1] See below.
[2] *Oz* magazine had recently featured in an obscenity trial.
[3] *The Little Red School Book*, by Soren Hansen and Jesper Jensen, had just been translated into English.

To the Editor, the *Guardian*

Sir   *11 December 1971*

I am one of the Editorial Advisers of the new magazine *Children's Rights*. I did not see the proofs of it, nor can I read it owing to the small print. So I go on your report. I think that the editor's publication of a letter from the Angry Brigade was most unwise; it will give the impression that the magazine advocates violence, sabotage and uncreative rebellion in general. Were this the magazine's policy I could not remain on the advisory board, but with serious students like Leila Berg, John Holt, Michael Duane, Robert Ollendorff writing for it I am sure none of these would support violence of any kind.

I am all for children's rights ... the right to reject the barbarous cane, the right to have some say in their lives and studies, the right to wear what they like. But sabotage is not the answer; it is negative, destructive. In fifty years of self-government my pupils have spent much time condemning the sabotage of unbalanced children.

I won't go into the sex element in the magazine; I can only say that when children have real freedom books on sex are not necessary. Free children, when adult, are not likely to be interested in porn in broadsheets or films or theatres, but how to rid millions of kids of sex guilt is too big a subject for a letter. I certainly do not think that the four-letter broadsheet is the answer. Maybe sick sex is worse than repressed sex.

Yours, A. S. Neill

5

Heroes

HOMER LANE

To Homer Lane, whose first lecture convinced me that I knew nothing about education. I owe much to him, but I hasten to warn educationists that they must not hold him responsible for the views given in these pages. I never understood him fully enough to expound his wonderful educational theories.

Dedication in *A Dominie in Doubt*, August 1920

To Homer Lane

Kingsmuir, Forfar, Scotland
Dear Mr Lane   *6 August 1918*
 Can money save the Commonwealth?[1] I have interested one of my plutocratic friends in your work, a born advertiser and businessman.[2] If it isn't too late I shall try to get him to do something. Meanwhile, apart from the above, will you send every pamphlet you have on the LC to Mr Martin, Grand Hotel, Frinton-on-Sea, Essex.
 Yours sincerely, A. S. Neill

[1] The Little Commonwealth had been closed the previous month.
[2] Walter Martin.

To David Wills

My dear Wills   *16 March 1948*
 I confess that when Unwin told me you were to do a Life I thought of how Lane got into the hands of the religious blokes, Symonds, Bish of Liverpool,[1] then Lytton, to whom I had to protest violently when he sent me an MS in which he claimed that Lane admired St Paul. I thought: Wills is a Quaker, and the practice of making old Homer a plaster saint may go on. Your letter completely eases my mind, and now I look forward to seeing a fine biography.

Sure, we should meet in town, but I dunno if I have any good material to give you. Raymond,[2] I know, has strong views on me and my work, bitterly saying in effect that I was the Judas who misinterpreted the God's message, but then the Freudians say the same thing. Ma Lane[3] I fear won't give you anything. Long ago I gave up trying to learn anything from her. Story ran that L loved her sister (Ray's ma) greatly, and when she died he married Mum and never loved her.

I never thought for a moment that the Little Commonwealth affair had any guilt for Homer in it. I had doubts abut the later trial and banishment, and John Layard one night quoted the testimony of a few women patients who had told him Lane had slept with them. His stories sounded convincing. Agst that was the fact that Layard was in the midst of a negative transference to Lane when Lane died, and was left without a saviour, and tried me (I refused of course) and then Stekel. Layard should be worth contacting; for by this time he may have mellowed a bit abt L.

I have mellowed a lot abt Lane. In my book in the press now[4] I praise him a lot as the most brilliant intuitional child psychologist I have known. On the other hand, he was like Groddeck, a flash in the pan man. Lane would say in a study circle around 1918-19 ... 'Football fans have castration complexes', or some such statement, and we all sat with open mouths and took it in, never questioning where the Master got his proofs. Again, but here we didn't accept at all easily, he used to argue agst any sex intercourse between adolescents, and his reasons didn't satisfy us ... and then in our analysis hours he began to make out that our attitude was due to a complex! I recall the stern hateful face he had on when Raymond married the uneducated Evelyn, and when I found Connie, a Little Commonwealth girl of 19, in tears at his home ... 'Daddy has forbidden me to walk out with the postman.' I feared him too much then to ask him why.

I found it hard to be critical because I was so overwhelmed with wonder and joy at his treatment of his LC cases. He ought never to have handled adults. The man with the Sunbeam car that he was so proud of was a different man from the one I saw in the LC in '17.

His attitude to me was a complex one. I dined at his house every Sunday night for about two years, and when he died took Olive here,[5] unofficially adopting her. He liked me but had an attitude I couldn't fathom. Later a woman patient said (to Layard I fancy) that he was jealous of me, but I can't believe that, for I was a nobody, a very weak disciple knowing my inferiority to him. I didn't do any good work until he died; then I had to feel: 'I am on my own now. I can't run to Lane for advice and guidance. I've got to stand on my own feet.' I used to quote him so much that he said to Radclyffe (another patient) that Neill is just a bloody sycophant.

But we must talk. Writing is too slow. You should try hard to get the full story of James the Italian boy who was insane. Lytton quotes abt him, how L got him from an asylum. Sad that Miss Ludolph died. Lane said to me she was his best pupil. The poor soul died of cancer, refusing to believe that she couldn't cure herself by psychology. (...)

I have no documentary stuff at all. Lane hated writing and I never had more than a postcard from him. But I know that Layard had many pages of typed stuff that wasn't used in either of the books. He got copies from Symonds or Lytton. Symonds shd be your man for MS and maybe Dr David. Lytton is too much Lane lyttonised. I rather shocked Lytton one day lunching with him when I told him that Lane thought that Jesus dined with pub keepers and sinners, which he did.

I hope you'll show Lane as the genius he was but also as the ordinary human being who was too naive to get into a Sunbeam Car circle.

Yours, A. S. Neill

[1] A. A. David. [2] Raymond Lane. [3] Mabel Lane.
[4] *The Problem Family*. [5] Olive Lane.

To David Wills

My dear Wills   *20 March 1948*

Yr 2nd letter today. Blokes you shd contact are Layard, but where he is now I dunno, Oxford or Cambridge. He wrote a Jungian book about the Hare[1] and if you could trace the publisher you could get at him. Another disciple of my era was J. H. Simpson who wrote *An Adventure in Education*, trying out self-government in Rugby, now Principal of College of Preceptors, Bloomsbury Sq. Then there is J. D. Radclyffe, also of my time, who had a long analysis, the man who after years of analysis said to Lane: 'I've come to you for three years and haven't understood a bloody thing you've said.' R said to me: 'Lor, Lane's mouth gaped in dismay.'

How are you to overcome the snag about offending living relations? How can you give a really true biography if Mum Lane is to read it and be ashamed? I wonder how much you'll get from the family? Cora and Raymond were first wife, Polly and Allen 2nd. Bar Raymond, the others, to me, were amiable without ideas.

It doesn't matter a cuss if Lane did sleep with his patients, but it may matter to Cora etc.

You use the word alas when you say he wasn't religious. I dunno what the word religious means anyway, but I'm sure that L kept his New England puritanism. Again and again he lectured us on the danger of having any emotional contact with women patients ... 'If you kissed one of them you'd never be able to analyse her further.'

Your argument (comic as you say) about Nemesis doesn't hold water. Else you'd have to prove that Keats died young cos he was a miserable sinner, while I live to 64 because I was a good lad who feared the Lord. I think that his New England conscience killed him ... wrote that to Dr David in 1926 and he indignantly opposed the idea.

I didn't even know that L was a mason, or I forgot it. I doubt if Sandwich and Lytton were masons, and surely Lady Betty Balfour wasn't. Nay, I doubt if the masonic had anything to do with it. I think his charm and genius caught them ... as it did me and the others. (...)

Yours, Neill

[1] *The Lady of the Hare.*

To David Wills

My dear Wills   *7 November 1955*
Thanks. Page 192. Dunno what meetings you mean; I never attended any with Nunn. MacMunn etc. Include me out of that part.

251. Not sure if I like your publishing 'bloody sycophant Neill'. Hearsay evidence anyway; came from Layard who perversely delighted after L's death in making as much mischief as possible. Re others I took Layard with a grain of salt e.g. when he told of a woman teacher I had been analysing and handed her over to Lane when I went to live in Dresden in 1921. Layard's story was that while Lane was having intercourse with her and she appeared to be less interested than he thought she should be, he got furious and shouted at her: 'You are wishing that it is Neill here instead of me.' Is that evidence of anything? In any case what the hell anyway. But I think you must be careful about hearsay reports.

293. Man, I wonder if Lane did free me from an inhibiting neurosis. His brilliant analysis of dreams and their symbolism (when I look back now) never touched me below the neck. Later when I went as a patient to Stekel in Vienna I found him also brilliant, but again never touching my guts. But who can assess therapy of any kind? How can I say I'd have run a Summerhill even if Lane had never lived? My own opinion is that I got a hell of a lot from him, but how much was personal (analysis) and how much social (ability to work) I can't say.

I don't know if today I'd say Lane had no religion. I think he had a New England Puritanism. I recall in his seminars when we demanded why he didn't allow love affairs in the LC his answers were never convincing. If he had replied: Cos the Home Office would have closed us down, we would have accepted that, but his involved argument that it would be bad for adolescents to have a full love life didn't satisfy us.

By the way sometimes you write Neill and sometimes Mr ... cut out the misters.

Only thing I'd like you to cut is the sycophant one, unless you can print every nasty thing Lane had said of folks ... according to Layard who at that time was in a hell of a state. Mind you Lane may have said it. In late 1919 Lane attacked me because I had given a lecture and had spoken of his LC work. Someone reported to Lane and he was wild, said I had misrepresented him and ordered me never to mention him again. I retaliated with anger too and for a few months took my analysis to Maurice Nicoll the Jungian (and got damn all out of it too). Meanwhile I continued to dine at Lane's house every Sunday night. He was quite friendly, asked me how I was getting on with Nicoll, and when I told him said: 'You'd better come back to me.' What I mean is that if the sycophant story is told this ought to help explain it.

Many thanks for information about schools for delinquents.

Good luck with the book.

Yours, ever, Neill

P.S. Hell, I lunched with Auden in New York five years ago, and we didn't know of the Lane link.[1]

[1] Auden, through his friendship with Layard, had become interested in Lane's ideas.

To David Wills

Dear David   *28 July 1962*

Chief fault of the MS is the beginning. Lanians are few, and the gen. public, opening the book, would say: what the hell is this about? I'd open it with a few stories of Lane's dealings with kids ... Jason one etc. I'd cut much of the family history which can't interest even me. I feel the book must dramatically get hold of the new reader or for that matter the publisher's reader. This is Lane the child psychologist, ran the LC, treated with love. The reader must first of all get interested in the important aspect of the guy.

I found the story fascinating, marvelling how you have done so well without ever having seen him. Yes, a well-told yarn, and a most fair and sympathetic one. There really shd be one volume with his Talks[1] and B's LC[2], ending with your Life, but Allen & Unwin wd never do it, I fear.

I dunno where you got all that abt the marvellous therapy he did. The

Lane I followed was the LC one, not the analyst. He was so keen on his symbolic interpretations that not a bloody thing he ever said to me awakened any emotion whatsoever. It was a head analysis to me. To Lytton, Osborne, Layard etc it seems to have been in some way emotional, for his death left them gasping for breath. My dear laddie, he didn't cure me of an inhibiting neurosis. Fact is I didn't think of analysis. After my visit to the LC in its last days the family took me to its bosom, especially Mabel, and when they lived in town I had supper with them every Saty night. It was after one of these suppers that L said to me he'd like to analyse me ... 'You must know yr unconscious if you want to deal with children.' I didn't then know I ever had a neurosis! I had analysis later with Stekel, but again it was a head one. (...)

L told us he had been analysed in USA but we didn't believe him, nor do I now. On his advice I took on a young woman for analysis. When I migrated to Dresden I asked him if he'd take her on. He did. After his death she told me that when he was making love to her he often said: 'You are not thinking of me; it's Neill you want to sleep with.' I hasten to add that possibly I hadn't done so because she didn't attract me. I saw many sides to him, his anger when I asked him abt Raymond's marriage to ... I forget her name now. That marriage pained him much. I was sure that he never loved Mabel and I had a lot of liking and sympathy for her. I don't think she understood a thing he did or said. (...)

I liked the family a lot. Polly and Allen Lane were sent to King Alfred School cos I was teaching there. But someone told me much later that Raymond called me a lowdown thief who cadged his Daddy's ideas. True, yet if he had lived he would have disapproved of Summerhill. (...)

After his death Symonds sent me his unpublished pages, the ones you quote about religion. They didn't strike me as being of much value. His interpretation of the Lord's Prayer and the Sermon on the Mount were just arbitrary and fanciful. But you are right abt his charm. He radiated warmth, and must have been a great attraction for women. I think we all had an ambivalent attitude to him, but in my own case I think that the love I had for him overbalanced the hate. I think it was Layard who said he called me a bloody sycophant. What he used to say abt Layard & Co to me was pretty awful. I didn't forgive him for telling one patient what another's complexes were. No good rationalising it and saying he did it to help one; no, it was just boyish love to gossip.

I don't know how much he read. The first book he lent me was Pfister,[3] then Jung's Psc and the Uncs.[4] He didn't speak to Adler but I feel now that he was maybe nearer to Adler than to Freud ... *vide* his early and late desire to have boys conquer difficulties. It was not true to say that given a sphere in which he would excel, a problem boy wd mend. His practice in giving kids love made nonsense of his theories. Jason didn't get cured by smashing cups. There is no dramatic cure in psychology, and you must know it too.

Let me hang on to the MS for a bit.

Yours, Neill

[1] Lane's ideas were collected after his death, and published as *Talks to Parents and Teachers.*
[2] E. T. Bazeley wrote *Homer Lane and the Little Commonwealth.*
[3] Oscar Pfister, *The Psychoanalytical Method.*
[4] Carl G. Jung, *Psychology and the Unconscious.*

To David Wills

Dear David   *9 August 1964*
    Kinda shy of a Homer Lane Society. Hate labels, hate the guy who claims to be a Freudian, Adlerian, Steinerite, what not. Any named socy will tend to stagnate ... our founder didn't do this, so we musn't. E.g. Steiner was a very bright laddie, but in Stockholm after a lecture the head of the R.S. school there said to me: 'I didn't agree with anything you said tonight. You educate for this life, while we educate for the lives to come.' I don't think old Steiner wd have said that. Think of the followers of Melanie Klein, how bigoted, how narrow in their acceptance ... 'Every child shd be analysed at four,' said Melanie, and they all agree.
    Or think of what I said abt our blind acceptance of all Lane said. Hence I fear a Homer Lane Society, fear a looking back, fear any anchorage. If I have a motto it is this: Take from every man what you feel is good. Lecturing last winter to the psychoanalysis dept of the British Medical Association I said: Why are you all so narrow? If you follow Klein you refuse to see anything of value in Adler or Jung. And that is true. (...)
    The best, Neill

To David Wills

Dear David   *14 August 1968*
    A paperback of the *Talks* is coming out in USA and they have asked me for a Preface. I sat down to reread your Life. How good it is, how fair, how clever ... yr tracing of Lane's downfall to his masochism all the way from the sister's death on. How the hell you collected all the material baffles me, how you met the expense of it I simply can't guess. Of course when I knew him I had no idea of his background. Time has blunted my

memories of him, less so with Mabel. I thought even then that he did not love her. I dined with the family every Sunday night for two years. Homer was often sour and grumpy and never spoke; at other times full of laying down the law. I'm sure he lied when he said he had had a Freudian analysis in USA; I doubt if he ever read Freud. He introduced me to analysis by lending me Pfister's book. Your idea that he might have gone off the deep end if he hadn't died is plausible; he certainly had a Christ identification and unconsciously sought his Cross.

I am often annoyed when I mention him in lectures. Most students and teachers know him not. So with USA. Twenty-two years ago I wrote the preface to the USA edition of *Talks*. I heard most were sold as remainder copies. My fan mail from USA averages 60 a week and I feel a little embarrassed that the man who was my master is almost unknown. I wonder if he had lived would he have approved of Summerhill. I doubt it. He was nasty about other men. I recall when Norman MacMunn sent him his book I asked him what he thought of it. 'It's chief fault is that the paper is too stout to use in the w.c.' He had to be king.

What a life he had. Was he seducing the girls in the LC? Could be if he had no sex life with Mabel. It doesn't matter to me one way or the other. I don't think the Home Office will publish the Report in our time, at least not mine at nearly 85. Pity tho. A friend of Lord Birkenhead who was Home Secretary asked him about Lane. He said the file showed he was guilty, but as you say, why then let the seducer go on living with the girls for six months?

They didn't ask me to give evidence at the trial. I could have counteracted their accusations of his exploiting patients by saying that he refused to take any money from me for at least a year of five days a week analysis ... bloody poor analyst he was too. (...)

Best wishes, Neill

WILHELM REICH

I was a friend who loved you, who recognised
your genius and also the Little Man in you, but
I never was a 'Reichian' who accepted all you
said and did.

Letter to Wilhelm Reich, October 1956

Dr Wilhelm Reich, the psychoanalyst, fled from Germany to Oslo,
where he has lived for the past few years. He has published many books
on psychology, including his brilliant *Massen Psychologie und Fascismus*.
It is possibly because of his attack on Fascism that the reactionary forces
in Norway are now trying to get his permission to reside in Norway
withdrawn at the end of December. His friends in England want to try
to help him. We think that if the authorities in Oslo had evidence of the
appreciation of his work, they might think twice before they put him out
of the country.

I myself am so taken with his new book on character analysis that I am
going to Oslo to study with him in the Christmas vacation. I am asking
as many well-known people as I can to write to him congratulating him
on his books, which are unfortunately all in German so far. If you happen
to know his work, please write him about it. If you haven't read him,
take it from me that he has struck something big and new in analysis,
using patients' bodily movements as a means to get at the unconscious.
I'm asking for much, but the victims of fascism require much.

A. S. Neill[1]

[1] This circular was included with the letter to Curry, and sent by Neill to a
number of his friends and acquaintances.

To David Barton

Dear David   *14 November 1948*
    (...) Must censure you for your conventional attitude to things you
don't understand. Why sneer at Reich when you don't know? I saw him
work a motor with cosmic rays or whatever orgone is, work without any

electricity attached, but when stimulated with 2 volts it went at possible 1000 revs a minute. I met doctors who put cancer patients in the accumulator and in 14 days the breast lump disappears, altho they don't claim the basic cancer is cured. So why sneer, boy? In 20 years Reich will be hailed as greater than Freud or Einstein. So come orf it, David.

   Love, Neill

To Alexander Katz

Dear Mr Katz   *27 April 1950*
   Thanks for MS, letter and copy of *Complex*.[1] It puzzles me why you ever asked me to contribute; it must have been because you read something I'd written, and therefore must have known my attitude and style.
   Looking over *Complex* I see that I cannot contribute to it. Trying hard to discount my disappointment at having a MS sent back after being asked for, I may fail to see your journal objectively. But it seems to me that it is a magazine for highbrows, for intellectuals who love to skim along the surface and ignore the deep flowing tide. (...) I don't see a line in *Complex* that points to a new orientation to life and psychology. You say my MS isn't up to the level of your readers, but how many are up to my level? How many know a damn thing about self-regulation or for that matter stiff stomachs? (...)
   To me the journal is in the past tense. If you haven't realised that Reich has killed psychoanalysis and that the new era is a biopsychological one, then *Complex* will appeal only to the learned and the American equivalent of the London Bloomsburyites. No, sir, it ain't dynamic.
   Yours sincerely, A. S. Neill

[1] A new magazine which aimed to relate psychoanalytical issues to society.

Paul Goodman[1] to Neill

Dear A. S. Neil   *5 June 1950*
   I assure you that most of our readers, who are largely 'progressive' academics (including some Reichian practitioners, by the way), know 'about' self-regulation and 'approve' of self-regulation of children. Obviously this kind of crude information and preliminary propaganda is not useful. What we hoped (and hope) for from you would be detailed implementation, concrete social invention, drawn from your considerable experience. Consider a simple but difficult debated problem: the witnes-

sing, or not-witnessing (and participation, or non-participation, and what degree of participation or censoring) of children in the first years of the sexual intercourse of the adults. This is a pressing issue in most of our homes. Suppose your best evidence dictated privacy: this would occasion a vast and revolutionary change in the arrangements of our physical environment, and this should then become an immediate major political issue, to the best of our ability to make it so. Suppose, on the contrary, the privacy is inessential if the general education of small children is altered accordingly, then *how* accordingly, and what about the issue of participation etc? We are trying to get a description of this problem among the Mohave Indians (where the privacy is inessential) – would you say, as you do of Ashley Montagu's article,[2] that 'it does not matter fundamentally'? Or consider the problem of defecation. Agreed that nothing may be done about it so far as 'training' is concerned – and thousands and thousands of persons in America agree to this and practise it – a simple physical contraption that would eliminate diapering at night would be now of more use than re-hashing a general theory ... Or tell us something in detail about when small children will go to bed – when their rhythms may or may not coincide with the adults' convenience, and the adults likewise have needs. I don't know any of these answers – I should like to be informed about them.

The bother with you, Neil (let me say it as a friend), is that you think that, theoretically at least, your revolution is over; or, to a degree, you are willing to let Reich do your thinking for you. But it is the essence of a dynamic theory that it at once, applying itself, gets involved in new troubles that make the old ones pale and recede. Nor is it the case that there's no use in going on to the new points till the old ones are 'accepted'. For it is just in the new points of concrete detail that the principle becomes inevitable and accepted.

You imagine that you are very practical; but you must know that what is narrowly practical is not practical at all. It is a system of bio-social resistances, avoiding true creativity. I'm damned if I know what is practical in the long run, so I judge by my tact for the interesting and concernful. Reik's paper on France's irony[3] struck me as very inward and interesting, because obviously Reik is attuned to just this kind of attitude himself; now this happens to be a very common attitude among precisely the good heads in our coercive institutions; is it useless to give such persons a clue of what goes on in them? Humane studies are *always* practical, when they have inwardness and vitality in them; you'd be surprised how they come home to one. To put this another way: the best way of getting a new orientation is not necessarily, indeed it is almost never, by 'pointing to a new orientation', as you counsel.

The 'new era' is not a biopsychological one but a unitary one – unifying the psychosomatic unity and the interpersonal unity and the culturalentropological unity and the educational-political unity and the ecological-economic unity etc. Neglecting any part of this, and singly concentrating on one part, won't make a humanity according to my aspirations. And it seems to me that in its horse-and-buggy way the old analysis of Freud, Jung, Ferenczi etc has done more for this unification than anything I can think of in a couple of hundred years. Reich has extracted a marvellous thing from that matrix; and there's still more to be extracted from it.

Lastly, I am annoyed by your reference to 'highbrows', 'Bloomsbury' etc. You presumably do good work in education (I have no first-hand acquaintance with it), and certain uses of words and arts are not your look-out; but the kind of prejudiced contempt you express is simply ignorance and withdrawal grounded in suspicion and fear. Let me assure you that any new spirit will involve a reform in language from the present 'common-sense' abuse of speech; and this change will be, is being, worked out in its own context – not by looking thru microscopes or at tense-muscles.

Best wishes, Paul Goodman

[1] Paul Goodman acted as co-editor of *Complex*.
[2] Ashley Montagu had written an article on Sterility and Female Adolescence for the first issue of *Complex*.
[3] Theodore Reik had contributed an essay on Anatole France to the first issue of *Complex*.

To Alexander Katz and Paul Goodman

Dear Katz and Goodman   *13 June 1950*
(...) Your letter, Goodman, shows we are talking different languages. I am not interested in discovering e.g. whether a kid should see its parents having intercourse. There are too many unknown factors standing in the way. No one has ever seen a healthy child, and if one did see one, what effect would seeing intercourse have on it if the parents were not free? Your question involves the larger one: Is sex intercourse a private thing or is it potentially a communal affair? I don't see how we can know unless and until folks are completely free from sex inhibitions as animals are.

You fire a lot of questions at me, but I have written something like 16 books answering a thousand questions that you or others might think of, answering not in theory but in actual practice. There is the difference between us, that you theorise while I practise. (I know nothing about you and you may be dealing practically all day long; I am only going by your letter and the books mentioned written by you, Goodman.) You say I let Reich do my thinking for me, yet, you know, I started my school in 1921 and didn't hear of Reich until 1937, and knowing Reich hasn't altered my school practice one bit, although he has given me personally a hell of a lot. In him I discovered what I'd been looking for for years ... the link between the psyche and the soma, and, really, that was what got me annoyed with *Complex* for devoting so much space to the old symbolism of the Reik era. And in a way it applies to your own clever article on weeping etc, for it does not touch the somatic and might therefore be called dated. I think of the terrible weepings and angers I had when in 1938-39 I underwent what was then called Vegeto-Therapie with Reich in Oslo. Violent reactions that sprang from Reich's attack on my stiff muscles.

I don't understand your letter, Goodman. You are too learned, too clever for me. I am a very simple person who can't think abstractly. You accuse me of thinking 'theoretically at least that (my) revolution is over'. What revolution? If you do as I have done, stood as it were outside children for 30 years observing what children do when not under adult discipline, is that revolution? If I had the power to alter all state schools so that they fitted the child as I have seen the child, that would be revolution, but as I have 60 children out of a few million British children who are all being educated the other way, my 'revolution' simply doesn't exist. All I am is a kind of scientist observing and sometimes hating to accept what I observe e.g. the fact that no kid under 18 ever wants to work in a garden or tidy up a garden path. The fact that the usual conditioned child of 'modern' parents is incapable of having a satisfactory love affair.

Call it prejudice on my part; you write to me 'the kind of prejudiced contempt you express is simply ignorance and withdrawal grounded in suspicion and fear.' Fear of what I dunno; a guy who will be 67 this year shouldn't have any fear of the Reiks of life, but don't let's be personal any more. I put it this way (and it isn't contempt either): I read the Orgone literature, not understanding much of the physics-biology side, but in the main I say to myself: I like this; it touches something deep in me: it fits into my view of my own pre-Reich work. I read *Complex* no.1 and say to myself: This doesn't catch my interest any more than reading the *Psychoanalytical Review* would. It takes me back to the time I spent with dear old Stekel in Vienna in 1922-24, the days of symbolism and dreams and unconscious slips of the tongue etc. And now I'll sit down and con your last sentence for the umpteenth time and wonder what it means, and in case you are like me and don't keep carbon copies, here it is ... 'Let me assure you that any new spirit will involve a reform in language from the present "common-sense" abuse of speech; and this change will be, is being, worked out in its own context – not by looking thru microscopes or at tense-muscles.' Oh, Paul Goodman! What the hell does it mean? When I come back to New York in August to lecture and hold

seminars and attend the Orgonon Conference, I may have a chance of
hearing from you in person what you do mean.

    Yours, A. S. Neill

P.S. The old brigade Freudian in me asks: Why does Goodman spell my
name with one L? Answer (perhaps): When you give a guy 'ell you first
of all take away an L, and then compensate. Just about as mad as many
a symbolism, though.

To David Markham

Dear Markham   *22 January 1951*
    Yes, I agree. I am sending your letter to Reich now. Not only do
we need a Reich therapist in England; we also need some control of making accumulators. I have allowed a few people to copy the one I had direct
from Orgonon. (…) But we are all so ignorant. I wanted to make a 20-
fold but Reich wouldn't let me; he said it was too dangerous for a layman
to use. Rightly he feels it is still in an empirical stage.

  Can you come and see me at the end of this month? Easier to talk.
    Yours sincerely, A. S. Neill

To David Markham

Dear Markham   *18 June 1951*
    (…) I don't see anything that can be done about Reich until he sends
over a doctor who is an authority. Telfer, Eastmond, others can experiment as they will so long as they don't claim any authority, but the snag
is shown in the sort of letters I get asking me for addresses of Reich
therapists and mentioning Eastmond or Pommeranz, or some other
damned man who has read a bit of Reich and now claims to be able to
practise. On the therapy side this is bad and dangerous, but I don't see
so much danger in the physics-biology side, where, e.g., Telfer is growing seed in an accumulator, and I am experimenting with growing lettuce
in boiled earth (with giant-like results).

    I don't want to attend a meeting of all the crowd who claim to be keen
on Reich. It would get nowhere. But if you have the time to visit here
again, I'd be glad to talk it over. (…)

    Reich is sending me a new book on the Box telling the whole story.
    Yours, Neill

To Paul Ritter

Dear Paul   *18 March 1955*
    I think that that paragraph about me will make Reich approve of at
least one item in *Orgonomic Functionalism*. I read it with pleasure, wondering of course who the guy was but not really caring.
    Letter from Reich last week but nothing about your venture in it. One
para puzzled me and I wrote him at once asking him to clarify ...'You
didn't mention flying saucers in your last letter, Neill. They are *very ur-
gent.*' His underlining. *Warum*? [Why]...
        All the best, Neill

To Constance Butler

Dear Constance   *10 January 1957*
    (...) I dunno if Reich is in prison or if he has still a third chance of
appeal.[1] The news is quite shattering. And on the radio last night
Eisenhower talked of freedom for all men. I wonder if the Statue of Liberty blushed. (...)
        Thine, Neill

[1] Reich's appeal failed, and he was taken to prison on 11 March,

To Ilse Ollendorff Reich

Dear Ilse   *25 June 1957*
    Do give me news of Reich. I hear only indirectly via Norway. Latest
is that he is ill and very miserable, that he has been pronounced sane and
may be released on parole in November ... too long time anyway. Is he
allowed visitors? Letters? Has he decent food and comfort? It is just shattering to think of his tragedy. I have been rereading *The Murder of Christ*,
People in Trouble, *Ether, God and the Devil* etc and am again struck with
his genius. (...)
    Tell Peter[1] that the noted scientist Neill has discovered that the Roman
Catholic Church is run on Organ Energy.
        Yours as always, Neill

[1] Peter Reich.

To Ilse Ollendorff Reich

Dear Ilse   *12 December 1957*

(…) Re my article about Reich, I wrote it because I felt his death very much[1] and felt that others might like to hear of R as I knew him. I offered it to Ritter for the simple reason that no magazine or paper will publish a thing about him. The anarchist *Freedom* maybe, but I had a quarrel with them a year or two ago; I accused them of giving too much space to R's enemies. I have no illusions about Ritter. On the other hand I don't want to take sides and will not be involved in any way. Ritter can't be taken as a mouthpiece of Reich, but on the other hand his little journal has spread the news of Reich's work in many unexpected quarters; many have bought or read the books, many who would never have heard of Reich.

What I feared is taking place; opposite sides are to claim that they are the correct orthodox Reichians, and one side will call the other side Trotskyites, *oder so etwas* [or some such]. In twenty years (if our wise statesmen allow us to live so long) what will Ritter's name or any other matter? Reich's will, because folks will always go to the source of knowledge, not to followers.

I see your point which I think is this … Reich wouldn't have Ritter but when he dies his friend Neill rushes over to the side of the enemy and supports his paper. But it isn't that way at all. I am ignorant about orgones and can't judge if Ritter is not capable of understanding them either. All I wanted was to publish my sincere remarks on Reich. But if I am going to be drawn into warring sections I'd rather retire from the whole business and not write a thing about Reich. Frankly I have no interest in Ritter or Eva[2] or Steig or Baker or anyone else in the movement. The man I loved and respected and believed in is dead and I should just live on memories. I shall certainly never make any claim to being an interpreter of Reich. Like you I think Raknes the only man who can carry on his work.

Sorry that my news of Reich was so false. Difficult at this side to get to know anything at all. The difficulty now will be to separate what is value from what isn't. The idea that the trial was organised from Moscow is just bunkum, and we have no proof of flying saucers anyway. Why should Reich's great work be mixed up with either factor? That Reich later had some illusions I think right, but they don't do anything to lessen his work. We all have illusions, and maybe the greater we are the greater the illusions. But that Eva and Moise and Steig should go on having illusions is bad, bad for the future of Reich's acceptance as a scientist.

Last night I sat down to read the many letters I've had from Reich, but I had to give it up; too near the shattering blow, too sad at this stage. Later I hope to read them with some calmness. His death grows on me. Little memories come back at odd moments, dear memories of Orgonon and his warm smile ... and even his angry temper sometimes. You say it might have been avoided. I doubt it, Ilse. Only if he had compromised with the enemy and he couldn't do that. I can't remember knowing so honest a guy as Willi Reich. (...)

Glad Peter is taking the sorrow as well as can be expected.

Love, Ilse, and I wish I could speak with you. Letters are so inadequate. Neill

[1] Reich died in prison of a heart attack, on 3 November 1957.
[2] Eva Reich.

To Ilse Ollendorff Reich

Dear Ilse   *17 August 1960*

(...) I often think of Reich. Recently I have reread all his books that I can understand and they seem more brilliant than ever. But I halt at Orgone Energy. Gold and Hoppe swear by the Box as a curing means but I just don't know what to think. To Gold and Co I think any doubt is emotional plague. Anyway the world isn't going the orgone way; the other atomic way is too frightening to think about. I wish I could believe that the fools of internationalism can control their weapons. (...)

Ritter stopped his magazine for a year; I doubt if it will start again. I still think that it brought some people in touch with Reich's books. Hoppe hates it. I wish a mag could be run by someone who knew Reich and his work personally. I protested in the mag against Ritter and Boadella doing orgone therapy without having undergone it themselves. As for me, I am tired of therapy of any kind, and dear old Reich used to grumble at having to do it for an income. (...)

Oh I wish I could see Orgonon[1] again! But to me it would be a very empty shell now.

Love, Neill

[1] Reich's home in Maine where he carried out his scientific work.

To Ilse Ollendorff Reich

Dear Ilse   *14 January 1963*

Tidying up my office, I found the original Deutsch MS of *Listen, Little Man!* I asked Mickey Sharaf who was in charge of Orgonon if I might send it there to the archives. I guess he doesn't think much of the Higgins set-up, otherwise he wouldn't have suggested I send it to Peter for safety storage, and, having mislaid Peter's address, I contact you. It may be worth a million dollars one day. (...)

Out of touch with America now; no idea e.g. what Reich followers are doing in New York. My own opinion is that Reich was so far away from ordinary thinking that no one can follow his genius or the madness that is said to be another name for genius. Reminds me that Hoppe seemed disappointed with your views on Reich. He and Gold and other doctors get mad when anyone wonders if Reich really did get unbalanced, heaven knows why; if it cd be proved utterly that R was insane it wouldn't make a scrap of difference to me and my opinion of him. (...)

Love to you both, Neill

To Ilse Ollendorf Reich

Dear Ilse   *17 March 1964*

(...) I guess Peter is still in Paris. I hope he comes to see us. I thought he had developed wonderfully ... no signs of his having inherited his father's quick temper and impatience.

A guy sent me the nine booklets on the trial. Most just dull reading, all that stuff about shipping accumulators etc. Poor Reich was just crazy to try to fight lawyers. They spoke a different language. How cd he expect any judge or jury to accept his Red Fascism Moscow angle? His flying saucers? His Higs? Greek to them. Every time in court he tried to explain what his work was they shut him up. You gave yr evidence very well, Ilse.

Love, Neill

To the Editor, *Freedom*

Sir   *December 1966*

You either think that Reich was a genius (as I do), or you think he was a madman who invented a panacea for all evil – Orgone Energy. Most people who have heard of him accept the latter definition. Those who were nearest to him thought him a great psychologist, an absolutely honest scientist, a wonderful sexologist; we thought him the only successor to Freud.

In America he was hounded literally to death by smearing scandal makers. Sick journalists described his Orgone Accumulator as a means for attaining a sexual orgasm. Hence it was with some concern I read in the *New Statesman* the words 'Reich rites'. A weekly competition was about sex and the compiler mentioned some of the topics appearing in the answers. I at once wrote a letter to the *NS*. I didn't keep a copy but, as far as I can recollect, I suggested that the phrase perpetuated the American smear. I said that Reich was one of my best friends and I knew him well. I said that Reich was almost puritanical in his attitude to sex; he found sex stories revolting, and the word fuck drove him to fury, for, to him it meant the wrong sex, the male aggressive sex shown in the word 'laying'; sex without love or tenderness, sex without a thought of the pleasure of the woman. Masturbation on promotion in short. Anyone who has read his *Sexual Revolution* knows that the man who wrote it could never have had any connection with rites, with pornography. Reich was a great man and even his Freudian enemies had to admit that his *Character Analysis* is a classic.

Then how come that the *NS* refused to publish a word in his defence? But it wasn't the first time. At the time of Reich's trials the then editor, Kingsley Martin, rejected letters some of us wrote in defence of Reich. So did the *Guardian*. The fact that I am writing this for *Freedom*, a journal with a small circulation, shows that of the papers of the Establishment, none of them will mention Reich.

Why this boycotting of Reich? Why all the bitter enmity shown in the USA? A mere crank does not get abuse and hate. The man who believes the earth is flat is not hounded as Reich was. People laugh at him but they did not laugh at Reich. They smeared him in America; they dismissed him as a paranoic. If a paranoic can give us such brilliant books as *The Mass Psychology of Fascism* and *The Function of the Orgasm*, then it is high time that psychiatrists were redefining their definitions.

Personally I think that the Reich boycott springs from his uncompromising attitude to life and especially to sex. I am convinced that the question whether Orgone Energy exists or not has nothing to do with anti-Reichism. I don't know enough science to say whether it exists or not, and I do not care a button about it. But I do care for the Reich I knew and could understand, the man whose analysis of human character was deep and convincing. And I care a lot about the boycott, for it suggests fear of the truth, fear of being considered unorthodox, fear of life itself.

The *NS* and the *Guardian* are Liberal. I begin to understand what Reich said to me in one of his last letters ... 'Beware of Liberals. They sit on the fence; they are neither one thing nor the other. They are liberal only in words.'

Yours sincerely, A. S. Neill

To Elsworth Baker

My dear Baker   *9 January 1968*
Thanks for the Journal, which arrived by the same post as Reich on
Freud,[1] a presentation from a friend. The former I read with sadness;
poor Reich trying to make the law understand him and failing utterly.
Elsa Lindenberg said to me nearly thirty years ago: Reich *hat keine
Menschenkenntnis.* [Reich has no understanding of people.] It was true and
puzzling. The man who tore me to pieces on his sofa in Oslo was a child
when he met a Washington or a slick lawyer. The Freud talks to me were
marred by unwise statements by Reich about Freud's cancer being caused
by his more or less anti-genitality; I say unwise because purely speculative
and unworthy of a great man like R. The obvious retort is: What about
R's heart?
I am still all at sea about orgone energy. I can't see how one can use
it to cure human sickness, world sickness. I can't think that if the whole
world had perfect orgasms in the R sense that Arcadia would result. Anyway how to tackle the universal fear of the genitals ... if it is universal;
I don't know any anthropology. Talk won't do it, therapy won't as you
know, politics are out. I see only the slow way of education, slow because
age brings conservatism, and the hippies today who seek freedom will
many of them be Goldwaterish by the time they are fifty. Reich diag-
nosed brilliantly but he did not know the practical answer, how to get
at the perverts who kill the kid in the cradle. And if there were a method
the enemy would kill it. (...) That is what I cannot get at, the why of mankind's hate and war and discipline. I can't find an answer to what made
man go that way. If R gave me one I didn't understand it. S'hill proves
that freedom brings out good and that kids can grow without being made
anti-life, but why? Why can't the whole world treat kids that way? I wish
I knew.
In the Journal you bring up again the question of R and sanity. I never
could get excited about it; to me it doesn't matter a damn if he had a streak
of paranoia ... who doesn't? When Peter came here as a boy with Ilse and
Ola Raknes and sat in my garden he said: 'Those American planes up
there are there to protect me.' I told him they weren't. He went home
and must have told R what I said because R sent a cable to Grethe Hoff
saying Don't trust Neill, he is disloyal. I wrote him a letter and the dear
old man replied with much regret and apologies. But I understood his
distrust of people, possibly stemming from his mother's tragic death.[2]
What was wrong was his loneliness. When we parted in '48 he said: 'I
wish you could stay. I have no one I can talk to as an equal. I cannot talk
about myself and my problems to the doctors I am training.' The loneliness of prison must have been hell. I think it was as much the Little Man
in him as the great genius that appealed to me, the R who stormed at Peter

and Ilse, the warm man with whom I emptied many a bottle of Rye or Scotch, in short the human guy who enjoyed an exciting film Western as if he were ten years old. (...)

All the best in a Happy New Year of Vietnam and Egypt and the nice politicians. Neill

[1] *Reich Speaks of Freud.*
[2] She committed suicide, after Reich had caught her in bed with his tutor, and betrayed her to his father.

To Lois Wyvell

Dear Lois   *25 April 1968*
(...) So you want to blow a contrary wind, you nasty lassie.[1] How dare you! If anything my article meant: Don't let Reich remain in the consulting room and the sick patients, but I didn't expect it to rob them all of their paying patients. I was fishing for a solution I cdn't get myself, hoping that the next number would have some brilliant suggestions how to use Reich among unsick people. You see, Lois, I am not nearly clever enough to understand things like superimposition. I have often wondered why Willi R wasted his time arguing with me, explaining to me. One of those guys who feel more than they think. (...)

I wish the clock could be put back and we were all in Orgonon again with dear Reich.

> 'Time, you old gipsy man,
> Will you not stay?
> Put up your caravan,
> Just for one day.'

It won't.
Love, A. S. Neill

[1] Lois Wyvell disagreed with some of Neill's arguments in an article he wrote for the *Journal of Orgonomy*.

To Elsworth Baker

Dear Baker   *28 February 1969*
Ta for letter. Ilse's book is being published over here and I read the proof copy.[1] I can see why Ilse didn't ask me for a preface; my name occupies the whole bloody book, mainly because she took so much from

my letters from Reich. Alas, I didn't keep copies of mine to him. I asked Higgins if I could borrow them for I knew he [Reich] kept them. I got a stiff unfriendly letter with a big No. I think the book will make a stir among the Reich fans, for she has told of his drunken bouts and violence, but not saying that he beat her about or that Ranger Hamilton[2] said he wouldn't have a meal in her house in case she were poisoning him. I think she was right in telling of the Little Man in Reich, even if it adds fuel to all his enemies, who, taking a long view, don't matter a bugger. When I say that I can't recall what Goodman wrote it means that he said damn all to me. Reich might turn in his grave to have a noted anarchist write about him.

All the best, old friend, Neill

[1] *Wilhelm Reich: A Personal Biography*.
[2] Eleanor Hamilton.

To Elsworth Baker

My dear Baker   *5 April 1969*
    Yrs today. I couldn't myself detect much bitterness in Ilse. Even in '48 in Orgonon I cd see how Reich bullied her and drove her to tears, generally over nothings. I think she softened as much as she could ... not telling how he beat her up when drunk etc. I am glad she wrote so bravely for it was just silly to keep pretending that R did not go off the deep end in the end. (...)
    I try in vain to find out if R ever solved the mystery of why sex became taboo. Why the Christians made it the big sin. R's free sex for adolescents was an impossible view to hold a hundred years ago when there was no contraception, but why the Trobriand lasses did not get pregnant Malinowski didn't discover. (...)
    I am still confused abt the role of sex repression. I have had pupils from homes that approve of masturbation, nakedness, cursing and still the little buggers bullied and destroyed, tho to be sure not so much as the kids of stupid parents. All so confusing. R who lived out his sex life fully and was filled with insane jealousy. When Ilse went back from visiting us R's first words were, Did you sleep with Neill?
    Ilse, Grethe and a Viennese woman I had as a music teacher[1] all lived with R and had to give up because of his jealousy, just as Elsa Lindenberg had to. So that when R used to say that the proof of a finished therapy was the right orgasm, I just wonder why the hell his own orgastic life ended in misery to all. I am not a deep enough thinker to grasp his genius, but I feel that his message about the ruination of kids in their cradles is right and hellish. He was so right about a Freudian analysis dealing with

words when the damage was done long before a baby knew words ...
the best justification for his O Therapy I can think of. (...)

Yours, Neill

[1] Ilse Ollendorff Reich, Grethe Hoff and Erna Gal.

To Elsworth Baker

My dear Baker   *8 September 1969*

(...) Disturbed by a report in a letter that Gold, Raphael and Oller
have issued a statement agnst yr Journal. I haven't seen it, but if you can
get a copy do send it on. I hate all this bickering in the movement, all
this mud-slinging. Why can't folks differ and leave it at that?

Orthodoxy be damned. Reich broke from Freud, so did Jung and
Adler, but who cares now? Here sectarianism is rife. The London analysts
stand on their dung heaps and hate each other. Live and let live. I dunno
where Paul Goodman for instance stands on Orgonomy, or Lowen. All
I know is that Goodman has criticised me in the *Village Voice* and I don't
care a damn. I have no idea what it is all about. The genius Reich is there
and each must make of him what he wants to. When Gold had his daughter here I criticised something in Reich and he shouted, Emotional
Plague, Neill. I'd like to write a short article for the journal on this whole
infantile business. Why Reich shd attract so many little men I don't
know, but Jesus collected them and still does ... cf Ulster. Cf the many
Christian sects hating each other.

Anyway, I'd like to see that pamphlet of Gold's.

Warm greetings, Neill

To Ilse Ollendorff Reich

Dear Ilse   *14 July 1970*

(...) Surprised to hear you're in Orgonon; thought the top lady banned you if without Peter. Oh, what a crowd of little men and women
there is ... her, Gold, Raphael, etc. And the Baker lot have gone all establishmental. I look at the gorgeous gown they gave me and wonder when
I can wear it. Can't understand why they have to go in for pageantry and
conventional robes. Dunno what Reich wd have thought of it all.

Baker sends me the journal but most of it I can't read for I have no interest in therapy now or case histories. I dunno if O Energy exists and anyway what can one do with it, whether it is called Orgone, Libido, Life

Force, what not. Seems to me they are all bogged down in words and theories. (...)

About that cold. Once there was a guy who made a Box. Have you tried it?

Lots of love, Neill

To Lois Wyvell

Dear Lois   *18 September 1971*

(...) Okay, R was mad, but Nixon, Reagan, Wallace are sane, so I am all on the side of madness. Hoppe was angry with Ilse, but I saw only a brave attempt to see R as she saw him, and my two long stays in Orgonon bear out much of what she says. The alternative to seeing him as a genius plus a little man is to make him a god. I hate gods unless they have feet of clay.

R hated the word fuck, which to him was aggressive male sex without tenderness or love. 'Women don't fuck,' he said to me once, and if the film[1] even uses the word fuck it is a barbaric insult to a great man. (...)

At times men write asking me if they can make a film of me and S'hill. I refuse, although I know they can do it without my permission. After my death some sick fool will make one showing S'hill as a free fuck community. But it won't cancel out what a few millions have read about me and the school. Maybe the bad film of R will lead many to read abt him, read what he wrote. The other kind don't matter. The doctors who fought agnst Darwin and Freud are dead and forgotten. No porn film can really harm the message of a genius. Wilde's plays were banned for years because he was a homo; today, when to be a homo is almost normal, revivals are frequent. So cheer up; no film can kill old Willy Reich. The poisonous yellow press headlines abt S'hill 30 years ago had no effect at all. Only the sick read them or remembered them.

Love and pagan blessings, Neill

[1] *WR: Mysteries of the Organism.*

To David Markham

Dear David   *8 May 1972*

At 88 my memory ain't that good and I can't recall telling you about orgone boxes. I never had enough faith in them to go on trying regular sittings. Can't recall ever seeing Reich use his own in Maine but maybe he did before I got up. He was one of those German five a.m.ers.

Dunno what you mean by writing I have something poor Reich never had. If you mean humour I agree; R had none that I could see which made our friendship kinda limited in a vital sphere. He was far beyond me; even today when I reread him I fail to grasp a half of what he is saying.

He is slowly being known. German and USA youth is keen on him. But he wd have turned in his grave had he seen the film.

The best, Neill

To Ben Morris

Dear Ben   *24 September 1972*

(...) You are wrong abt Reich, laddie. The Reich film would have shocked him to despair, with its blazing FUCK all over the screen. He was a puritan in sex. Fucking to him was male aggressive sex with no thought for the partner. Sex stories he abominated, as, by the way, did impotent Barrie, Lawrence, Joyce. R did not have the whole truth. I told him I knew oldish men and women who never had sex in their lives, but were happy and charitable and doing good work. And I can't see the connection between genital suppression and a boy of ten breaking 32 of my windows. Meaning that at the end of my life I know bugger all. (...)

Yours sincerely, A. S. Neill

H. G. WELLS

> Old saying: One should not meet one's heroes.
> I worshipped H. G. Wells when young. I met
> him when he was old, arrogant, peevish,
> squeaky voice. Feet of clay.

Letter to Henry Miller, October 1968

To H. G. Wells

Ffestioniog, North Wales
Dear Wells   *26 February 1943*

Ever heard of Dr Wilhelm Reich? Discoverer of Bions and Orgones. Doing cancer research in New York now. Opinion of him divided ... genius or mountebank. I am no scientist and can't judge. You are and could. May I send you the first three numbers of his magazine *International Journal for Sex Economy and Orgone Research*? No payment wanted in cash or puff or any damn thing: all I want is to catch your interest, knowing that you can look at a new thing without preoccupation.

As a layman I can't describe much. Reich heats material (blood, sand, gold) to incandescence and then gets a culture that looks like life and attacks cancer cells. He calls this Bions. Orthodox science so far has been sceptical, but as it was with Freud and Darwin and Pasteur. (...)

Yours sincerely, A. S. Neill

P. S. Haven't forgiven you for guying me in your Dictator book.[1]

[1] Probably *The Holy Terror*, published in 1939.

H. G. Wells to Neill

Dear Neill   *[February] 1943*

I shall continue to guy you as long as and in so far as I think you are wrong. A teacher who can't learn can't teach. There's no such thing as a 'scientist'. There are mathematicians, physicists, biologists – all working in different disciplines in perpetual pursuit of the truth. I may not be able to form any judgement on this Reich, but send the stuff along by all means.

Yours, H. G. Wells

To H. G. Wells

Ffestiniog, North Wales
Dear Wells   *1 March 1943*

Good. Just a little about Reich in a nutshell. Was one of Freud's inner circle for many years; came a day when he said to Freud: 'We all agree about repressions, but where are they biologically?' F didn't know. R said they get fixed in the muscles, and every neurotic has a stiff stomach; every neurotic is fearing any orgastic pleasure, and his muscles go stiff as an armour. So that round about the solar plexus he has a Maginot Line that stops all natural sex urges. (His book *The Function of the Orgasm* I have in English, but am not including it now because I don't want to shove too much Reich on you at a time.)

He saw that until psychology linked up with biology there would be no post-Freud advance, so he took up biology, declaring that the cell proves his point about muscle armouring (I can't follow him here, knowing damn all about biology). In Oslo where I knew him the 'scientists' cried: 'Let the cobbler stick to his last. The man's a psychoanalyst ... what the hell can he know of other sciences?'

R has had a roving life. Fled from Berlin when Hitler came, went to Copenhagen but was expelled because of his book *The Sexual Struggle of Youth*, in which he argued that sex must follow biology and intercourse should be free to adolescence. (I first met him after I had lectured in Oslo. Later he said: 'Neill, you are right to make masturbation free and guiltless to kids, but why do you stop there? Why don't your adolescents have a real love life?')

He got away from Oslo just before Hitler moved in. And as a price had been on his head from 1933 onwards, they would have flayed him alive.

My own opinion is that in psychology he is the only original thinker since Freud. For years I had been saying lamely and helplessly that psychology must join up with physiology and biology, and when I met a man who was working that way I was ready to fall for him.

As for your guying me ... that's o.k. by me. My postscript was only to remind you who I was. I guess I must have written the tripe that you guyed me on, but about 20 years ago. Since I have learned from Freud and Homer Lane, and at nearly 60 take up the new theories of Reich, I have no conscience about being a teacher who can't learn.

I have a special regard for you, Wells. You had a tremendous influence on me when I was a youth, and, I blush to say it, but in a history of Eng Lit I wrote for a *Popular Educator* in 1912, I claimed you as the greatest writer of all time (if I remember aright). I still think *Kipps* and *Polly* are masterpieces, and your only claim to immortality, but I realise the tactlessness of this comment, for when any man praises my *Dominie's Log* (1915) I see red, for I lose interest in a book the day after it is published, rightly so, for it is out-of-date. Yet that doesn't or shouldn't apply to art, and *Kipps* and *Polly* are art creations independent of time. Psychology is at the stone age and anything fresh today is stale tomorrow.

Yours sincerely, A. S. Neill

H. G. Wells to Neill

Dear Neill   *[March] 1943*
    You have sent me an awful gabble of competitive quacks. Reich mis-
uses every other word and Wolfe is a solemn ass. There is not a gleam
of fresh understanding in the whole bale. Please don't send me any more
of this stuff.
    Yours, H. G. Wells

To H. G. Wells

                                          Ffestiniog, North Wales
Dear Wells   *8 March 1943*
    I cannot understand why you are so damned unpleasant about it. I
considered you the man with the broadest mind in England, and sincerely
wanted light on a biological matter I wasn't capable of judging myself.
Your Black Out letter might have been written by Colonel Blimp. I
hoped that you would give an opinion on Bions and Orgones, whether
they were a new discovery or not, and all I got was a tirade against
Wolfe's translation of Reich's German. You apply the word 'quack' to
a man whom Freud considered brilliant, a man who has slaved for years
in a lab seeking truth.
    I grant that I asked for it. I intruded. I apologise, and ... being a Scot
... refund your postage. Your reputation is of a man who can't suffer
fools gladly. Apparently you can't suffer sincere research gladly either.
When a New York Medical School is trying out Bions and Orgones on
cancer patients, your 'no fresh understanding in the whole bale' sounds
odd.
    But this is no quarrel, and I won't bother you again about Reich or any-
one else.
    Yours sincerely, A. S. Neill

H. G. Wells to Neill

Dear Neill   *[March] 1943*
    No. I decline your stamps, but this business is quackery. You call
me a blimp. I call you a sucker. Bless you.
    Yours, H. G. Wells

HENRY MILLER

> I think I love you, Henry ... the most human
> guy I have ever met.
>
> Letter to Henry Miller, October 1968

To Henry Miller[1]

Dear Henry   *11 December 1958*

Can't call you Miller after just having read Perlès' Life,[2] *Tropic of Cancer*, *Big Sur* in that order. No use calling you a genius for what the hell the word means I dunno. Better simply to say, Here is a good guy who gives out much more love than hate; you both have very much the same view of the Little Man, but Reich has more bitterness – understandable after being chucked out of so many countries. When in Maine he said: 'Neill, I'd like to chuck the whole bloody business and come and teach in Summerhill.' I replied: 'Reich, I wouldn't have you within yards of my brats. You'd scare them.' And yet if anyone loved humanity, Reich did. (...)

What a style you have, man! And what erudition – you mention scores of writers etc I never heard of, but I don't know a word of French which is a bit of a handicap when reading, for no one ever translates French passages; they always do German ones, which annoys me, cos I know German. (...)

I think you know Jimmy Stern, a very good pal of mine. I note that he reviewed one of your books in the *London Magazine* some months ago. But having common friends ain't enough. Why shd you and I be so widely separated? I can't come to USA ... one of the few guys who have been refused visas by USA and Russia. But if you ever carry out that idea of sending your lassie to Switzerland, you must touch down in England and have a jaw and a drink. One of my boys defined masturbation as the pale shadow of sex, and I think we can call correspondence the pale shadow of friendship.

I am posting this sea mail for I want it to arrive with a book I am sending you – *The House with the Green Shutters*, which I hope you haven't read. It is the only Scottish novel I consider of any merit. I've read it twenty times because of its raw Van Gogh elemental style. There is no sex in it and no love. Douglas Brown wrote it and died before it was acclaimed a great book. And I hope it doesn't mean your saying: 'Christ, why the hell do blokes send me books?' By the way, the Scots dialect may handicap you; it didn't when my brilliant sister-in-law by my first wife, the Australian novelist Henry Handel Richardson, read it. Note that in the book bodies is pronounced buddies.

You puzzle me when you speak of God. Brought up in Calvinist Scotland and later having dropped the idea of a heavy father God, the word doesn't mean a thing to me, meaning that I can't visualise or fantasy any Power that is external to me. Like Reich, I can see no purpose in life. I guess that the godly argue that God slew millions of men in two world wars and 4 million Jews in order to chasten his creations. But I am no philosopher, no thinker. My head never was in the clouds ... my typing gets worse every day. I was 75 last October and what typing will be like when I'm 85 or 105 the good Lord only knows; wrong expression, I guess, like the man finishing an argument on religion with 'I'm an atheist, thank God.' Speaking of chestnuts, I guess this is one: Two students in Paris. One: 'Christ, we've been in Paris a whole week and haven't once been to the Louvre.' The other: 'I think it must be the hard water.'

Well, enough of rambling. It is a joy to me to have any contact with you at all.

With warm feelings, Neill

[1] Some earlier letters of Henry Miller appear on pages 140–42, under 'Authors Books and Writing'.
[2] *My Friend Henry Miller* by Alfred Perlès.

To Henry Miller

Dear Henry   *8 October 1961*

Now what exactly does a guy say when another guy sends him 500 bucks? There isn't any vocabulary that fits. Thanks ... okay for passing the mustard, but inadequate for passing the buck, so to say. Best simply to say: Damn your eyes, Henry; you're a pal, and leave it at that. (...)

It was grand meeting you, Henry. Just exactly as I pictured you. Why must kindred souls have to live miles away from each other? No Ritter next meeting, no anyone.

It would be interesting to know if anyone with pains in his guts buys a copy of *The Tropic of Cancer*. Could be ... like the local movie manager, who advertised a coming feature – *A Doll's House*, by Henrik Ibsen ... bring the kiddies. The title *Problem Family* has changed since I wrote that book. Now it means a family in economic difficulties, bad housing etc. I guess that quite a few have bought my book hoping to read about new drains, and getting a big disappointment. My *Free Child* was catalogued in Edinburgh Library as *The Free Church*. I like to imagine what some Free Kirk Minister thought of it when he opened it.

Love and blessings ... pagan ones, Neill

To Henry Miller

Dear Henry   *19 January 1962*
   Now I know my mission in life ... to bank 1000 dollars and dole it
out slowly to a poverty-stricken Henry Miller, ruined by many law-
suits.[1] For if you lose you'll need the cash; if you win your sales will make
you a millionaire. (...) I fear very much that you will lose. All the death
merchants – the Pentagon, H bomb shelter folk, lynching mob, the Catholics will slay you if they can. Every anti-sex person in USA will be on
your top, and I guess that sort forms the vast majority ... *vide* Kinsey.
Yet things are moving. In a mixed party the other night a young woman
told this story and all laughed heartily:
   Young parson is giving a talk to the parishioners. At the end he said
he would be glad to answer any questions. Pause, then a woman:
   'Do they have babies in heaven?'
   Her husband, *sotto voce*: ' Do they fuckin' hell!'
   The parson: 'One question at a time, please.'
   I can use the word bugger when lecturing, or shit, but not fuck or cunt.
   Note that I ramble, trying in vain to say thank you with some feeling.
You promised to come over in the fall. Are you coming soon? Our short
talk wasn't enough for me.
   The Summerhill book is coming out here in April, published by Gol-
lancz. I said to him: You must use Henry Miller's blurb for the USA edi-
tion.[2] Answer: No, no, it might put many people off. So that silly buggers aren't all confined to America. What old Reich called the emotional
plague is universal. And because 99% are anti-life they must destroy the
world sooner or later.
   Well, Henry, you are a pal. Bless your heart.
      Yours ever, Neill

[1] Miller had given Neill a second cheque for 500 dollars for Summerhill. Miller's
Tropic of Cancer had 75 court cases pending against it in the USA.
[2] For the US edition of *Summerhill: A Radical Approach to Child Rearing*, Miller
had said: 'I know of no educator in the Western world who can compare to A. S.
Neill. It seems to me that he stands alone. The only possible revolution, the only
worthwhile revolution, must be created not by politicians or militarists, but by
educators. Rimbaud was right when he said that "everything we are taught is
false". Summerhill is a tiny ray of light in a world of darkness. Its aim is to create
happy, contented people, not cultural misfits dedicated to war, insanity and
canned knowledge.'

To Henry Miller

Dear Henry   *14 April 1963*
    The announcement that the *Tropic* isn't to be prosecuted here gives
me a great warm joy. I thought of cutting out all the press notices I saw,
but guessed that your London publishers will send them to you. (...)
    I smile when I recall that Hart in New York and Gollancz in London
refused to use your name in ads because it would kill my book. Half a
mind to tell Gollancz to seize the moment and use your publicity to ad-
vertise Summerhill. I refrain cos he wouldn't.
    I don't like you. What the hell did you mean by being in Edinburgh
and not calling in to see us? Unforgivable sin, sir. (...)
    Well, I set out only to say how glad I am of your success on both sides
of the ocean. I fear I use you ... 'Henry Miller? Oh, a pal of mine. Good
guy.'
    Go on getting your books across ... I was going to say message across
but dunno what your message is. I hope you haven't got one, for you
are not the guy to be in the company of Billy Graham and the Pope. Your
life is your message.
    Warm affection, A. S. Neill

To Henry Miller

Dear Henry   *18 May 1965*
    A research group of Phoenix, Arizona, sent me a copy of your letter
to them. In it you say: 'If I were running a school I wd begin with games
of skill, with song, dance, acting, boxing, wrestling and a knowledge of
the handicrafts, etc.'
    Of course, man. If the bloody exam system did not exist I'd sack all
my teachers of History, Geography, English, Maths, and staff up with
guys and guyesses who would teach exactly what you prescribe. Of my
eight teachers only three do creative work ... woodwork, art, pottery.
I do acting myself.
    I wish you would revisit England. I want to see Henry Miller see S'hill
before I peg out. More than that I want to see you again, you warm,
humorous bugger! (...)
    Come again, friend.
    Warmest greetings, Neill

To Henry Miller

Dear Henry

(...) I keep hating the fact that miles separate us. Old saying: One shd not meet one's heroes. I worshipped H. G. Wells when young. I met him when he was old, arrogant, peevish, squeaky voice. Feet of clay. When I met that villain Miller he came up to expectation, *echt* [genuine], warm. Glad I never met Shaw. Guy I'd have liked to have met wd have been Oscar Wilde to hear his talk about Whistler. Dunno if I'd have liked to meet Jesus, certainly not that anti-life guy St Paul ... I always think of his going thro life trying to hold down an erection. (...)

Damn you for dwelling so far away. I can't even hope to see you in the next world, for I won't be allowed to go below visiting.

I think I love you, Henry ... the most human guy I have ever met.

Neill

6

Politics

Neill challenged controversy by saying that
schools cannot be founded on either Socialism
or Communism. To do so would still be to im-
pose something upon the child, with the con-
sequent neglect of the unconscious. Schools
should be founded on the child itself.

New Leader, August 1932

To David Barton

Dear David   *29 April 1948*
    I haven't the time to write at the enormous length you do, but briefly
... Reich and *The Sexual Struggle of Youth*.[1] When I was there an official
from the FBI[2] came abt a poisonous article agst R in *Harpers*, how he
was corrupting youth etc. If he is soft-pedalling on it it will be because
he was hoofed out of three Scandinavian countries cos of it, and his books
were banned in USSR. A disciple gave lectures on sex to youth recently
in Copenhagen; some CP members came and were charmed. Party told
em: Cut out this stuff (sex); it is side-tracking. One or two gave up the
Party rather than cease sex economy. I go parallel to R here. We hold that
the sickness of humanity is primarily due to castration via sex repression
in babyhood, and that communists ignore this factor and concentrate
only on the economic one. Hence the latest rules for kids in USSR schools
... stand when teacher enters; obey instantly without question; don't
smoke or swear etc. In short, communism in practice is the opposite of
S'hill, for any council school would think the USSR rules damn fine. So
would Eton.
    Reich traces sex repression to patriarchal society where father must cas-
trate in order to have obedience, and father capitalism does ditto so as to
have oxen as workers. I hoped that communism would bring a combination of patriarchal and matriarchal rule, freeing youth sex ... and it did
in 1917 onwards for a few years. I see it going the same old way of our
fathers. In schools Stalin is the ideal father image.

You say I accept the newspapers as a father voice. I say that you blokes do it more effectively by seeing right in everything USSR does. Kravchenko may be a neurotic, but *all* his books can't be a lie, yet most Party members dismiss him as a bloody Trotskyite. You must know that S'hill couldn't possible exist under communism as it shapes today ... see our kids salute any flag or portrait?

Grant that I could as easily criticise the Truman side. It is bad, very bad. I want communism, i.e. a non-profit society *plus* what S'hill stands for ... independence of the individual. How you after a life in S'hill can approve of the USSR telling musicians what they mustn't compose, I dunno. You rightly condemn it in capitalism ... as when in New York they cut out of my broadcast a bit abt no wholemeal bread in USA, cos the white flour millers own part of the commercial radio. (...)

My new book in the press[3] elaborates this letter, and I fear will give the impression that I am an anti-communist bloke. So that when *der Tag* [the day] comes you may be commanded to shove me up agst the cottage wall and say Fire. A wise guy like you shd see that I am aiming beyond communism, aiming at humanity whether it owns factories or not, aiming at complete freedom to be free from all moulders whether communist ones or not. Ultimately communism will give freedom to youth. I want to speed up the process. (...)

Neill

[1] A pamphlet by Reich published in 1932.
[2] In fact it was the FDA, the Federal Drug Administration.
[3] *The Problem Family*.

To David Barton

Dear David   *27 June 1948*

Dunno why I have to be the one you practise your clever debating powers on. Fact is you are too far ahead of party members in general ... t'other day at a Party meeting in town S'hill was mentioned, and all the teachers present were agin it cos they thought subjects etc were edderca-tion. One or two parents remained behind interested to ask questions of the one who had spoken for S'hill ... a parent of course. (...)

I am puzzled why the Party here in England is so consistently agin S'hill, for the fact that it is a class affair ain't deep enough. Most of em can't stomach the truth that every kid ever born shdn't work until he or she is at least 18. They shd play up to then. (...)

Thine, Neill

To James and Tania Stern

Dear Both   *1 December 1952*

Pleasant surprise to know you are still here. Yes, I can understand your mixed feelings in going back now. If at the age of ten you attended a peace meeting or ever waved a flag for the Spanish Left ... Gord elp you if Mr McCarran catches you.[1] I feel most depressed now that the fire-eaters are in the saddle, not because I can't ever get to US again (don't want to go now anyway), but simply because of the appalling fear now that reaction rules openly. (...)

Be seein' yuh, I hope, we hope. Bless you both. Neill

[1] The McCarran-Walter Act had been invoked to prevent Neill from returning to the USA in 1950. The Act allowed entry to be refused to anyone who advocated doctrines or was affiliated with organisations held to be subversive.

To the Editor, the *Guardian*

Sir   *4 February 1953*

Mr Blair Mitchell says: 'No one is prevented entry to the United States because of his political convictions...'. In 1950, after having had two lecture tours in the United States, I was refused a visa because of political convictions I did not have. I have never been a Communist. I admired the Russian system of education when it was going my way, the way of freedom for children. Now that that education has become authoritative character-moulding, it is the opposite of all I have done and written about for years. So that, if I had got that visa, the only things I might have said in my lectures about Russian education would have been strongly 'anti'.

It seems obvious that the act, originally intended to keep out Communists, is now being used to keep out anyone who has liberal opinions on any subject. Indeed I am so alarmed that I hesitate to write to any of my teacher friends in America, fearing that Mr McCarran might put them in the pillory as dangerous persons who correspond with a foreigner who was refused entry. I suppose I am not the only one to sigh at the thought that a few thousand Americans will enter Britain this summer without any visas whatsoever.

Yours, etc, A. S. Neill

To Nina Kai Nielson

My dear Nina   *24 October 1954*

(…) As for communism. My dear, I have read oceans of pro books; took the *Daily Worker* for years, and gave it up long ago because I couldn't stand its hate. My dislike of communism is simply that it is nothing new; it moulds kids all the way. One teacher visitor says in nursery schools a child is not left alone; must always be educated to be a crowd unit. Dunno, but it fits in with a Pavlov nation. One of our MPs just back from USSR says she saw a nursery school with a basin of red flags in the centre. It isn't my conception of freedom any more than McCarthy's is. You say you are reading *The Sexual Revolution*. Good, but there hasn't been one in USSR. Yes, in 1920 or so, then back to the western idea of the family, abortion, divorce, refusal of love life to adolescents. Just that point that Reich broke with communism on.

Love to you both from us both, Neill

P.S. Solve this riddle. Communism says economic factors form man's character. Reich says the character structure of man determines his economic system.

To Gordon Leff

Dear Bunny   *3 March 1962*

Shelley puts it:

'Most wretched men are cradled into poetry through wrong;
They learn in suffering what they teach in song.'

You are saying much the same thing, that resistance, fight, rebellion spring from a cramped environment. In my own case the fight against my narrow Calvinistic youth and its stupid authority. But here is a snag. All my seven brothers and sisters remained in the Establishment. Why did I rebel? I don't know. You and others had not the urge to find a better life; S'hill was easy, pleasant, even to some lotus eating. Things like slums, criminality, prisons, the under-privileged were outside your ken. In a way abstractions. Hence the awkward question at my lectures … why hasn't any old pupil decided to follow in your footsteps and reform education? The answer may be: because to them education *is* reformed. They never knew the misery of barrack schools. Summerhill doesn't give a big enough grouse. Note that the only rebels really are the Communists – Mike B,[1] Barton, Johnnie Collier, who accepted the home grouse; their communism has nought to do with S'hill. They can't even see the paradox – S'hill freedom of the individual v. the Russian moulding of character from the cradle. So, laddie, there is a deep problem involved. Does freedom lead to indifference? Not quite. Possibly every old pupil is anti-bomb; quite a few take part in the marches. (...)

Love, Neill

[1] Michael Bernal.

To Brian Stanley

Dear Stanley   *21 September 1962*
I dunno what anarchy means. I subscribe to *Freedom* simply because it is always on my side and that of Reich. Some anarchists claim that fundamentally Summerhill is an anarchist community. I dunno. (...)

Yours, Neill

To Seishi Shimoda

My dear Shimoda   *21 January 1966*
(...) I hope you and your family will have a good New Year, but how any of us can be happy in a world of Vietnam, Rhodesia, colour hate I do not know. The voices of you and me never reach the war makers and the statesmen. L. B. Johnson never heard of us I'm sure. They have the power and we have only our dreams of freedom for mankind. But it was always so. The haters killed Christ and they don't kill you and me simply because they don't think us dangerous enough, dangerous to their hate view of life.

Yours ever, Neill

To Elsworth Baker

Dear Baker   *22 October 1967*
What a wonderful surprise to get your birthday gift, and what a joy to get a book from USA that isn't dull to read.[1] (...) The only criticism I have is that I think you are a bit unfair to the liberals. I don't care a cuss if they are compensating for hidden impotencies or what not, but it pleases me to see them, over here, pressing for reforms on laws on homos, on abortion, on divorce, but being stopped by the conservatives

... and not only the political ones. The House of Lords is trying to castrate the Abortion Bill. Also, the majority of teachers here are conservative and in a recent Gallup Poll 86% voted for the cane in schools. But I grant that the liberalism of – say – the *New Statesman* is as anti-life as hell. I had long arguments with Reich about this. After all the parents of my kids ... 42 from US and only 22 from England ... are of liberal mind. I was puzzled when R gave me a year's sub for a magazine with a name like *World Views and Reviews,* for to me it was all that was anti-life. It might have been published in the Pentagon. (...)

Yours, Neill

[1] The book Baker had sent was his own study of Reich's psychiatric ideas and techniques, *Man in a Trap*.

To John Aitkenhead

Dear John   *13 December 1967*
(...) I wish I cd share yr enthusiasm about Scots Nationalism. Have a House in Edinburgh and it will be full of all the buggers we are up against, the wee self-important men who take up politics ... I wonder if any really great men were politicians. Can you imagine a Freud, a Darwin, an Einstein sitting in Westminster? Mind you, to start with you might get good members with vision, but politics corrupt and of course attract the anti-lifers. Who cd call Wilson or Brown or Heath big men with vision? I gave up faith in politics when Russian politicians killed the freedom of youth there. Will a Scottish Educn Dept in Edinburgh be on the side of Bob Mackenzie or his governors? Ye ken dawm fine which side he'll tak. (...)

Love to you both, Neill

To Elsworth Baker

Dear Baker   *15 February 1968*
(...) I have long ago given up all interest in politics. Our Labour Govt has the same views on education as the Tories ... better science, higher level in exams. Yet in the main the Tories want to keep capital punishment, the cane in school, rigid censorship of films etc. And today our home Tories are almost openly on the side of Ian Smith and their Rhodesian 'kith and kin'. Still I shd vote Tory for as long as the Tories ... the real ruling class ... retain their Eton and Harrow, Summerhill will be protected by their 'independent umbrella'. (...)

All the best, Neill

To Gordon Leff

Dear Bunny   *24 November 1969*

You are too deep for me, but thanks for casting your pearls.[1] I think you are too diffuse; a synopsis of each chapter giving the main points would have helped a layman like myself. Puzzled about page 60, where you discount psychoanalysis. Hitler's origins etc are *unbedeutend* [unimportant] I agree, I am sure that history will concentrate on the causes of Fascism ... war defeat and subsequent poverty etc. But will it take into account the deeper causes? Reich's *Mass Psychology of Fascism* tells of the reasons why 60 million Germans, agnst all their own interests, followed a madman ... the castration of the masses, by the Establishment's making them guilty abt sex, making em obedient in infancy so that they could never really rebel or even challenge. You might like the book ... I can lend you the only copy in England. True, it can be asked: why then do the castrated millions in other lands not seek Hitlers? They could given the circumstances, and, after all, the docility in this country, the acceptance of the Establishment, international finance etc cd be traced to the killings of the emotions of the young.

Take S'hill. Some future historian will tell of the progressive movement following the first war. I can see the sentence: 'The most radical school was Summerfield, run by an Irishman, A. C. Nail.' But it won't say how we differed from Bedales; it won't tell of the influences that made S'hill different ... my stay in Vienna amongst the analysts, Homer Lane, the failure of politics to give freedom for kids ... cf the original wave of freedom in USSR schools and its evil indoctrination today.

Take anti-Semitism, how to trace its origins. In Dresden in 1921 the big shops had notices, *Keine Juden werden verdient* [no Jews will be served], but it began decades before then. Who knows why? Reich held that it was mainly sexual ... the circumcised Jew was paradoxically a good lover. Myself I don't think that can be a main reason. What I am trying to say is that crowd psychology shd loom largely in history. Leslie Morton tried it, but ignored the psychological and made the economic the main factor.

Thanks a lot for giving me a headache, you learned bugger.
      Neill

[1] He had sent Neill a copy of his book *History and Social Theory*.

To James Young

Dear James   *24 June 1972*

(…) I lost interest in politics years ago, partly cos of the enforced insincerity. Possible that Wilson thought Vietnam a crime agnst humanity but he had to support USA for dollars, arms etc. And with many Roman Catholics in his constituency he'd have found it difficult to support, say, an abortion bill. Also I think I lost interest when early communism, with its school and sex freedom, ended in the present police state. Democracy? A few million workers who think of nothing but football and never read anything higher than the *Mirror* are the voters. Only when kids are free all the way will a democracy work … no one cd lead my old pupils. (…)

Yours, Neill

To Joseph Kirschner

Dear Joseph   *19 February 1973*

(…) Anarchy. You know I never knew what the damned word meant. If it means literally without law, S'hill is miles from that with its self-govt. Maybe significant that Paul Goodman was one of the severest critics of my system. On the other hand, if anarchy means being anti-laws made by authorities, I am an anarchist. (…)

I often think that USA is on the verge of Fascism. Since the fascist mentality controls the mass media – press, TV, radio – and feeds the masses on kitsch, I tremble for the future. I fear that Fascist Reagan reaches a much wider public than I do, and I don't get much comfort in thinking that Summerhill will live long after he is forgotten. (…)

Alles gut, Neill

7

Authors, Books and Writing

A Dominie's Log (Herbert Jenkins, 2/6d) is the title of a volume of some interest that has recently come to hand. It might be described as the revelation of the soul of a teacher struggling to emancipate himself from the shackles of formalism and tradition ... It is to be hoped that we have not heard the last of the author.

Times Educational Supplement, December 1915

To the Editor, *New Age*

Sir   *16 December 1915*
    Anyone of average intelligence would guess that I want to try an experiment.[1] I have read out in school a few verses of Little Jim, and then a few verses of La Belle Dame Sans Merci, in order to convey to my bairns that there are such things as good verse and bad verse. On the same lines I want to try them with a popular tune and an acknowledged masterpiece.
    Now I want to know where the cant comes in. I take it that cant means hypocrisy, and most people take it thus. If the compiler of your column sees any attempt at hypocrisy in the passage quoted, I should not be surprised if he looks upon the Sermon on the Mount as an advocacy of polygamy and vegetarianism.
    I don't really mind his little joke, but I contend that it is quite pointless and very silly. His interpretation of the word 'cant' must be the one that is not the usually accepted one. I beseech him to define 'cant'. If he does not, the column will continue to be the mystery it is now.
    Yours, A. S. Neill

[1] Two weeks before, the *New Age* had featured the following passage from *A Dominie's Log* in its 'Current Cant' column: 'If I could play the piano I should spend each Friday afternoon playing to my bairns. I should give them Alexander's Ragtime Band and Hitchey Coo; then I should play them a Liszt Rhapsody and a Chopin waltz.'

To W. B. Curry

Dear Curry   *19 January 1935*

(...) I've taken to playwrighting, and have produced a damn good one I think. Know of any producers? I'll try Maurice Browne, I think. I was tired of writing about psychology, and wanted to do something more creative. (...)

Yours, Neill

To W. B. Curry

Dear Curry   *12 February 1935*

I got Maurice Browne to read the play. He sees a good play in it, gave me some valuable suggestions, told me to re-write it and send it back to him. So keep your hopes on that box.[1] (...)

Yours ever, Neill

[1] Curry had asked for a box for the play's opening night.

To J. R. Ackerley

Dear Ackerley   *22 April 1937*

I'm damned sorry ... for you. To be unfree to work in your own way is simply bloody.[1]

Confidentially between ourselves would it damage you if I got another paper to publish the review stating that it was rejected by the *Listener*? I'd like to. But only on condition that it doesn't hurt you in any way.

I'll return the cheque when it comes to the Editor in Chief, with a neat note of thanks. Shall I send the books back?

I don't know who the powers in the BBC are now. I used to meet the late editor, Lambert (?)[2] at Prof Flugel's.[3] He argued with me about education, taking the diehard angle.

I think you ought to join the *Daily Worker* ... you'd be comparatively free there!

Yours sincerely, A. S. Neill

[1] The editor of the *Listener*, Sir Stephen Tallents, had refused to let Ackerley publish Neill's review of three educational books, in which he had written in scathing terms of the heads of some of the major public schools. 'I won't have all this cocking snooks at the bigwigs,' Tallents observed.

[2] R. S. Lambert.

[3] J. C Flugel's house in London was a meeting-place for leading psychologists and public figures of the day.

To Lilian Morgans

Ffestiniog, North Wales
Dear Lilian   *22 June 1942*
    I thought you a bright-minded person when I came to Saxmund-
ham, but now you spoil the picture by liking *Is Scotland Educated?* which
I personally think is a poor book, full of padding to hide my gross ignorance of Scotland today, or rather 1935. Too much ASN in it. However,
I can only conclude generously that you liked the few wee diamonds in
the mass of blue clay. (...)
    Yours sincerely, Neill

To Lilian Morgans

Ffestiniog, North Wales
Dear Lilian   *11 December 1942*
    (...) Enclosed article shows a new interest, one that is driving me to
Ayrshire to get material for a life of Brown.[1] I presume you know the
book. If not I can lend you a copy. Odd that at long last I leave education
to justify my Hons English degree! (...)
    Yours, Neill

[1] George Douglas Brown, author of *The House with the Green Shutters*.

To Lilian Morgans

Ffestiniog, North Wales
Dear Lilian   *30 March 1943*
    (...) I get along too slowly with my book,[1] impatiently too, for I
long to write a long-planned *Diary of an Ugly Woman*, a psychoanalytic
detective yarn, a life of G.D. Brown, lots of plays ... in short a 50 yrs
plan, and I am 59. Time is the most deadly enemy in the world. In young
years when we have time we are full of love and ambition and conceit
and we do so little, and then when we feel inspired to do much, Father
Time steps in and says: 'Put your toys away, child, and come along.'
    But one knows that nothing is lost. What will it matter in fifty years
whether I write a book or not? That is looking at it from a society viewpoint; from a personal one it is different. The joy in doing something one
loves doing is the main thing. It is all a variant of a woman producing
a child, but much easier in this way, that if I paint a picture, creation is
finished, and the result remains. You produce a brat and your creation
grows away from you, forgets, must forget you in the long run, as we
all come to forget everyone. No woman can rightly look at a genius son

in glory or a criminal one in the dock and say: I did that. Yes, she must have done a lot for the lad in the dock – the wrong lot, but for the creator son I wonder how much? It is the doing value that matters. I think that the feeling your man gets when he has done a good job of bridge work is essentially the same thing as that which followed the writing of *Hamlet*, and just as important to the doer even if he pleases one individual while Shakespeare pleases millions. (...)

Yours, Neill

[1] Neill was having difficulties in completing *Hearts not Heads in the School*.

To James Stern

Dear Jimmy   *3 April 1947*

Good of you to offer help re editions in USA. International Universities Press Inc. brought out my *Problem Teacher* over a year ago, but up to Dec last sold only 140 copies, which is a bloody sale anyway. They haven't approached me re an edition of *Hearts not Heads* (I'll post you a copy ... no, better get it when you come, for it may miss you) and it seems unlikely that they will after so bad a sale. By the way, McBrides published my *Problem Child* in '27 or so, but when one or two papers said it was obscene they hastily stopped selling it. If I could get a lecture tour in USA I think I could get a public for my books. (...)

Ethel.[1] See her once in a blue moon. Drifted apart a lot I fear. I mean if I stay a night at Oak Cottage we are both delighted to talk and laugh, but in the morning I (and I fancy she also) feel that we have nix more to say to each other. She is over-determined with anarchism and ILPism and a most persistent belief that Britain is always in the wrong, and out-gestapoes the Gestapo in India and colonies in torture etc. N.B. she is having a new edition of *Commonsense and the Adolescent* and asked me to write a new preface. I did, casually mentioning a young Nazi who threw a baby agnst a wall cos it kept him from sleeping. Ethel indignant asked me to cut it out cos it is time we stopped writing about the Nazi sadists when we ought to write of our own treatment of natives etc. But apart from opinions, we do like each other a lot. (...)

All good things, Neill

[1] Ethel Mannin.

To George Ives

Dear Ives   *10 February 1949*
    My very warm thanks for the gift of your book which awaited me at Norman Haire's. It kept me completely interested on my train way home. Your erudition is wonderful; you seem to have read everything of importance and remembered it. But to me the important factor is that, behind all your quotations, there is your own personality standing forth clearly, that of a man who loves infinitely more than he hates, a man with charity to see the other fellow's point of view even when that view is a dangerous one. For all I know you may be a fire-eating general in person, but I very much doubt if you are.
    That trick of yours of making chapters sometimes as short as two pages is a very good one and quite new to me.
    My latest book came out last week,[1] and I have much pleasure in sending you a copy. Possibly we may differ on minor points, but we are both similar in the big ideas in life. You are older than I am ... 65 the other day ... and I only hope that at your age I shall be able to write and live the 'alive' way you do.
    Yours sincerely, A. S. Neill

[1] *The Problem Family*.

To Seishi Shimoda

My dear Shimoda   *2 October 1950*
    My most humble apologies. I offered to send you the MS of my autobiography,[1] knowing that I had it, but after a long search I found it with many of its pages missing. It has lain since 1939 and has been through the moving of the school when war broke out. So I had to sit down and try to complete the missing parts. Then I got into personal trouble. I was booked to go to USA to a conference and to lecture, had my passage booked, then suddenly the American embassy held up my visa, and for ten weeks I sat waiting to see if the visa would be granted. The other day the consul wrote saying that I could not get a visa. You can imagine that working at a MS while I had this nasty worry was not easy, and I fear I had spells when I couldn't write a thing. However I have completed it, and on second thoughts have sent it to an agency to have two other copies made. (...) Now that I'll have two copies to keep, please keep the other copy with you. And if England is wiped out by atomic war, there will be some record left in the Far East, so that future

educationalists may read something about the background of Summerhill. That sounds pessimistic, but the world situation is so very black today.

Yours sincerely, Neill

[1] This manuscript eventually formed the first part of *Neill! Neill! Orange Peel!*, published in 1973.

To James Stern

Dear Jimmy   *7 March 1953*
I've been ill with flu for weeks and read every book in the house. Then came your wee parcel of salvation. When I say salvation, I am not ignoring the fact that there is some doubt whether it is good for a guy with a high temp to read about biting mamba heads, fever rooms, hunting deaths, yet the temp didn't jump up. It did next morning, when three shorts of my own came back from a Scots paper as unsuitable.

So as one guy to another, a guy who can't write stories to a guy as can, I ask how the hell you do it? I know it can't be taught, can't be learned, the skill of restraint, the covering of a large canvas by one small sweep of a wee brush. *Die Stimmung* [atmosphere] e.g. of that new governess story, the brilliant way you got the younger brother to kill himself while you and dad jumped together without seeing the kid. No explanation, none, a bloody gift, that's all. I ain't no judge, only took 2nd Class Hons English M.A., but I'd put you among the few top shorts writers today.

Love to you both, Neill

To James Stern

Dear Jimmy   *30 March 1953*
Just back from Edinburgh and Nature Cure which bucked me up a lot. Then your sad letter came. I dunno; have had no experience of a creative lamp running short of oil. Old men repeat themselves, become poor in art ... Kipling, Jacobs, Wells, Chaplin (to judge from *Limelight*), *aber* [but] a young man like you isn't in that category. The Happy Marriage theory I reject, on the ground that it fits into the Freudian view that sublimated sex makes art. I agree with Reich that a sex, or better, a love life helps a creative life all the time. (...)

Love to you both, Neill

To Paul Ritter

Dear Paul   *18 March 1955*
    (...) Will you do something for me, Paul? Various people have suggested that I might make a book called Neillisms, wisecracks etc culled from all my books. Might be an idea, but I feel kinda shy at approaching the publishers myself. Would you write em a letter suggesting the idea ... Herbert Jenkins Ltd, 3 Duke of York St, St James's, London SW1.
    All the best, Neill

To Harold Hart

Dear Mr Hart   *24 April 1958*
    My publishers have sent me your letter. They have nothing to do with foreign rights.
    Your plan sounds excellent, and if you can come over to discuss it with me I shall be glad.[1] (...)
    I doubt if you can use *The Problem Family* which was published about ten years ago by Hermitage Press Inc in New York. It sold badly and I think was sold out as remainder copies. I understand it is out of print now. *The Problem Child* (1927 or so) contains much that I'd now disapprove of; I was then too much influenced by Freudianism.
    I think you are a hero to try to abridge the lot ... it would break my heart to make the attempt.
    Yours sincerely, A. S. Neill

[1] Hart had proposed bringing out a new volume in America, containing the essence of some of Neill's earlier books.

Henry Miller to Neill

                                      Big Sur, California
Dear Mr Neill   *9 July 1958*
    I've been hearing of your wonderful school for years and finally, through Mrs Ann Perkoff who has corresponded with you, I got hold of about five of your books and read them with jubilation.
    I have a girl of thirteen whom I will have to send to another higher school shortly. I wish I knew of one remotely approaching yours – in this country. Is it possible there is such a one? I imagine you would know better than any one. I can get nowhere here through my inquiries.

There is an Ecole d'Humanité in Goldren, Switzerland, but that's so far away! (...)

I know you must be a very busy man. Just a postcard will do, if you have a school to suggest.

Let me say in closing that everything you say strikes me as absolute common sense. The trouble is that only a man like you can undertake such a radical project. You may not have a successor for a thousand years. I mean it!

Warm greetings to you – carry on!

Sincerely, Henry Miller

To Henry Miller

Dear Henry Miller   *25 July 1958*

I know of no school in USA that resembles Summerhill. During my two lecture tours (1947 and '48) after answering many questions I always ended with a question to the audience: 'Have you anything resembling my school in USA?' The answer was always a negative shake of the head.

The Hart Publishing Co are bringing out my last two books in one volume in a cheap edition. They want me to suggest a sponsor to write a preface (to me a silly American convention, for a writer shd stand on his own feet). I'd like very much to ask you if you'd do it, I'd be as proud as Punch to be backed by a man of your stature; my doubt, however, is whether the publisher would agree on the ground that your name would frighten off all the people of shall we say Dulles mentality, i.e. the guys who buy books. (...)

Yours, A. S. Neill

Henry Miller to Neill

Dear Mr Neill   *31 July 1958*

Thank you for answering – I know how plagued you are right now. I would be happy to write a preface for that American publisher – don't know them, incidentally – if he wished it. *And*, of course, if he'd accept what I wish to say.

Since reading you I feel I must make an effort to say something – to Americans – about you, your work, your aims. How we need you!

I started a book recently, and shelved it temporarily, on children versus adults. I'd like to close my own life effort – all these banned 'autobiographical' romances – by making a desperate appeal to save the children of this world – save them from the stupidity and cruelty of their elders. I have two wonderful kids of my own and it sickens me to see what they are up against.

What I want to say, in connection with you and your work, is that the only real revolution is the one you are carrying on. We'll make no radical change in our way of life thru political changes. Education seems to come last on the calendar – even with revolutionaries.

Everything Reich said in that vituperative little book of his, *Listen, Little Man!*, is so very true. Everything you write – and from the depths of experience! – likewise. But where is the genius who can make em listen?

I may get to see you some day. I'm not fond of England but I want to explore (before I die) the land of Avalon. King Arthur is still a great name for me.

Blessings on you and your good spouse.

Henry Miller

To Henry Miller

Dear Henry Miller   *3 September 1958*

Alas, the Hart Publishing people seem to think that your preface wouldn't draw the public. A great pity. Of course I don't know the situation in the USA. I guess no publisher here would think my name of any value in a preface ... even one to the New Testament.

I wish your books were available over here. Yours and Reich's are almost impossible to get. It would be good to escape into your works in the pauses between brinkmanship.

Yours, A. S. Neill

To Harold Hart

Dear Hart   *24 December 1958*

I'm sending the MS by airmail. I've made a few smaller corrections. Only thing that worries me is the going so far back to *That Dreadful School*; it reads as if my first wife is still alive, and the names of staff are names that went from the school many years ago. I don't suppose it will make any difference to American readers anyway. I dunno if you'll keep the few additions when I mention pupils who are now grown up and are university lecturers etc now. I think you've done wonders so far, and the above is my only criticism. (...)

You don't say who the sponsor is. Sad that it couldn't be Henry Miller.

I've just read his *Tropic of Cancer* and *Big Sur* and he sure can write, moreover he is a warm-hearted man ... but then I am prejudiced cos he writes me letters praising my books.

Why not break that silly tradition that a book needs a sponsor? Or can't I be my own sponsor? I could easily begin thus: 'It gives me misery to write a preface to this bloody book by that damn fool Neill.' Better of course if John Foster Dulles would do it, or that Ike should sponsor it from a Sputnik. Hell, cut them all out. Just say, This book doesn't need a sponsor. (...)

Neill

To Harold Hart

Dear Hart   *31 January 1959*
  I am worried. Reading my own work is shattering, and that is the real reason why I suggested that you carry on without sending me the MS. It is most depressing to read what I wrote, say, twenty, or in the case of *The Problem Child*, thirty years ago. Books are bloody milestones on a journey in which one does not want to go back. Seriously, I suggest that you do exactly what you like with the MS, while I write either a preface or an appendix saying how I differ or agree with what has been written before. (...)

I am filled with wonder and admiration for your patience in picking out so many things from the books. I'll have another go at the MS and then return it. (...)

Now what about your having a free hand about the MS? I trust you; I can see you have done a difficult job well. You say nothing about that preface by some well-known guy.

  Alles gut, Neill

To Harold Hart

Dear Hart   *21 February 1959*
  I'm still not recovered from flu but have managed to go through the MS again. I am still concerned about the mixture, and it would be grand if you did come over to thresh it out with me here, but is the huge expense for you worth it? It is possibly too late for me to say: Cut that bit out cos I no longer use that method. A lot is from my Freudian period of child analysis which I wouldn't use now. E.g. today I would never interpret – say – a phallic symbol in a child's picture or dream. And you, poor

devil, have the awful task of reconciling different attitudes due to my growth (or degeneration). Your query about conflicting ideas about bed-wetting is right. I've marked that short chapter Delete, partly cos I have never had much success with enuresis. (...)

I see your point about my writing an appendix stating changes in my attitudes or rather my methods, because my attitude to freedom has never changed. (...)

Yours, Neill

To Willa Muir

Kingston Clinic, Edinburgh
My dear Willa   *Christmas Eve 1959*

Your cheering letter lightens the sombre gloom of a nature cure diet. But even here there is relief. I sit daily in the National Library (once the Advocate's) reading the original MS of the *Green Shutters*, hoping to do an article on the mysterious fact that, outwith the *House*, Brown never wrote a vivid line or phrase. If it weren't for his actual handwriting in the MS a case could almost be made out for this prose Shakespeare having his Bacon. I am seeing James Veitch who wrote the Life on Sunday. Hope he doesna speir hoo [guess how] I liked it.[1] (...)

No good my suggesting you write Edwin's Life. He dunnit himself.[2] Mind ye, I dinna hold wi' lives; I think that only what one does matters. Sed he after his own autobiog has been rejected by three publishers, including Jenkins. (...)

Lots of love, dear, and pagan blessings for 1960. Allie

[1] When he gave up the idea of writing George Douglas Brown's life, Neill passed the material he had gathered to James Veitch.
[2] Edwin Muir's *An Autobiography*.

To Harold Hart

Dear Harold   *15 April 1960*

Fromm's introduction is a Wow. Wonderful. But do send me his address so that I can thank him.

I am still worried about your Reich complex. I shudder to see an index without his name, for, as I told you when you were here, I cannot claim to have discovered that neurosis shows in stiff necks and stomachs. I must give Reich the credit for that. (...) Haven't you just been a little cowardly about Reich? The majority condemned him, but you don't strike me as being a majority guy. Otherwise why issue *Summerhill*? (...)

Nothing more to say, only to repeat that I am so glad and proud to have a man like Fromm support us.

Yours, Neill

To Harold Hart

Dear Harold   *14 June 1960*

(...) Fromm sent me two of his books. He is more of a philosopher than a psychologist I think. His words don't touch something deep in me as Reich's did. A clever guy to be sure; his analysis of society fine and true, but so far I can't discover what he wants to do positively about social evils.

The Menninger book you sent me months ago I have just read. Some good ideas in it, deep ones often. But how is an ordinary guy like myself to know what truth is? All bright men – Reich, Freud, Menninger, Fromm – all giving their views on truth, and all different. Moral: abolish all books and allow publishers to earn an honest living sweeping streets. Same with authors.

All the same I'd like to meet Fromm, but will never be likely to visit Mexico. Mind you, I know nothing about him. How he stands in the States I dunno. I won't be able to assess him til I have read him more and digested his books.

Thanks for kindness about that generous royalty arrangement, I mean giving me a break ... my God, I need it. Can't now afford a car or a gardener. Why should all these writers like Fromm and Henry Miller and Huxley make a packet while I can't?

All the best, Harold, Neill

To Ilse Ollendorff Reich

Dear Ilse   *17 August 1960*

(...) Hart Publishing Co New York is bringing out a volume called *Summerhill*. It is made up from my last five books. I had an argument with Hart about Reich. He cut out every reference to him, saying that his name would ruin the sales. I insisted that I could not claim the discovery of stiff stomachs and that he must say the idea was Reich's. He tried to get Margaret Mead to write a preface and she said: 'This man Neill is a Reichian; I won't touch a book that mentions Reich.' He got Erich Fromm to write one. Fromm has sent me a few of his books, *aber* he is not a great man like Reich. Hoppe says R told him that Fromm has stolen his ideas without acknowledgement, but I can't see it, for Fromm denigrates sex all the way. (...)

Love, Neill

To Harold Hart

Dear Harold   *2 November 1960*
(...) I had the book sent to the BBC, and if they take it up and interview me it will be grand, only I fear that they can only deal with books published here, so that listeners or rather viewers can buy a copy. Will it mar your sales coming out at election week?[1] (...)

I shall be with you in spirit on Sunday night ... no, it will be bedtime over here. I wish I could be there. Interesting that *Summerhill* and *Lady Chatterley's Lover* come out (I hope) this week. But the jury may refuse Lady C. I wish I could get as much publicity as she had.

I am most anxious to hear as soon as you can tell me how the sales go. You deserve bumper ones.

All the best, Neill

[1] *Summerhill* was published on 7 November, during the week John F. Kennedy was elected President of the United States.

To Harold Hart

Dear Harold   *21 November 1960*
(...) I eagerly watch each mail to see what USA is saying about the book. The BBC hasn't answered; I think they won't touch it until it will be issued here.

You will have to decide which publisher here you want to publish it. None of them, the nearest Gollancz, has the drive and initiative and the boldness that Harold Hart has. They are sleepy publishers.

Someone suggested I shd approach Penguins to issue my last four books in paperbacks, but I don't want to spoil your sales here and won't do anything about it. I know Sir Allen Lane and years ago suggested to him my books, but he didn't agree.

Were there any press reports of the Sunday launching meeting?

Everyone who has seen the book praises the way it has been got up.

The best, Neill

To Ilse Ollendorff Reich

Dear Ilse   *27 December 1960*

Of course you must not buy the book; I told the publisher to send you a copy. I left it to him what to select from my past books and I soon noticed he did not want Reich's name to be prominent; he said that so many reviewers are against Reich that his name would spoil the sales. I was sad about it but, after all, it is about Summerhill, and Reich came too late in my life to influence the Summerhill set-up. I hear the first edition was sold out in three weeks and that another 5000 are being printed. Americans must be *Meschugge* [mad]; I wouldn't pay £2 for any book! (...)

Neill

To Livia Gollancz

Dear Livia   *17 June 1961*

(...) Ask Read if he will consent to cutting out the name of Caldwell Cook for his blurb.[1] ... Cook wasn't a real pioneer, only in teaching English, not in living. I really don't think the book will make the same impression here as in the US, for if my other books didn't, why should a symposium break the record?

Yours, Neill

[1] Herbert Read had written: 'Summerhill is the name of a small school, but it signifies a great experiment in education. In the forty years of its existence its founder has proved (despite much discouragement and revilement) one simple truth – *freedom works*. I place Neill with Pestalozzi and Caldwell Cook among the great reforming teachers, bringing light and love into places (the home as well as the school) where there was once tyranny and fear. Summerhill is a name that will never be forgotten in the annals of education.'

To Elna Lucas

Dear Elna   *12 May 1962*
    I am going to have a treat.[1] In the past Peter's books have made me
feel so small; I know so little, have read so little, and his erudition gave
me an inferiority complex. Now I can face the man, for since 1908 Ibsen
has been my hero, and at last I'll know what Peter is writing about. As
for Strindberg; I've read and re-read him since the night in Berlin, 1922,
when, knowing not a word of German, I saw the *Totentanz* [*The Dance
of Death*] and was thrilled just by its tenseness and sincerity.
    I'll sign the book[2] and post it to you. It has sold 30,000 in America and
is in a second edition over here after two weeks. *Nicht so staubig*! [Not so
dusty!] But I don't like the book much, for the American publisher
Americanised my style, split all my infinitives, and made me say: 'Never
derate a child.' The only meaning I know for that word is to lower someone's rates. Also he included Freudian things I grew out of years ago. But
in the main it sums up what I have done. (…)
    I'll write after I have read the book. Many thanks for sending it. Why,
with all his books and his good sense, he isn't Prof of Eng Lit in Cambridge I dunno. Too radical I guess, too much outside the dear old Establishment. (…)
    My friends live a few miles from Skien and usually drive me over to
see Ibsen's birthplace, and I am always annoyed, cos the fools have done
it up; instead of showing the big pot on charred sticks they have painted
the damn thing. Anyway I can never go back into the past by looking
at ruins, only in Holyrood can I dimly see David Rizzio being stabbed
to death, but here agin they washed out the blood stains. Vandals.
    Love, Neill

[1] Elna Lucas had sent him a copy of *Ibsen and Strindberg* by her husband F. L.
Lucas.
[2] *Summerhill*.

To Brian Stanley

Dear Stanley   *21 September 1962*
    I am sending you the beginning of an autobiography I started but
didn't go on with, mainly cos I don't think I'm important enough, partly
because I can't publish to the world all my shortcomings. (…)
    Yours, Neill

To the Editor, the *Guardian*

Sir   *12 December 1963*

Mary Crozier's review of the television Wesker play *Menace* tempts me to reveal my out-of-dateness. Reared, as it were, on Ibsen and Strindberg, I can see nothing in modern plays of any dramatic significance.

In *Waiting for Godot* two tramps talk and talk and get nowhere; all they convey to me is the known fact that it is a sick world. So in Pinter's *Caretaker*. Here three misfits talk and talk and stay put. *Menace* the other night almost put me to sleep ... gabble, gabble, gabble.

True, all the modern plays show character, but I take it that character in drama should have action and growth. Nora grows from a baby doll in the first act to a woman in the last one; Hamlet does something, Prospero burns his book. The characters in *Menace* simply were there, futile, aimless, not half alive most of them.

It is usual to talk of kitchen-sink drama. Fine, good to get away from the middle class of Ibsen & Co. But ask a million housewives what a kitchen sink is and I guess the reply would be: The shabby symbol of my lifeless life.

Yours sincerely, A. S. Neill

To Bryn Purdy

Dear Bryn   *5 March 1964*

I dunno if Dent and Co wd want to do anything. In his *To be a Teacher* he called me a towering genius (poor devil ... I mean him). James[1] likes me personally but is a religious guy. Clegg in a review of *S'hill* was half and half. Auden? I dunno. Lunched with him in New York 1948 but, alas, didn't know he had been influenced by Lane. Burt is out. I haven't met him since the late twenties. He chaired a radio talk between me and another man and stole the show. Nicholas Bagnall, ed of the *Teacher*, is friendly to me. Why not ask him to run yr MS as a serial? Ben Morris, Prof of Educn in Bristol, is a great pal of mine. I go abt once a year to lecture for him. *Id*[2] isn't widely enough read for you.

Best if you don't need puffs from other guys. You have em in plenty on the American side of course. But the names don't mean much over here.

I never heard of the Charles Causley you mention. But I can't read poetry.

Write to Bagnall. Or the editor of *Anarchy*, which is having a Lane no. in April, with extracts from David Wills' Life of Lane.

Alles gut, Neill

[1] Walter James, editor of the *TES* at this time.
[2] The magazine of the Summerhill Society.

To David Wills

Dear David   *4 August 1964*

I feel the same way about the *New Statesman*. Never have I seen it back up anything vital, like freedom for kids. Worse under Freeman, but K. Martin was not more advanced.

I am not like you; I get all reviews via an agency, and had I kept them all I'd have had a tome since 1915. I keep none, for or agnst, but I like to see what is being said about me in case the *Mirror* tells of my having been seen in the arms of some noted homo. (...)

The Lane book[1] is too dear. I always boast it when I lecture but know that no student can afford 40 bob for a book. By the way, I reviewed it for the *New Era*, not yet out, also for the S'hill Socy roneoed *Id*. I guess that I am about the only one of Lane's circle left, barring John Layard maybe. (...)

Well, well, laddie, I hope the Lane book brings you some royalties. I suggested to A & Unwin that my New York publisher, Hart, might be approached for a USA edition, knowing that he might turn it down on the grounds that Lane is unknown in USA. In '48 I got the Hermitage Press, New York, to issue the *Talks*. I wrote a preface. It never sold, and the firm is now extinct, I hear. But then my books *Problem Teacher* and *Problem Family* didn't sell in US twenty years ago, while today *S'hill* is out in a paperback edition of 35,000. USA has advanced ... cf Goldwater, Little Rock.

All the best, Neill

[1] Wills's *Homer Lane: A Biography*.

To Josie and David Caryll

Dear Both   *14 September 1964*

You've said it: I havena. How the hell to make Bunkie[1] into a theatre piece I dunno. It is an outside story of sea and golf and a village band.

Only the last cd be brought on to a stage. I can't remember much about the book and dare not reread it.

I hold the copyright of all my books, but in practice I get my agent to deal with contracts, translations etc.

Bunkie is Lunan Bay near Arbroath. Would yr lyrics be in dialect or wd Bunkie be English?

Sorry I canna see the musical. MacMunn's arguments to villagers yes, the growing town, no, unless combined with film. Anyway carry on, bless you, and make a kirk or a mill o't. (...)

Love to all three, Neill

[1] *The Booming of Bunkie*, written in 1919.

To Antoine Obert

Dear Tony   *16 December 1964*
(...) Now about that book you sent me. You know what happens to books in S'hill. It disappeared, 'borrowed' by someone. Luckily I found one of the staff had it and I re-read it. What I liked was the story of the young man, not so much the psychology given in explanation. Fact is that, after knowing Reich, most books on psychology bore me ... *Gott*, I get so many sent by authors in USA, mostly Sullivan school. After Reich they are mostly dull, un–dynamic, not going deeply enough. Truth is that I've had too bloody much of psychology in the last 50 yrs. Today I'd rather read a book on hammered brass work. Here I am looking a gift horse in the mouth, but you are a guy who says what he thinks and you will understand. (...)

Yours as always, Neill

To Harold Hart

Dear Harold   *1 April 1965*
I have asked a Miss Claire Wong of New York to get in touch with you. She wants to translate *S'hill* into Chinese. But I don't know how you are placed. Would yr consent mean appearing before an anti-American committee? In fact I don't know who has translation rights, you or me. If you had political difficulties I cd do it via my agents and you would not be responsible. I'd like very much to reach some of China's 700 millions. I have asked her if China pays royalties.

Shimoda writes: 'Instantly I ask for Shibata to do his duty and request him to write direct to Mr Hart.' He says the book is selling poorly in Japan. He lays it down to reaction in Japan, for it is not selling nearly so well as former books of mine. (...)

Warm greetings to both of you, Neill

To Elna Lucas

Dear Elna   *21 August 1965*

(...) I am writing a new book[1] answering the questions visitors have been plaguing me with for years. Wot a bloody life! (...)

Oh how I suffer from American profs and analysts sending me their books. They are so dull I can't face them and anyway I can't read a book on psychology now ... but I've been dipping into Stekel to keep up my German; he writes so simply. I wish writers had the easy style of Peter[2] and, modestly, myself.

Love, Neill

[1] *Freedom not License!*
[2] F. L. Lucas.

To Tom Eagle

Dear Tom   *25 February 1966*

A sad day when the old firm has to reject the MS of old Herbert's third writer.[1] I think that Wodehouse and Baden Powell were his first two. But I see your point. The MS was written primarily for USA which seems to love questions and answers. Hart expects it to have a many dollar sale there and I hope he is right. I may or may not try another home firm like Allen & Unwin, Constable, Gollancz, but most probably they'd have the same judgement as your lot has.

One benefit of old age ... the rejection of an MS seems to mean damn all, but if H. J. had rejected – say – my *Dominie Abroad*, I'd have been cast down and bitter.

All the best ... and one nasty thing is that now I'll have no excuse to drop in and see you when I am in town.

Neill

[1] Jenkins had turned down *Talking of Summerhill*, eventually published by Gollancz.

To Willa Muir

My dear Willa   *25 May 1966*

(...) Nother three chapters to write, but how do you ken? I've never been able to think in chapters, but then I never wrote anyone's Life, but maybe *Carroty Broon* was mine.[1] I take it you are sure of a publisher; [2] you ought to be anyway. Owing to my complete inability to like poetry I wonder how Edwin will stand in history, and who decides if a man is a major or a minor poet? Crashaw was minor: Pope and Tennyson major. *Warum*? [Why?] Is Scott a major and George Douglas Brown a minor novelist? For that matter, who decided that Bach was major and Ravel minor? Intrigues me. Obviously Ibsen is greater than Pinero or Coward, but then I have a sense of drama and none of poetry or music ... but I do prefer Chopin to Irving Berlin ... or shd one say prefer 'before'?

You and I won't likely be immortal as writers, but what matter? As Sam Goldwyn cried, when asked to think of posterity: 'What the hell has posterity done for me?' Keats lamented that his name was writ in water, but had it been writ in great golden letters, would it have eased the agony of leaving life so young? The thought that one day I may be put in a book of famous educationists does not give me the smallest thrill. In short, im-mortality be buggered. (...)

I liked yr Dorothy Parker's phrase. The other one was her review of Katherine Hepburn in a film. 'Miss Hepburn runs thro the whole gamut of emotions from A to B.' Nasty wumman. Another from her. A fellow woman journalist, back from England and mad about England, spoke of schedule and not skedule. Dorothy said: 'Schedule. Skit.'

Odd letter this, may be due to my regret that I never became a scholar. Had I taken the Hon Eng medal I might have written a Life of Congreve. I failed to write up Geordie Broon.

Love, Allie

[1] *Carroty Broon* was the fictional account of Neill's childhood published in 1920.
[2] Willa Muir was writing a Life of her husband, Edwin.

To Henry Miller

Dear Henry   *23 December 1966*

(...) Henry, it was sweet of you to say what you said about my new book. Off the record I think the book lousy. Hart changed my glorious Miltonic English into Americanese, splitting all my infinitives with an axe, in short making me into American journalese. And I feel a bit ashamed of impersonating Aunt Mary of the Washerwoman's Weekly, only I don't think she would have given the same answers. Hart says the book is selling like blazes, and I'll just have to content myself with the flowing in royalties, royalties I will never spend, for I never buy anything barring baccy and Scotch. (...)

With warmth, Neill

To Livia Gollancz

Dear Livia   *8 February 1967*

(...) Some publishers seem to be arrested authors. Herbert Jenkins from 1915 onwards used to tinker with my style, and I couldn't get him to stop it.

Yours, Neill

To Livia Gollancz

Dear Livia   *12 February 1967*

I regret very much that I only met your father once, at a pro-China rally in Ipswich. In the great days of the Left Book Club. My contact was reading his fine book on music, fine because it made a musically ignorant man enjoy every page. I think of him as a great man and not as a great publisher. He did so much for humanity ... no one can ever know how great an influence he was. Damn it all, I wish I had known him personally. (...) I hope that your sorrow and that of your mother is blended with pride and the feeling that Victor did more for humanity than all the politicians rolled into one. No one could desire a better epitaph.

Yours, Neill

To Penguin Books

Dear Sir   *13 March 1967*

For many years Allen & Unwin published two books – *Talks to Parents and Teachers*, by Homer Lane of the Little Commonwealth, and *The Little Commonwealth*, by his matron.[1] The latter has been out of print for some years. Lane's daughter tells me that A & U will not reprint the *Talks*.

Since Lane was a great child psychologist, I suggest that a paperback might be made incorporating both books. The *Talks* were published in

USA about twenty years ago and I wrote the preface, but at home Lane does not need any introduction. Think about my suggestion.

Sincerely, A. S. Neill

[1] E. T. Bazeley

To James Stern

15 March 1967

You bugger, Jimmy, sending me all that screed. (...) But I forgive you cos you sent me something that did grip me, yr chapter. I now just wish I were a Christian and cd pray to the Unseen Guy to let me live long enough to see the Autobiography in toto. *Tono Bungay* gave us the gentry from the below stairs viewpoint, but I can't recall any story from the upstairs angle. Get on with it, man.

Kafka. I shd blush to say I can't appreciate him; too reminiscent of Stekel's dream analysis, to me sick, but recently a temperature gave me hellish nightmares all night and I awoke to think: Christ, this is his *Trial*, his *Castle*. I always thought he was tried for Onanie, the unspeakable love as Wilde might have said. Edwin Muir and Willa adored him[1] ... by the way she has just finished Edwin's Life. (...)

I am sending you a TV play I have sent to the Wednesday Play people. Tell me if it has any merit ... I won't pay return postage in case you say it has none at all.

Love to you both, Neill

[1] The Muirs translated Kafka into English.

To James Stern

21 March 1967

You bloody Philistine ... I cast no more pearls, see? How dare you compare my effort with Chekhov? Ibsen and he cd get across without any character's explaining a thing, but the much lesser GBS spent pages on spouting, cf *Superman*. I can't see any dramatic way of making Jenny pinch without letting the audience into the why of it. Barrie cd do it, say in *Dear Brutus*, but he had bugger all to say anyway. I have read Ibsen a score of times with almost worship at his art and skill. Chekhov ... I get so confused with the character names. Chap is Petrovitch and then someone calls him Little Sonovabitch, and before the scene is over he is Shostavitch. No, give me Ibsen every time.

Anyway, I know that the BBC will take your perverted opinion and send the thing back. One merit it has ... bloody good dialogue, snappy, even witty on occasion.

Anyway what's wrong with the dirty woid love? The other Jesus used it. And now I have to get my halo repaired.

Love to you both ... specially Tania, who is a better judge of pearls.

Neill

To Robert Hutchison

Dear Robert Hutchison   *24 March 1967*
It will be wonderful if the general public has the chance to know about Lane. Alas, even teachers know little about him, but they aren't interested in living, only learning.

I hear ... possibly from Hilary Rubinstein ... that Gollancz had offered your people *Summerhill* and they had refused it. At a loss to know why if they did, for it seems to be selling well in its fifth printing, and I guess that publishers don't seek paperbacks until the hard covers have dwindled to nothing. Why firms like Gollancz don't do their own paperbacks I dunno. As a Scot I'd like to see books at ten bob rather than 40/- ... by yr name you must also be a Scot. (...)

Yours hopefully, A. S. Neill

To Bill MacKinnon

Dear Bill   *5 May 1967*
Do ye ken that lad who plays the undertaker in *Dr Finlay*?[1] His elastic face fascinates me. I have written him a sketch making him the centre and I'd like to contact him, but I dinna even ken his name.[2] If I send it c/o the BBC they open all letters and decide for themselves if they shd be forwarded, so I am told. Who is he? I'd like to send him the MS ... it is damned funny, tho I say it as shdn't ... style of our Border Customs sketches.[3]

Love to Käte and self, Neill

---

[1] *Dr Finlay's Casebook*, a popular television series about life in the village of Tannochbrae, based on a series of short stories by A. J. Cronin.
[2] Robert James.
[3] A sketch performed by Neill and Bill MacKinnon at Summerhill.

To Gwen Horsfield

Dear Gwen   *14 July 1967*

Ta a lot. Yr play is in the tradition of action telling the story. An actor told J. M. Barrie that the action shd tell all even without words. J. M.: 'Then go to the front of the stage and tell the audience by action that you have an aunt in Brighton with rheumatics.' But why no explanation? Yr play needs none ... the goodies and the baddies are clear cut. All the Establishment will understand the selfish old bitch, the Carol bitch, the Janet weakling. In my play 90% of the audience would not have the least notion of what rewarding a thief was, and why not explain? When Finlay argues his vague Freudianism with Dr Cameron it doesn't add to the action, but it does show a gulf in character between the two.

I am not in touch with modern drama. The dialogues of Pinter, Wesker etc just bore me; they explain character that doesn't seem to matter. So in *Waiting for Godot* which again bored me stiff. Talk, character, if you like, little or no action. Yr own play ... must beware of sour grapes ... I didn't notice the direction words until I had read it ... filter at phone, what the hell does it mean? The play was the thing. Well written; good dialogue, simple if rather common situation of family hate and greed. But when I had finished I asked myself: 'Would these people interest me if I met em?' Only the convict, I thought. True, you are ahead of all the boring nobodies who haunt the TV screen ... *Newcomers, Coronation Street*, etc, all saying not a word of interest. Yet, you know, lassie, the great ones, the Ibsens, the Strindbergs, the Chekhovs, seem to get away from the homes we know and give us people who show a tremendous force in their characters. No, kinda annoyed with you for yr happy ending. Wrong. That old bitch would have won in real life. But dunno why the BBC rejected it.

My own efforts I'll scrap. I haven't got the drama talent, but I hate to scrap the really funny coffin bits. Anyway, I have ceased to aspire to being a BBC playwright.

Love to both, Neill

To Joseph Kirschner

Dear Joseph Kirschner   *6 August 1967*

It was good of you to offer to write my Life. Oddly enough I began myself to do so a few weeks ago, grudgingly, for I feel that the only thing interesting about a man is what he does, not how he got to do it. It doesn't seem to matter that Wilde was a homo or that Barrie and Carlyle and Ruskin were impotent, or for that matter that Dylan Thomas drank too much. I have often been glad that we don't know a damn thing about Shakespeare ... think of the reams of paper that would have been used up. (...)

Well, thanks for your kindly offer.

Yours sincerely, A. S. Neill

To Harold Hart

Dear Harold   *4 November 1967*

Cannot this business be settled amicably? I don't want to have to be in a position where I side with you or Watt-Gollancz. As I said in my last letter, my desire is to put Summerhill across, to reach the wide world. To me money doesn't enter; my share of royalties wouldn't amount to anything of value. You launched *Summerhill* and all honour to you for doing so. Psychologically I guess that the good ship *S'hill* was launched by you ... and now some other captain is trying to take the helm. But I don't see it that way. All I see is the chance to get a few thousand more readers over here. You see, S'hill is not known here as it is in the USA. Many American visitors say that they mention the name in London and no one has heard of it, whereas in USA (thanks to your good self) everyone knows about it.

All this talk about rights and copyrights is outwith my interest. It is all Greek to me. My only interest is to get S'hill known all over the world, a sentiment I know you share.

Watt says that Penguin wouldn't issue for at least two years, so that I might not live that long anyway. Or be in my second childhood.

All I ask is that this affair be settled as I say amicably.

Love to the two women, Neill

To James Stern

Dear Jimmy   *16 November 1967*

> And down the long and silent street
> The dawn with silver-sandalled feet
> Crept like a frightened girl.

Wilde, 'The Harlot's House'. I quoted this to a visiting literary man and he called it kitsch. Is it? I grant that it isn't on the plane of old Will Shaks.

And look, the gentle day ... dapples the drowsy east with spots of grey. or ...

Look, the morn in russet-mantle clad
Walks oer the dew of yon high eastern hill.

But to me it isn't kitsch. You are a good judge of language. What do you think?

Did you say you had *The House with the Green Shutters*. If not, I'll post you a copy to cheer your coronary nerves.

Love to you both, Neill

To Harold Hart

Dear Harold   *4 December 1967*

What is happening about Penguin? One of their men called to see me and it is clear that they are going ahead making a book of the two books combined.[1] I phoned Rubinstein, but he says that he has had no communication with you for months.

If your contract with Watt does not allow you to ban the plan, where do I stand? I wrote to Gollancz saying I did not want any agreement about paperback Penguin unless you and they settled the matter amicably. I want to have that paperback of course, but I don't want to be in the position of saying: 'Old Harold is a friend. He saved my school. Now I have to go against him and sign a contract against his wishes.' It is too much for a man of my age.

You see, Harold, I don't know the ins and outs. I don't know why you are agin the scheme. All I know is that Watt and you hate each other's guts, but why I can't even guess. (…)

I'd like to spread the gospel among the millions who can't afford hardback covers. I have no other aim; I told you the small royalty divided into four would mean nothing in the way of income. So, Harold, I beg of you to come to some arrangement so that this can happen over here; I beg you not to allow a situation to arise where I'd have to sign a contract and lose your friendship.

Love to the two lassies, Neill

[1] The Penguin editor was Robert Hutchison, the two books *Summerhill* and *Talking of Summerhill*.

To Carlos Kruytbosch

Dear Carlos   *20 December 1967*

Yr letter to Hart was fine, but he has such a hate of my *Talking* book[1] that he will never allow it to be published in US. I got led into the bad

F not L book[2] in error; I had sent him the full MS of *Talking* and expected
him to use most of it with the silly questions he sent me to answer. He
used about 3% I fancy. Sad that US can't get the better book. I feel
ashamed of *F not L*, and when Hart wrote me the other day saying he
was printing another 14,000 I felt bloody awful about it. (...)

    Alles gut, Neill

[1] *Talking of Summerhill.*
[2] *Freedom not License!*

To Bill MacKinnon

Dear Bill   *19 January 1968*
    (...) I sent to the Tannochbrae undertaker, Robert James, who lives
in Ipswich, my script for a play starring him. He was delighted and sent
it on to the producer, but I don't think he'll take it. Too much coffin in
it. Multiple firm sets up as coffin men advertising etc. The play was about
how to rescue him, but as I wrote it I thought that the dull buggers who
control most things wold think it shocking to many e.g. when he talks
of selling second-hand ones. James thought it screamingly funny. I dinna
suppose it will come to anything now that *Dr Finlay* has become a mixture of snobbery ... the big hoose ... and far too much medical stuff. (...)

    Love to you both, Neill

To Robert Hutchison

Dear Robert   *27 January 1968*
    It wasn't my idea to have a single volume; Hart angrily refused to
allow any parts of *Talking of S* to be in the book. He maybe had no legal
right to stop it but I couldn't go to law, and anyway he saved my school
by publishing *Summerhill* in 1960, for I was down to 24 pupils till the USA
book came.

    Yes, cut Fromm's preface, also dedication to Hart. Preface? How many
words? Why a preface? Myself I never read a preface to any book but,
if the book pleases, I can read an appendix.

    I hate to do it – read the book and cut out things I don't like, but I'll
have to, for there are things I wrote over 30 years ago when I was a Freudian. I have a hell of a lot to do, so tell me how much time I have to vet
the book.

    All the best, Neill

To Livia Gollancz

Dear Livia   *30 January 1968*
(...) Penguin want to go through *Summerhill* and cut. I have told them to cut Fromm's preface, dedication to Hart, and I want to cut Freud's things dating back to 1936. My feelings for Hart are ambivalent ... the man who got me so many pupils, and the villain who kept *Talking* from the US nation.

Some Americans wrote suggesting I made an omnibus from my 18 or 19 books. That would be hell on earth for me.

Yours, Neill

To Robert Hutchison

Dear Robert   *8 February 1968*
I tried to go through the book and had to give it up; made me too depressed to read it. All I have done is to cut the Fromm preface and dedication to Hart and an analysis of a girl that dates back to my Freud days and seems all wrong to me now.

I want to make the preface/appendix the tale of how I kept to principles but changed my belief in therapy. It is all in *Talking of Summerhill* but Hart won't give way. He hasn't answered my letter of a month ago probably cos it was rather a nasty one. If *S'hill* sells there might be a demand for *Talking of S*.

Book on way.

Yours, Neill

To Robert Hutchison

Dear Robert   *6 March 1968*
I find that according to my contract with Gollancz I get only one sixth of royalties. Have you any idea what the book will sell at? I always think of Penguins as 3/6d each, but I guess today they cost at least double that. And are you going to make it a preface or an appendix?

Just read with relish *Last Exit to Brooklyn*,[1] a terrible but necessary picture of a large slice of humanity. Its inspiration came too late for me to sprinkle my preface with a plethora of four-letter words plus a mass of sex perversions. But I never was a good business man.

The best, Neill

[1] By Hubert Selby.

To Robert Hutchison

Dear Robert   *16 March 1968*
    You can cut that para, but why you both want to puzzles me. I can
see a Colonel Blimp objecting to it but ... surely Penguin is big enough
to ignore dislikes by diehard readers. Meaning that I hate being cut.
    Price six bob. Royalty say 10%. Sevenpence a copy. I get one sixth.
If I believed in after life I'd be a publisher.
    Yours, Neill

To Tom Eagle

Dear Tom   *17 April 1968*
    I'll look for the book and send it on when found.[1] It is badly dated,
I fear. Hitler's submarines, Franco and the rebel war. I don't think it
would sell enough to pay its way. In any case, the illustrations by a
Spanish pupil wouldn't be worth reproducing. Poor lassie she is dead.
Dead also is one of the boys, Gordon, drowned bathing when we were
evacuated to North Wales.[2] David now prof of maths, Bunny of history,[3]
Michael a physicist, son of J. D. Bernal. Dunno if I could bring it up to
date by cutting Franco etc. And it was too vulgar for suburban parents
to give their brats. I recall a battle with the convicts. 'Take them in the
rear,' said one of the kids. 'Don't be vulgar,' said Neill.
    Anyway, I hope you can regress enough to childhood to enjoy reading
it again.
    The best, Neill

[1] *The Last Man Alive*, first published in 1938 by Herbert Jenkins.
[2] Gordon Nairn.
[3] David Barton, Gordon Leff.

To Tom Eagle

Dear Tom   *19 April 1968*
    I hae ma doots about *Last Man*. I doubt if I could rewrite parts now,
doubt if I'd tell a story today with so much bloody murder in it. Anyway,
lots of books are dated ... Dickens, *Kipps, Mr Polly*, Rider Haggard. True
they don't sell well, but I don't think *Man Alive* sold well in '39. But it
does have the merit that it was one of the few kids' stories a father can
read aloud without being bored stiff. (...)
    Anyway, I hope you enjoy your re-read, and won't find it too 'not with
it' as modern kids might say.
    Yours, Neill

To Livia Gollancz

Dear Livia   *29 January 1969*
    Reitzel in Copenhagen is doing a second edition of *The Last Man Alive*. Intriguing. Hart, Jenkins, Gollancz all say no chance of sales, yet Denmark buys it. Must be more primitive folks.
    Yours, Neill

To Ben Morris

Dear Ben   *11 February 1969*
    (...) Ah weel, be seein' yuh ... as my 40 USA pupils should say but don't. They know no slang. I ask a lad of 13 how many names for a re-volver. He says gun, automatic, pistol, never heard of gat, iron, rod, Betsy, John Roscoe, equaliser, never heard of Damon Runyan or O'Henry. Still, our home lot never read Jerome or W. W. Jacobs. Makes me feel my age. (...)

    Love to you both, Neill

To Robert James

Dear Robert   *24 April 1969*
    No, man, they didna gie you a chance in that film. I am getting tired of that *Finlay* show; it has no humour, and it concentrates too much on the medical side. And with age I miss a lot said by mumbling Cameron and soft-voiced Janet. Yr voice, like Finlay's, comes over fine.
    Alas, I can never hope to give you a part that would show your talent, not after my quarrel with Cronin.[1] I hear he is a Catholic, and I guess that he must hate his series being written by all and sundry. I would in his shoes.
    Aweel, I do hope some play writer will give you a part you can get your teeth into. They did it for Mrs Niven, and why not for you?
    No answer required.
    Yours, A. S. Neill

[1] Neill is probably referring to the BBC's refusal to use his script, rather than any difference with Cronin himself.

To Robert James

Dear Robert   *26 August 1969*
Tut, tut, I was playing with the idea of re-writing my sketch as a non-*Finlay* affair, and now my idea of a rival undertaker has come out. I thought it terrible, unreal, without humour and all out of character. Man, they didn't give you a chance.

I first fell in love with your acting long ago in the *Finlay* tale of the woman corpse who woke up and came down the stairs, but since then the script hasn't been good enough for you. Fact is that I am gey weary of the series these days. It has outlived its lifespan.

Aweel, I'll just have to stick to my last and leave drama alone, but I am glad to say that at nearly 86 I can laugh, and laugh too at myself.

Hoping they will give you better parts.
Yours A. S. N.

To Bill and Käte MacKinnon

Dear Bill and Käte   *17 October 1969*
Ta for the flattering snippet in the Neill book.[1] It will be out end of Oct, but Allen Lane, an old friend, sent me an advance copy for my birthday. Me an actor? Bloody amateur all the way. I hadn't yr native talent, your timing; I still gib at a chap like you being left out of things like *Finlay*. (...)

Get *The Progressive Schools* by Skidelsky, Pelican 7/-. I get a big write-up, pro and anti, as should be. I think he is right in saying the prog schools have had their day. (...)

Love and blessings ... heathen ones, Neill

[1] *Neill and Summerhill: A Man and his Work*, a pictorial study by John Walmsley, published by Penguin. Leila Berg collected impressions and memories of Neill from former staff, pupils, parents and others. Bill MacKinnon had observed: 'Had Neill chosen, I'm sure he could have made his mark as an actor.'

To Harold Hart

Dear Harold   *31 October 1969*
The Last Man Alive is excellent, a beautiful production. Gollancz won't publish it for a year or so. I wish they had your go-aheadness. (...)

Today a cheque for £3740 ... a bloody millionaire thanks to your enterprise.

Have no idea how the Penguin *Summerhill* sells. Home publishers have no go. I asked on six occasions for it on Liverpool St station bookstall. They had never heard of it. Still, I suppose with this balance of payments I shd support home industries.

All the best and lots of thanks. Neill

To Harold Hart

Dear Harold   *5 November 1969*

My press cutting people don't touch USA. I'd like very much to know what yr papers say abt *The Last Man Alive*, and if you mail them to me I promise to mail them back after perusal. I am reading it to the kids and they are enthralled, a good omen for its sale. (...)

So far I have had no knowledge of how the *S'hill* Pelican is selling. I know that, had I left it to you I'd have got more dough. On the other hand, I have a sort of nationalism outside money; can't explain it, but the book you gave me about the USA takeover of British industry kinda shocked me.[1] I know that home royalties are small, but I fancy that you yourself couldn't sell more books over here than Gollancz and Penguin do. For I am not known in England. (...) One woman said she phoned the Ministry of Education for my address and they didn't know it. Remember that you have four times our population. (...)

All the best, Neill

[1] Probably Vance Packard's *The Organisation Man*.

To Ilse Ollendorff Reich

Dear Ilse   *26 November 1969*

At last a decent review.[1] I think I sent you the *Sunday Times* one before. If the *Vanguard* is to review my paperback *The Last Man Alive*, I hope Peter writes it.[2] I fancy the humour in it will appeal to him and yourself. I gave Reich a copy in '38 but he had no interest; now I see why, for as you say, his sense of humour was poor. He said it was a subjective picture of myself, possibly it is, in part anyway. (...)

Love, Neill

[1] Of Ilse Ollendorff Reich's *Wilhelm Reich: A Personal Biography*.
[2] Peter Reich.

To James Stern

Dear Jimmy   *22 December 1969*

I told you I never heard of *The Purple Cloud*. When my book came out in '38 no review said it was a crib, so maybe this guy cribbed from me.[1] No idea what his book was about, if it slew humanity or not. You don't happen to have a copy, do you? Anyway it is the treatment that matters. *Hamlet* was a crib, so were lots of Burns' poems, so what the hell? My fan mail from USA says The funniest kids' book ever written. Anyway, I have no purple patches in it.

Merry Xmas *ohne* [without] fags, *ohne* booze, Neill

[1] Neill's book *The Last Man Alive* bore some resemblance to M. P. Shiel's *The Purple Cloud*. It was reissued in 1970.

To R. F. Mackenzie

Dear Bob   *17 January 1970*

(...) Try reading enclosed to your ten yr olds to see if in the new space fiction age kids' tastes have changed since the 1930s. Of all my 20 or so books, it is the only one I can dip into, maybe cos it expresses the deepest part of me ... the bairn, the laughter at life. (...)

Yours, Neill

To Harold Hart

Dear Harold   *5 March 1970*

I want to write to *Psychology Today* asking if they will take my review of the new book.[1] I forget what they paid last time but it was pretty good. It wd be the best medium, I fancy, for getting to many folks.

What do you know of that hater Rafferty?[2] Sounds Irish, an RC. I'd like to see one of his books if they are in paperback. Pity so much in the book is out of context quotes from my books. In the main they were fair and even kind, especially Fromm. The student leader[3] wasn't interested in S'hill; only his own student rebellion. And the Warner woman[4] with her reading complex said damn all to me.

Tell me if you think I ought to approach *Py Today* and what fee I should ask. You know my publicity value in USA and I don't. I guess a TV star wd get about a buck a word.

Let me have copies of book reviews. My mail increases now that Germany is S'hill conscious, but that Canadian boy's fan letter about *Last Man* is the only one I've had. Humourless lot of sods in USA!

When is French copy coming out?

The best, Neill

[1] *Summerhill: For and Against: Assessments of A. S. Neill.*
[2] Max Rafferty wrote: 'I would as soon enrol a child of mine in a brothel as in Summerhill.'
[3] Michael Rossman.
[4] Sylvia Ashton Warner.

To Evelyn Williams

Evelyn, my dear   *25 April 1970*

In case you have lost the copy of 33 years ago.[1] I have been wondering why Jean and you appear so little in it, while Robert, David and Betty get a lot of space. Maybe cos you were retiring kids while they were demonstrative. To me you were a bonny face with a sense of humour. Beauty dies but humour goes on. Jean had a sense of humour too.[2]

The book is coming out in autumn by Gollancz. It is having a big sale in USA and Denmark, and now the Germans are to publish it. I am pleased, for of all my books, I like it best: maybe cos it is the daft side of me. (...)

Read it again and get a few chuckles, if not belly laughs.

Lots of love, dear Evelyn.

Thine, Neill

[1] Of *The Last Man Alive*.
[2] The story featured, among other Summerhill children, Jean Allen, Robert Muller, David Barton and Betty Muller.

To Peter Owen

Dear Peter Owen   *13 May 1970*

(...) It wd take a hell of a lot of research to make a book called *The Early Neill* from many extracts. I couldn't do it, not at eighty-six. The only books of mine I like are *The Last Man Alive* and *Carroty Broon*, a kind of fictional biography of my childhood. It is marred for English readers by having too much Scots dialect. The *Dominie* books are curate's egg books, but that applies to any book.

Let me think about it anyway. And thanks for writing.

Yours, A. S. Neill

To Harold Hart

Dear Harold   *3 September 1970*
    (...) German invasion every day. Ten letters from there today, but
none from France, where the book does not seem to have caught on. (...)
I am unknown here. Penguin sold about 10,000 and Rohwolt getting on
to half a million. Yr total sales must be enormous. An Italian visitor had
a copy in Italian, but the publisher never sent me a copy. I didn't know
abt it. (...)
    What I earn from my books goes into the school, partly because of so
many bad debts. School lost £2500 last year cos of them. Bastards. But
it is only money.
        Love to Bea, Neill

To Elna Lucas

Dear Elna   *3 October 1970*
    What a lovely present ... or was it a loan?[1] It gripped me as a quon-
dam Barrie fan years ago. I grew out of him, and the book explains con-
cretely what I felt unconsciously, that he was a self-centred impotent man
who remained a Peter Pan.
    You sure gave me a treat with that book. (...)
        Hastily but warmly, Neill

[1] Janet Dunbar's *J. M. Barrie: the Man behind the Image*.

To Ivor Cutler and Helen Oxenbury

Dear Ivor and Helen   *3 June 1971*
    Thanks a lot.[1] But why let em call you reminiscent of Lear and
Caroll? Can't see their influence at all. Yet in a way an inversion of Jack
and the Beanstalk, but getting down to more roots as it were. I like text
and pictures, their unsentimentality ... shades of Enid Blyton. I confess
the humour escapes me; I only see sincerity and kindliness and, tho a dirty
word today, love. (...)
    Glad you made it, Ivor. Didn't surprise me, for long ago here you were
a mad bugger with crazy ideas. The sane ones, the Heaths and Wilsons

and all headmasters, never get anywhere that matters. Your dedication was most kind, since it may halve your sales in Establishment circles.

Have bumper royalties.

Thine, Neill

[1] They had sent him a copy of Ivor Cutler's first children's book, *Meal One*, illustrated by Helen Oxenbury.

To Harold Hart

Dear Harold   *19 June 1971*

I keep on writing and posted you pages marked Preface.[1] I am mailing a few more as I write them, bringing in a few stories which always please readers; if they do not know them they tell them to their friends and so spread the book. (...)

I want to know when you will publish. So far I have not settled on a title. My Life, by ASN, is too ordinary. Maybe what my small kids call me would do: Neill, Neill, banana peel, by ASN. There is time to decide. I want to live long enough to see the book. You will of course hive it off to England and Germany, and after I have gone the family will make a tidy sum I hope.

I think the book isn't much of a Life; too much about my opinions, I fear.

Love to both, Neill

[1] For his autobiography, eventually published as *Neill! Neill! Orange Peel!*

To Harold Hart

Dear Harold   *6 October 1971*

A farmer will haggle over the price when buying a horse from his best friends; nothing personal in it. Of course I don't think you a crook. You are a business man and I ain't, and if I had known the facts you have now given me I wouldn't have thought of challenging. It was a family affair. A recent visitor had talked about the big royalties good sellers got, and as I had 20% from Herbert Jenkins I was inclined to believe him. Granted that stopped with the Second World War. I think he paid P. G. Wodehouse more than he paid me. Of course I wouldn't think of going to another publisher, you silly man. (...)

Slightly bothered at giving up the copyright, for the Society of Authors' chief tenet is: Never part with the copyright. Still, I think it is safe in your hands. (...)

Well, Harold, pardon my feeble attempt to be a business man trying to make a horse deal. I guess you may be right in saying that I am over-optimistic about selling like hot cakes, yet in paperback the Germans sure will sell the book in thousands.

Love to both, and let's forget the rift in the loot.

Thine, Neill

To Jonathan Croall

Dear Croall   *13 October 1971*

Many thanks for the books.[1] The difference is deep. Wills deals with humans, but the two ex-educn ministers talk of politics and organisation and I don't see the word child in the book. I found them dull, lifeless, whereas my old friend Wills is full of pro-lifeness. I wish the guy who had asked the two ministers the questions had asked deeper ones. I guess to them education spells learning, exams, degrees, while to David it spells free character formation and creation. Sorry to look your gift horse in the mouth.

Oh, if you have time, drop me a note telling me what sales *Summerhill* has made. The German translation was 800,000 some weeks ago, and may be a million now. Britain doesn't know S'hill, but millions in USA, Brazil, Japan do. Puzzling. I have an idea that my native town in Scotland never heard of me. (...)

Yours, Neill

[1] *Spare the Child: The Story of an Experimental Approved School*, by David Wills, and *The Politics of Education: Edward Boyle and Anthony Crosland in conversation with Maurice Kogan*, both published by Penguin.

To Gordon Leff

Dear Bunny   *4 December 1971*

(...) *Last Man Alive* is now a best seller in Germany. They called it *Die Grüne Wolke* [The Green Cloud] and changed Spike into *Sargnagel* – coffin nail, why I dunno, and they buggered up most of my humour; still reviews say how funny the book is. It is being done in Dutch, Danish and I think French, yet in this land it fell flat, but so did my other books. S'hill Penguin sold 60,000 in three years, but the German one sold a million in a year, and the USA possibly double that. I can't quote a prophet is not without honour etc since I ain't no prophet. (...)

Thine, Neill

To Harold Hart

Dear Harold   *15 March 1972*

If that last lot of proofs was the total of the book[1] I am very much upset. You have edited my MS ... a thing no publisher over here would do. You have judged what is important, something I should have done. My memory is now bad, but in the galleys I failed to see my chapter on my attitude to my old books. You cut out that I pick my nose. I recall writing about my pet aversions but I don't recall seeing it in the proofs. More than once I disclaim being a guy of much importance. I wanted the public to know my weaknesses and my strength, and yr editing has separated me from that public. I can't remember if you pruned my chapter on my writing Eng. Lit. for a self-educator. Harold, the book is half me, to judge by what has been set up.

I loathe rows, but better a row than bottled-up resentment. In bad health I laboured to give you as much material as I could and hate to see it wasted. If the MS was too long, why pad it with excerpts from my *Log* and *Times* articles?

It may be that I have forgotten what I have read in the proofs, but I am sure that you have cut lots that were important to me. I didn't want a book Neill, Neill, Castrated Neill.

And now tell me your side of the argument. I have a suspicion that you have cut the parts that showed me up as a common or garden guy, wanting to give the image of a noted educator. In the London edition I would like the cut parts to be retained.

Bless you and damn you, Harold, Neill

[1] *Neill! Neill! Orange Peel!*

To Harold Hart

Dear Harold   *16 April 1972*

Your letter is most pleasing re all you have done for publicity etc, but my grouse is still there. Apart from the editing, which still annoys me ... can you imagine Hemingway or Steinbeck allowing editing? ... I feel you have left me out too much. Had you consulted me about the *Log* I'd have said that it should have been *Carroty Broon* instead, for it was fictional autobiography of my boyhood. And I think you might have given me a say in choosing an English publisher. My original publishers Jenkins and Gollancz did me well. You think primarily of the USA public, which is different from my home one.

I'd like Weidenfeld and Nicolson to use the original MS with my own editing where necessary. I think that you cut much that an English public would appreciate, also the scholars. Example: I quoted a verse from Oscar Wilde mainly to add a comment by a USA professor about it. By cutting the comment you spoiled what I wanted to convey to English scholars. I can't of course recall all I read in the galleys but feel that much that was important to me was cut ... my hopes, fears, aversions. Why cut my notes on my failure as a dramatist, as a pen picture artist? I tell you, Harold, the book is not fully me. And in spite of the fact that you put me on the international map, I really regret leaving the whole business to you. Publishers and authors should not be expected to have the same values. (...)

Thine, Neill

To Ben Morris

24 September 1972

Damn you, Ben, what do you mean by casting pearls?[1] You must know that I am a peasant; I haven't read a tenth of the chaps you mention. After being called a follower of Rousseau for 50 years I have just read *Emile*, and with some disappointment, for the blighter wanted his pupil to have freedom within the ideas of his tutor. I liked best yr chapters on violence and sex, great stuff but kinda confusing to a man of 89 next month. Fifty years ago an invitation to spend a weekend with Greta Garbo would have been heaven, and most likely the lustful weekend wd have left me with a mad passion for her. Of interest is that my old pupils don't seem to be promiscuous; I know of none who go fornicating all around, nor would any of them I have asked go to see a porn film or play. 'Too bloody boring,' is the usual answer. The whole Longford crowd can't see that the answer isn't censorship, but a sex orientation for the young that does not link sex and sin. Nice fantasy – what would Mary Whitehouse have coughed up on Freud's couch? I can guess. (...)

You give me an inferiority complex; you have read so much, thought so much, and I am neither a reader nor a thinker. I told both Russell and Herbert Read that I loved their conversation but their books were too deep for me.

I like yr violence and sex chapters because they are so positive, while in the earlier part of the book I feel you are being the conventional lecturer giving yr students both sides of the question. Man, you have the uncommon gift of being highly readable. Every bloody prof in USA seems to send me his latest book on psychology and they are so dull in prose that I can't read em. A letter from Herbert Marcuse says he thinks children shdn't have self-government, not until their twenties when they can reason. And Margaret Mead hates my guts.

Yr students are lucky when I think of the dead lectures I had to sit under by guys like Saintsbury. Still, laddie, your book doesn't 'place' you. Meaning that it doesn't show where you stand, so to say, in the big controversy which might be called the Summerhill-Rotten gulf. Obviously you are nearer S'hill freedom than Elizabeth's morality, and you see farther than us both. At least than I. For I have gone my way knowing little of what others have done, e.g. Dewey and Kilpatrick, tho I have read some of the new lot, Holt, Illich, Dennison, Goodman etc ... Goodman died recently of a heart attack, by the way. In other words, Ben, you have a perspective that I haven't got, a sort of educational *Weltanschauung*. If you had run a school I wonder what it would have been like; being a cannier Scot than I am ye didna dae it. (...)

My Life, *Neil, Neill, Orange Peel!*, has been out in USA for some weeks. I don't like it. Hart cut chunks and printed three quarters of my *Log*, which I never wanted to see in print again. Weidenfeld & Nicolson are to print it from my original MS and the Germans are to use that version. How ignorant are Yanks. To tell how my father had a school board I wrote that the chairman visited and in the logbook wrote 'numbers presant 89'. The fools printed it 'present', thereby killing the illustration. And he defined 'grat' in brackets as 'grieved'. Your book shd be published in USA but watch the publishers. Mine even adds what I never said or knew ... a bit on an Egyptian religion I never heard of. Demand galley proofs. I'd like to help by telling my Hart man abt you, but am afraid he'd castrate you as he did me.

Love to you both and heathen blessings, Neill

[1] Morris had sent him a copy of his book *Objectives and Perspectives in Education*.

To Bill and Käte MacKinnon

Dear Both   *2 November 1972*

Many tas for the MacD book,[1] even if half the bloody words I never heard of. I have never been able to judge poetry and really don't know why he is acclaimed as a genius ... on TV he was just a thrawn [stubborn] auld bugger. (...)

Love to both, Neill

[1] A book of poems by Hugh MacDiarmid.

To Dora Russell

My dear Dora   *6 December 1972*
    (...) Glad Hemmings got a fairly good write-up in the *New States-man.*[1] So far the dailies and weeklies have ignored him. Snag for the poor lad is that they review me instead of the wonderful job he has done. I am past being thrilled by any review. Did you see the long symposium in the *New Humanist* on BR?[2] If not I'll send you a copy. (...)
    Love, Neill

[1] For *Fifty Years of Freedom: A Study of the Development of the Ideas of A. S. Neill.*
[2] Bertrand Russell.

To Michael Lynch

Dear Mike   *1 February 1973*
    (...) Dunno when Colin's Reich book will be out.[1] I like the Hem-mings book, but think he wasn't critical enough. Got few reviews. My own *Neill, Neill, Orange Peel!* comes out mid May and I keep hoping I won't have a heart attack til then. Puzzled why at home *S'hill* is almost unknown or known only by stupid hearsay, while in USA the book is required reading in 600 colleges. And the name in Germany is a house-hold one now. (...)
    Love, Neill

[1] Colin Wilson's *My Quest for Wilhelm Reich* was published in 1981.

8

Humour

'I saw a lad in a temper break twenty-four windows of the school in one day,' said Mr Neill.
'I pointed out to him one pane he had missed.'

Daily Mail, August 1932

To David Barton

Dear Mr Barton   *11 March 1943*
    Do you consider it a good idea to inform the staff of this establish-
ment exactly what you passed in and why and which subjects and how
many and what 1st Div means? I ask because there is a vague suspicion
here that you have stolen one of Hitler's Divisions from the Eastern
Front, hence the USSR advance. Do not hide your light under a bushel
(*Bible*, 1604, Herbert Jenkins Ltd, 5/- net). Townshend Minor, inspired
by your attainment, wants to know what you scored in maths e.g. Corks
Senior would also like to know. *Ergo – honi soit qui mal de mer*, as Vos,
Roger, Bobe might phrase it. In other words cough it up, me lad. Thou
canst not do that there here.
    For the Headmaster, R. Supwards, Secretary

To David Barton

                                                        [1944]
This youth has been at this school for too many years, and during that
period he has been generally (i.e. not particularly) honest and industri-
ously indolent. He has a taking way (cf General Meeting Annual Reports
on Honesty, 1930-43) and is never at a loss in company, although the
company generally is.
    Politically he is Left ... at the Post (*vide* Monk, *passim*), and he invari-
ably sees Red when there is no second helping. He admires the Hammer

175

& Sickle when these implements are in the hands of the other fellow, and he would gladly die for Russia, knowing well that it is many steps away ... steppes away: *verst* thoughts are not always the best (old Ukrainian proverb).

In love emotion he is at sixes and seven, but also at sixteens and seventeens. He has personal attraction comparable with that of a Summerhill Lab magnet after treatment by Tookie & Co.

His intelligence quota almost compares favourably with other quotas (oranges, bananas etc), but his intelligence quotient is still being investigated, the trouble being that a 4000X microscope cannot be obtained. A slide shows some faint blueness with some greenness. Professor Corkhill is of the opinion that with care the young gentleman may, in the course of a few years, show a glimmer of intelligence. (See Desai on *Glimmerings in Apes*.)

It is a great joy to his school that he has passed Matriculation with the same nonchalance with which he passed full dustbins and the buck generally. I am sure that he has a great future behind him, one that may find him a seat in Parliament. Interested in the feminist movement (especially the snaky and seductive kind), he will always stand up for women, everywhere save in buses and tubes.

In a well-blitzed area he should rise in the world, and he should hold down any job by his long-used method of sitting on it. His hobby at school was Damp-Collecting, but he had also some considerable interest in mud-slinging, a hobby that should help him later in the C. P. underground work if his political aims are right (*vide* Bunny on The Leff Wing).

He has done some original research in English Literature, taking the proverbs as his magnum opus. It was he who discovered that many had been mixed up in the past, and he may attain immortality, or it minus the T, by his demonstration of the truth that A Bird in the Hand Keeps the Doctor Away, a truth realised from another angle by Freud, Reich and Newton. He also demonstrated by example over a number of years that Silence is Golden is a fallacy.

Born of poor but dishonest parents, he should go far ... with his accustomed half ticket.

A. S. Neill, Headmaster

To Douglas Neill Thomson

Dear Sir   *5 November 1944*

I learn on comparatively honest authority that you have arrived safely, and, as you are new to your environment,[1] I hasten to give you some information.

Your horizon will be bounded by two (comparatively) human figures, both of whom will gurgle and coo at you as if you were the village idiot: they will give you the misleading impression that you are of all people THE cat's whiskers, whereas, apart from your middling illustrious name, you are just a brat indistinguishable from a sheaf of other brats. I presume that your face is red and that your voice is unmusical, therefore, when mad women croon over you and call you sweetums and similar fatuous names, take them with a grain of salt ... not the celery variety either. And when you reach the speech stage make sure that you demand everything that your parents desire that you do not have ... pickles, fags, pepper, and later beer.

The picture is not all evil. Your parents have certain minor merits of course. Your dear mamma will never slap you and she will, when you are old enough to come home with the milk, believe every tall tale you like to spin. Your dear papa will smile at you every time you use a hammer on his transformers, even though behind the smile is cobalt murder. For you are the HEIR, the hope of the hopeless family. Peace is on the horizon, but not for the T family. The war has begun in the pacifist homeland, and God help the Right (and the family).

Take these precepts to your bosom.
1. Scream like hell till you get all you want.
2. Scream also when you've got it.
3. Distrust all honeyed words and vow to slay all who call you wassums or diddums and who ask you to kiss old ladies.
4. See that the new cat gets more than its share of blame for breakages.
5. Love your mother and pray for your father.
6. Beware of your aunties ... *timeo Danaos et dona ferentes* [I fear the Greeks even when they are bearing gifts].
7. Join the Liberton Golf Club so that your father may be shamed into being a he man.
8. And refuse to be a teacher or a naturopath.
9. Also refuse to be house-clean until you come to years of indiscretion. Your dear mamma loves to do odd jobs, and I take it heredity will make you also do odd jobs about the house.
10. Finally, don't try to live up to any of your names; rather try to live down to the last one.

Your wellwisher, A. S. Neill

[1] Douglas Neill Thomson had just been born.

To David Barton

Dear Bartie   *8 February 1945*

Psychological. A mad attempt to prove that you have not missed the bus after all.[1] I wonder just how badly damaged that bus was. Now if you had any inclination to maths you would have, like Neville's pal Adolf, missed the bus, for as I see it from the diagram a bloke as enters a main from a side road at speed on a vehicle, to wit a cycle, is of the opinion that the intersection of the lines is a point(less) collision. Howsoever, there is of course no possible chance of any BRAIN injury ... but to revert to that bus. My friend Watson has just phoned me from my flat in Baker Street asking the name of the driver, conductor, bus-cleaner, passengers. I laughed scornfully into the mouthpiece and informed him that he was on the wrong line (Green Line), that the vital clue was the colour of the bus. YELLOW. Why yellow? Ah! *Vide* Howard on the Compost Heap.

Nuff said on this topic. I picture you on your back, calmly ordering sundry more or less picturesque nurses to fetch you Pêche Melbas and jellies galore. Caught the bus all right, this guy, this time.

Jonesie seems to want me to write cheering you up. Good. News, and this is still me writing it ... it rains here. Several water pipes bus(pardon the painful letters)t, coal shortage. Lastly, Gallop comes today on a visit. Nice if Trotter turned up at the same time, what?

How to cheer this bloke up ... oh, heard of the *ersatz* prompter at the Old Vic (in hoarse stage whisper from the wings): 'Or NOT to be!' Three folks have written to me asking where the joke is.

New Govt here. Catch, Kyng, Betty, Neville, etc. Hon members etc. Opposition alleged to be led by Shagger is so far speechless and planless. Usual mud-slinging on wall-paper.

Well if this letter helps ... remember the film *A Slight Case of Murder*, where at a gangster party Edward G. Robinson likes a gangster's song so much that he gets it relayed by phone to a pal in hospital. After song is over you see two nurses slowly draw up a sheet over the pal ... you know.

Cheer up, Neill

[1] David Barton was seriously ill in hospital after being run over by a bus.

To W. B. Curry

Dear Curry   *11 July 1947*

Need a housemother? Mother of two kids here has been one in a school called Formosa, and has resigned because it ain't progressive at all.

Good looker, nice, capable, social: Phyllis Harris. If you have a job for her, let me know: she's good.

Off to USA in August with enough lectures to pay my fare of £82 third-class return. My dog-track old parent went last week first class, at £250. Moral: go to the dogs and not the kids. (...)

All well here barring the bank balance. You don't know of any sick millionaire who would sign a will in my favour, do you? But you are the sort of sod who would bag him yourself, I fear.

All the best, Neill

To Richard Marcus

Dear Richard   *13 July 1955*

Tut, tut, if you will let the old school tie get smudgy you should keep it dark. However, every cloud has a silver lining, and during question times after lectures, when the old favourite crops up ... And how do they fit into a disciplined world later ... I can now add: In addition to a Cambridge don and two lecturers in London University we have an ex-pupil in Bristol ... no, sir, I said Bristol, not Borstal ... etc.

I dunno how you do it, frankly. I recall a maths pupil who was, so to say, kinda *durcheinander* [confused], incapable of tense concentration, always of divided mind. I don't like to guess the answer, for I know how difficult it is to snaffle exam papers the night before. I'll put you in the next circular, i.e. if a modest subscription is forthcoming. (...)

Thine, Neill

To Jacquie Elvey

Dear Jacquie   *30 October 1959*

It was kind of you to remember my birthday. But very unkind to try to get wed without my being able to put the chosen guy through an examination ... you know the sort of questions, like this one: Yr wife gives you cold coffee each morning. State clearly your preference for taking care of her ... arsenic, cloak and dagger, pushing off a ship (say around Aden), but the honeymoon will be too early for all that, I fear. Ulla[1] says the guy is a nice guy so maybe you'll be safe. (...)

Well, old dear, I do hope you will be happy. You always were a nice person and had I been two years younger ... well, well.

Love, Neill

P.S. I suppose Ivan has discovered how lovely are the eyes of his lady love. But maybe they have changed in this hard world.

[1] Ulla Otte.

To Peter Russell

Dear Rusty   *10 May 1962*

It was great to read of your success.[1] Seems as if you've made it, and now I can answer the idiots who ask: Have any of your old pupils made a success on the stage?

Oddly enough I re-read the whole play a few weeks ago. I saw it first in Berlin in 1922 ... *der Totentanz*. I didn't know a word of German but it was all so tense I was thrilled. But, *mein Gott*, the hate in the play!

If it comes on in the West End I naturally shall expect a couple of stalls and of course a programme, all free, but the latter isn't so important; I can borrow one from some sap of a mere Englishman sitting near me.

Nice to have successes in ex-Summerhillians. Bunny[2] sent me his latest book, so deep I have to read each sentence twice. Barton sent me a 63/- book on maths, and so far the only bit I understand is his name on the cover. Evelyn[3] wins first prize of £500 for sculpture, and Tishy[4] has exhibitions and sells pictures. But I won't crow until Tookie[5] is in the Cabinet and Philip Townsend a bishop. Then I'll have to become Lord Summerhill just to keep my end up.

Good luck, old sausage, Neill

[1] Peter Russell had appeared in Strindberg's *Dance of Death* in a performance by the Royal Shakespeare Company in London.
[2] Gordon Leff   [4] Ishbel McWhirter.
[3] Evelyn Williams   [5] John Tooke.

To Eva Leff

Dear Eva   *23 July 1963*

Tut, tut! For years I have been thanking you for money gifts and have found it difficult to say something new in doing so. Of course there is one way. ... Look here, you silly woman, what the hell do you mean by wasting good money on a Scot who is a failure (financially only I hope)? Or: Madam, how dare you? Don't you know there are Cat Homes that need money? Or again; Make the sum big enough to let me get into the Paddington–Rachman racket. No, that wouldn't do; I am too old to entertain Christines and Mandies.[1] So it will have to be the conventional: Thank you very much, kind lady.

Love and blessings (pagan of course) to both of you, Neill

[1] Christine Keeler and Mandy Rice-Davies, involved in the 'Profumo Affair'.

To Janina Popenue

Dear Janina   *5 February 1964*
So your convent school is very strict. I thought that convents were following Jesus who loved children. Dear me! Summerhill has no religion, yet every child loves it.

We are full up, but there is a chance that a bed for a girl your age may be vacant when we open again in May. But it is a long and expensive way from Malaysia to here, unless of course you walk and swim it.

Let me know soon, because lots want to come here. Already we have 28 Americans and we are trying to learn their language; but I can't yet call a bawth a beth or a dawnce a dence, but I do know a sparrow is a little boid.

Cheerio, Neill

To Stephen Shapiro

Dear Stephen   *25 May 1964*
Nice of you to write me, nice to hear of all the subjects you are studying. I am now teeching speling and i like kids to rite ritely and to have good gramer. And speaking of riting well how do u expect me to read yr addddddderresss? It can be Sarnia, Trania, Sornin. Dunno how I can address this letter.

School as usual. Very full with many new ones you wouldn't know. The big ones have left – Malory, Freer, Cara, Irene, Zoë, but that big one Neill is still here. I keep telling him to leave but he won't.

Well, Mister Shapiro, you sound as if you were happy. Good. Ena and Ulla and Harry and Peter send their love. Me too.

Cheerio, Neill

To Daphne and Robert Byng

Dear Both   *22 December 1965*
    A_s y°u c^an see I have opened your bottles, and now request you to
send me as many hangover pills as you can muster. But I did not mix
the gin with the whisky. You are very kind folks and it is a tragedy that
you have such a terrible daughter. This is just a hint to her that, if she
wants to redeem herself, she can bring me a nice present, a modest one
like a Jaguar or even a TV set that will get BBC2. I'll help her to carry
either when I meet the brats at Liverpool St.
    May you all have a festive Xmas with lots of booze and grub.
        Yours with thanks, Neill

To Barbara Grigor

Dear Barbara   *8 August 1967*
    Kids return on Friday 29 September, and if you can come about
Wedy or so you would have two days to get your room and teaching hut
eingerichtet [organised]. Maybe not the word but it sounds kinda Deutsch
anyway. You said you would bring yr Mini ... car not skirt but both will
be welcome, only there is no garage available, but we often leave our cars
out in wet and wind and they don't seem to suffer.
    Vague memory that you asked me for advice in teaching English.
None necessary; we have a few modern books that will guide to that
paradise we call O level.
    Be seeing you then later on. My wife Ena may write you telling you
about domestic factors that a mere man never sees.
        Yours, Neill

P.S. I heard you visited Kilquhanity and that they liked you there.
Good, but of course you were not to know that *die ganze Familie Aitkenhead ist meschugge!* [the whole Aitkenhead family is crazy!]

To Sean Ames

Dear Sean   *22 April 1968*
    Ta for a very nice letter. (...) Sorry for you and other old Summerhil-
lians being badgered by questions. Why not pull their legs and tell them
of our savage beatings and our religious converts? Snag is they wd believe
you. You mention drink. It ain't a problem really; end of term sniffs at

the corks and then intoxication. Staff are the swiggers of beer, not the kids. Dunno how I'll cope with dope if and when it comes ... bag it for myself maybe to escape into a world where there are no visitors.

Love, Neill

To James Stern

Dear Jimmy   *6 February 1969*
    (...) Yr diet. What in hell does the guy eat instead of bread and butter? Sleeping pills. Never take em, bad hangovers they tell me. I count sheep ... millions of em, and then it is time to get up. (...)
    Love to both on ye. If that is true Lancashire. Like the two servant sisters being photographed. Man puts his head under black cloth.
    'Wot's he doin', Bess?'
    'He's goin' to focus.'
    'What? Both on us?'
    Neill

To Gwen Horsfield

Dear Gwen   *19 February 1969*
    Snag is that with sometimes 40 visitors a week the kids made a law only on Saturdays. Don't want to hear at a meeting: I charge Neill with breaking the law. Fined his pudding. But if yr friends can't come on a Saty I'll risk it, but looking out of my window I ask who the hell wants to see S'hill this weather? (...)
    Love to both, but do you deserve it?
    Neill

To Barbara Longbrook

Dear Barbara   *6 September 1969*
    Now why do all the pretty girls tell me they love me when I am 86 next month? They didn't do it when I was 26, bless em. (...)
    If yr middle name is Rockefeller send me 3 or 4 bucks for our rebuilding fund and I'll send you my latest book *Talking of Summerhill* which can't

be sold in USA. I make a modest charge of ten grand for autographing it.

You sound a nice lassie, but any lass who likes Summerhill must be nice.

Yours, A. S. Neill

To Leslie Thomson

Dear Leslie   *28 October 1969*

What stunning photies! Better than last time. You must have a very quick camera. (...) Thanks a lot, laddie. You may be a flop as a nature cure healer but as a photo guy you are great ... meaning that a snap shows immediate results while any bloody cure is largely intangible. I attribute my longevity to the fact that I believed in nature cure ... and didn't live up to it, but how can I when my birthday party in town last week gave me five bottles of the best malt whisky? But I will say that the Kingston diet wasn't ignored all the same. Wish I could have it all the time but in a school not easy to get it ... like the Scot who was refused entry into heaven on Peter's objection to making porridge for one.

Thine, Neill

To Ivor Cutler

Dear Ivor   *10 August 1970*

I accept the compliment with joy but with reservations.[1] My *The Last Man Alive* (pub 1938) comes out again by Gollancz in Oct and I simply refuse to have my sales cut by your bloody book, so I want you to postpone publication until 1999 or so. Got me?

So you are teaching again? Dunno why they keep you, cos any teacher with a sense of fun is anathema to the Establishment. We had an average of 100 visitors weekly all term. Oh to live in Texas where one can buy a gun in any shop.

I expect a signed copy of that ere book.

The best, Neill

[1] Ivor Cutler had asked Neill if he could dedicate his children's book *Meal One* to him.

To Diana Butler

Dear Diana   *5 October 1970*

I don't usually give advice but in your case I do. Don't spank Daniel more than twice a day. Take his hand away from his genitals and if he doesn't stop tie his hands. Teach him his prayers when he begins to talk, and never allow his unholy grandmother to get near him. Then when he is a real problem send him to Summerhill. (...)

I envy your and David's life of being kept awake the whole bloody night. However in about five years you'll get a decent sleep.

Love, Neill

To Ulla Otte

Dear Ulla   *27 November 1970*

(...) Why not try to make a few DM by writing abt S'hill to *Die Zeit* or *Eltern*? You could make a nice sensation ... I spent many years in Summerhill and it was hell. Neill made a fortune by starving the kids. u.s.w. I could make a great stink if I wrote an article, 'Summerhill is a Swindle', or better still, 'How I Became a Roman Catholic'. But the school has made enough sensation already. It is too respectable now. We had a visit from the Earl and Countess of Stradbroke in their Rolls. So we are respectable at last.

Tell us how you are and how *das Leben geht* [life goes].

Love, old friend, Neill

To Ilse Rolfe

Dear Ilse   *11 January 1971*

How nice of you to write me. I cannot recall how I saved you from the Nazis, only have a vague memory of your applying for a job from a Koncentrationslager. Had I known what a terrible woman you were I'd have left you to Mr Hitler's tender mercies!

So yr lass is taking her MA in English. I took that degree just on 60 years ago. I have forgotten all I learned. (...)

Warm wishes, Neill

To Gwen Horsfield

Dear Gwen   *24 June 1971*
     How sweet of you to send me flowers ... damn the woman, too premature, yet I at least saw em and smelt em, which I won't be able to do at the cremmie. (...)
     So what do you think of the school that made your brats guys with strings of letters after their names? Don't try to reply via the *Guardian*. They generally print my letters but never any that are pro or agin them. *Times* ditto. But the *Telegraph* gets 300 letters a day. *Sunday Telegraph* didn't publish one of mine last week on penis envy, mentioned in a book review of Spock. Penis isn't yet as respectable as learned words like shit and fuck, showing that soon one can say shit in a drawing room, but not excrement.
     Love, bless you all, but no prayers please for my recovery. They could easily annoy the Angel of Death and make him speed up his visit. Got me, you heathens?
     Neill

To Beryl McAlhone

Dear Beryl   *3 July 1971*
     How good of you to send me *Where* copies; how evil of you to encourage me on the way to chronic alcoholism. Gord, it took so long to unwrap that bottle that the consequent thirst almost emptied it.
     I didn't realise you were the editor. I'd have shown you more deference.
     I know I should become a subscriber, but hesitate owing to age and heart, like the Aberdonian who was sent by his doctor to see a Harley St specialist on hearts. 'I hope you live to complete the journey.' He booked at every station on the way ... to the next station. That is how I feel, but, dammit, I enclose a yearly sub and if I pop off will try to claim a repayment from hell. (...)
     Thine, Neill

To James and Tania Stern

Dear Both   *19 July 1971*

(...) Is this a chestnut? Deaf judge to prisoner. 'Before I sentence you have you anything to say?'

'Bugger all, my lud.'

Judge to clerk of court: 'What did he say?'

'He said bugger all, me lud.'

'Really? I could have sworn I saw his lips moving.'

Love, Neill

To Beryl McAlhone

Dear Beryl   *3 August 1971*

Yes, Edward[1] is a likeable guy, but you are a nasty guyess ... fancy asking me to leave writing my Life to give you a measly article! Orrid wumman, but, being a saint with a halo, I forgive you your trespasses.

Friendly criticism ... not enough about kids in *Where*, but I have seen only the last number. And of course not enough four-letter words to make it really popular. Out Oz Oz^2 and I'll protest when they cut your hair in stir.

Thine, Neill

[1] Edward Blishen.
[2] *Oz* magazine had been the subject of a celebrated obscenity trial.

To Tom Eagle

Dear Tom   *4 January 1972*

Hurrah! Thought you might be dead. Guy phoned from California yesterday. 'Now that Neill is dead who is running Summerhill?' 'I am.' 'And who are you' 'A. S. Neill.' Sounded like a collapse at the other end. (...)

Thine, Neill

9

Fatherhood

We were very close, and we loved each other
very much. He was as soft as lights with me; I
could do whatever I wanted with him. Can't
you always – especially being the only daughter? I would always prime him up before asking
Mum something.

Zoë Neill

To Angus Murray

Dear Angus   *25 November 1946*
    (...) No special news to give you, for you don't know the new pupils
at all. No news ... except, oh yes, I became a father last week, a girl Zoë.
Kinda late at 63. (...)
    Yours as ever, Neill

To Wilhelm Reich

*November 1946-January 1956**
Many thanks for your good wishes for Zoë. She is a pretty kid without
a blemish on her skin. So far I don't feel possessive about her, and won't
until she begins to take notice. Luckily Ena agrees with me that
timetable feeding is the devil, and is very likely the cause of so much modern thumb-sucking. Zoë is making her own timetable, I notice.

* Neill regularly kept Reich in touch with Zoë's development and his and his
wife's feelings on the subject. Yet often he wrote no more than a line or two in
lengthy letters dealing with other topics. I have therefore run these together to
form a ten-year 'report' on Zoë by her father.

Zoë flourishes and already is trying to bully us both at seven weeks. God help a poor father.

Zoë is a darling. Taking a few steps now, and, alas, waking us at 6.30 a.m.

I long to show you Zoë, who under self-regulation is fine, but we have to go against her when she wakes at 2 a.m. sometimes and yells because we won't take her up to play games with her. She has a tremendous will, but is 95% quiet and happy. No signs of her wanting to play with faeces and urine.

Zoë flourishes, walks about everywhere and is no trouble at all, a fine example of self-regulation.

Ena and I get great joy out of Zoë, although here again I often look at her and wonder sadly what life has in store for her. We had a Danish girl as housemother, an admirer of Philipson. Zoë was sleepy and Ena lifted her to take her to bed. The Dane said: 'You talk of self-regulation, but you do not practise it; you should let her fall asleep on the floor and then put her to bed.' Ena said: 'She wouldn't fall asleep; she would cry for an hour with tiredness; what would you do then?' The Dane didn't know.

Most wonderful is self-regulation with Zoë; she shows no sign of hate or destructiveness. It is a joy to watch her grow. One of the staff has a girl of two and the difference between the bodies is great. Zoë is as loose as a kitten; P— as tight as a drum.

Ena and I often say we should start a home for mothers and children of a week old. The more I see of stiff stomachs the more I feel that the start should be made with infants. Ena has been an ideal mother for Zoë, and the result is just excellent.

I fear that it is going to be impossible for Ena to go back to USA for therapy. One joy is that, without therapy, she hasn't made a single mistake in Zoë's case. The result is pure delight to me. She is talking quite a lot at 16 months. So Peter [Reich] is reading! Both cases make me think there is nothing in heredity!

Re Peter. Have you considered the sleep angle? Recently our kids have been breaking all bedtime laws. A meeting was strict about them, and for a week they have gone to bed early. Result: most of the bad tempers, destructiveness etc have lessened greatly. Zoë, if too late up, owing to the exciting life here, is a problem next day, whining, ill-tempered ... and in her case there is no question of anything genital at all. Peter goes to bed far too late. Here in the Cottage he'd be bedded by 6 or 6.30 ... and in Orgonon he was often up till ten. I'd play the heavy parents about sleep if I were you. Self-regulation be damned sometimes ... today is very cold;

Zoë wanted to go out in her thin frock. Ena said no; must wear overalls.
Anger, tears, but Ena insisted and put on the warm things.

Zoë tiresome at bedtimes, keeps getting up. Ena suggests owing to her
genitality not breaking through. Since there has been absolutely no repression and her genital interest hasn't awakened, I wonder if it is due to
the fact that Ena's milk gave out after three weeks, so that she missed the
oral orgastic phase. There is no boy her age or a little older for her to make
play with. I am so ignorant about babies that I simply don't know when
a girl reaches genital interest. A boy earlier surely, for his apparatus is so
outstanding.

Oh dear, you run away from me again; I can't follow you. You say that
genitality is a total bodily function with special qualities of energy dis-
charge. I try to think in terms of Zoë. All her interest seems to be in
things, in making toys work, in seeing how and why everything is there.
Her play with little boys and girls is all out-going. Now that the kids have
come back after the vacation she is so excited that she can't wait to eat
a meal, and wakens at night unusually often. Watching her makes me
convinced that I don't know a thing about kids or human nature. She
seems to me to behave almost exactly like the kittens we have ... just delighted to be alive to chase a bit of string. So that the more I think of the
word genitality the more confused I get. All I see in Zoë is Life-ality.

Zoë always a delight, but we both worry about her having no chance of
good sex play. In the train I read part of a book on Oedipus, giving a
synopsis of Freud's ideas. It struck me that much of Freud's theories
about babies are just wrong, for instance, a baby's attitude to father's
penis and mother's envy of boys' penes seems to me to be based solely
on a family with authority. Indeed, all Freud's *Realitäts Prinzip* [Reality
Principle] seems to be based on the family as it is now. Castration seems
to Freud to be a normal fear in every boy, but will it be in Peter? Will
Zoë fantasy that someone has cut her penis off?

Zoë running all over the place. *Daily Herald* woman coming today to see
her and to ask about self-reg. *Picture Post* wants a woman photographer
to spend eight days here photoing Zoë, saying: 'Nowhere in England has
any baby the environment and chance to be self-regulated and we ought
to make a record of it.' But I fear that all this worship will be bad for Zoë,
for up to now she has shown no narcissism or self-consciousness. Our
unself-regulated boys are too sadistic and rough.
    Budda Leunbach talked rot when she said a baby self-regulated itself
in cold weather re clothes. Zoë would die of all the acute diseases in the
world if Ena didn't insist on her wearing warm things.

Ena and I both have that exhausted feeling we get after a heavy term giving out to the kids all the time. And I begin to feel my age now, find it difficult to get up when Zoë makes me lie with her on the floor. Yet I can dance all night.

We are concerned about Zoë getting fears and complexes from badly reared kids in the Cottage which houses the smallest children. A trying problem to you and us and all the other believers. It makes me furious to hear a kid say to Zoë: 'Let's shit here but don't tell your mummy.'

I am much troubled with a riddle ... A child frightens Zoë by saying cows will eat her. We tell her that is nonsense but she doesn't believe us ... the word of the badly reared child of 5 has more weight than anything we can say. Why? In spite of her fearless life of 3 years she is prone to accept fear even though it does not stiffen her stomach. What structural feature in a baby reacts to fear? Tell me the answer, but even if I know I can't eliminate that fear. I took her to the zoo yesterday with a girl of just six. A lion roared. Amarilla fled in fear. Zoë who hadn't minded the roar saw the other's alarm, and she also showed fear. I wish I knew even the elements of child nature. Puzzled too when Zoë sometimes says at bedtime: 'Go away, Daddy, I don't *like* you.' Maybe I am not a good father, distributing my love to 70 children, but that would apply to Ena too, even more so. Ena asked her who said that about not liking Daddy and she answered 'P—' ... the 'trained' stiff-stomach girl of 5 who makes Zoë taste her shit and threatens to beat her if she doesn't. Again apparently the self-regulation child accepts what the spoiled brat says even about Daddy. Makes me long for an island with only Zoë, Peter, Pussy[1] etc on it, but even then I guess fears would appear. Prophylaxis has its snags I see.

Zoë grows big in every way. Demanding reading lessons every day and far too bright for my taste, for she never lets up, simply goes on energetically all day till she gets tired, which I suppose is the normal thing to do in life. No interest in having a sweetheart yet. I wonder if Peter will have any interest in her this summer. Maybe too young for him.

The joyful side of life is Zoë, who has at last reached the Daddy stage and makes me play with her for two hours. I'd rather she played with other children, but only one or two had self-regulation and she finds the others unwelcome. They are so prone to frighten her with stories of wild animals and bloody deaths. Death of mice and rats etc doesn't seem to affect her; she accepts the fact that they are dead, but in fantasy stories she asks me to kill some animal or person and then bring them alive again.

I have decided to write another book, mainly about Zoë, but not giving her name;[2] it is embarrassing for adolescents to find as infants they were 'cases'. Your own daughter said at my Hamilton Seminar: 'I'm tired of being called the Result of the Function of the Orgasm', said it with humour, but enough suggestion of truth to make me hesitate to use Zoë's name.[3] Apart from embarrassment, if we say too much about Zoë and Peter and their like, the poor things will feel it difficult to live up to what we say of them.

I wish I knew more about the contest between the world and you for Peter's soul. Here our trouble is the world of un-self-regulated children who infect Z with their fears and hates and sadisms, but so far, not making her sex conscious in a wrong way. She still doesn't want much of me; I am only the man who can tell her stories of animals. Her identification of self with animals persists all the time; she wears out all her stocking knees and shoe points crawling on the floor as a zebra or a horse or a Bambi. One thing I have learned, that the Freudians are wrong when they say that fantasy is a flight from reality, for Z is at home in both. Still her identification with animals may be a flight from the wrongly reared human animals around her. No, for now during vacation she plays animals more than ever, so that I have to scrabble about the floor as a 'friendly lion what doesn't eat people' twice daily. Again, pax old Freud, she has never shown any desire to be a boy, and in play all her animals must be female.

Just as the Freudians found much aggression in every child they concluded that aggression was the norm, but I find in Zoë little or no hatred. She wants to give out love, to ask for love, and because in her environment she satisfies both wishes she is no hate person. Later when she finds her love attitude met by hate she will react in hate, but would this be necessary if all kids were free and loved? Why no real fights among Summerhill children?

Zoë will be 5 next month. Our headache is a girl of 6, 'trained' to be clean at 9 months, whom Zoë follows all day. She tells Z that witches are in her toy cupboard and keeps talking with guilty giggles about shit and piss. We feel like telling the parents to take their trained brat away, but can't face the row that would follow our 'sacrificing' their brat for our own. Get me a visa and an island out in the lake at Rangeley[4] ... and then my worry would be Zoë falling into the lake. In other platitudinous words ... there is always a bloody snag somewhere.

Zoë will soon be six. We seldom see her all day, for she is so busy with her own gang. I wish you could see her now, and that we could see Peter. Unfortunately we have no boys her age who were self-regulated.

Zoë is now 6 and nice to look at and clever and easy to live with. She now lives in the school while we are in the Cottage. She brings the usual plague remarks from other kids ... 'Daddy, it is rude to say cock, isn't it?' Damned annoying all the same to find how strong a hold the other side gets on a kid. Ena and I counteract all the time, of course.

Why, why, why? Why the hate of genital life? The origin doesn't matter much, but the perpetuation does. Theories of father jealousies, patriarchal states, suppression of sons simply don't click, and if they did one would still have to go behind them and ask why, why? Five minutes ago Zoë was undressing to go to bed. Our history master came in; she told him to shut his eyes till she had her nighty on. She didn't get that from us, but from other adults (domestics) and kids, but why the devil does she seek Barabbas? Why is anti-life so easy to be captured by a child?

No special news from here. Zoë was 8 the other day; she is tall and bonny and quite clever. She has little interest in grown-ups (including me) but enters fully into the group life of her pals. She has just come to me reciting a very obscene poem a boy taught her, and last week said she liked hymns and would like to go to church. Just shows how far a journey it is to a self-regulation world.

We should never be proud of our children. Zoë, now 9, will eat nothing but bread and potatoes, refuses all greens and most fruits. *Bockbeinig* [Pigheaded] about it too. She gets catarrh and ear-trouble and looks pasty-faced … and one can't do a damn thing about it. Self-regulation! But I hope it is just a necessary phase, when the growing body needs mostly starch and sugar. I dunno.

[1] Theodore Wolfe's daughter.
[2] This became *The Free Child*, and Neill eventually did use Zoë's name in it.
[3] Neill spoke at a seminar at the Hamilton School in Massachusetts.
[4] The location of Orgonon.

To Constant Butler

Dear Constance   *5 May 1956*
      (…) Zoë didn't want to go to Scotland with me; she knew she would be bored. I have simply got to lump it and it was easy, for I knew she was being sensible and right. Possessive love is such a bloody curse. (…)
      Yours, Neill

To Constance Butler

Dear Constance   *10 January 1957*
      Zoë told me of your book and Nobby's sugar[1] when I returned. Not being the kind of father who says: 'Now you must write Constance a nice

letter of thanks,' I wait and make the guess that she will thank you without prompting. (...)

Thine, Neill

[1] Nobby was the name of Zoë's pony.

To Harold Hart

Dear Hart   *24 December 1958*

(...) Zoë delights in the books you send her, but I don't suppose she ever thanks you. At that age who ever thanks without prompting? My sister sent her ten shillings for her birthday, and my remark that she was a fool cos she wouldn't get anything for Xmas didn't affect her. *So ist das Kinderleben* [Such is childhood]. (...)

Neill

To Seishi Shimoda

My dear Shimoda   *2 March 1959*

(...) We are sending Zoë to a school in Switzerland for a year. It is too difficult for her here; as my daughter, staff and pupils expect her to be perfect and the result will be a problem child if she stays here. But I hate to have to part from her. (...)

Your friend, Neill

To Edith Geheeb

Dear Edith   *23 April 1959*

Dear, dear, I blush to think that I once wrote that a child is homesick when it comes from a bad home. Zoë's letters tear my heart and I long for the day she will write that she is happy with you. My wife has told us all about your school and it sounds fine, just as I imagined it would be. *Aber...* Zoë has so many difficulties and is a headstrong girl. My wife has told me she explained Zoë to you, and when I come to fetch her at the beginning of July I may be able to tell you more. I am sure that in your kindly atmosphere she will soon settle in. If she does not then we shall have to think again, but I think she will. I was sent away to work in an office 100 miles away when I was barely 14 and had many months of absolute hell with homesickness, so that I know what it can be. But in a school it cannot last so long. (...)

Yours most sincerely, Neill

To Constance Butler

Dear Constance   *6 July 1959*

(...) Zoë's coming home has been lovely; she is charming and kind and she talks German well. I love her. I want to be fit to take her back to school ... which she loves. I'm so happy abt her.

All the best, Neill

To Paulus and Edith Geheeb

Dear Paulus and Edith   *15 July 1959*

After six weeks in bed I can now sit up to write you telling you how delighted we are with Zoë. You have worked wonders; she is restful, happy, sweet to one and all. She *Schwarms* [is wild about] Ecole and seems to have only one grievance ... she can't dance until she is 14 and she loves to dance. *Sonst ist alles wunderbar, sagt sie.* [Otherwise everything is wonderful.] The first two days she talked to us in German and she is certainly fluent for the time she had with you. She speaks of you both with love and admiration. (...)

It is a delight that she has liked being with you, for it would have put us in a horrible position if she had not wanted to return to you. Makes me glad that I decided to send her to you.

Ena sends her love and Zoë *auch* [also], A. S. Neill

To Edith Geheeb

Dear Edith   *10 September 1959*

So sorry I could not hear well enough on the phone. But I heard that Paulus thinks I should not come now, but that you think it might be good to come and get everything clear.

I have always said that when parents differed about Summerhill I would not take their child because he or she would never settle. Ena and I differed about sending Zoë away. I thought that in the end she would do well in our school, while Ena was of the opposite opinion. I consented, saying that there was no school in England I approved of, and if she went she should go to Ecole. I don't think that Zoë *knew* of our difference of opinion, but she *felt* it, and I feel sure that that is the main reason why she will not settle in Ecole. I think it would have been the same in any school.

I think I shall risk coming but not on Monday, towards the end of the week better. I have a selfish reason also ... I have so much looked forward to meeting you both.

Es tut mir leid [I am sorry] that you are having so much trouble with her. For me to have a *Problemkind* [problem child] is terrible. I want to tell you all about her and her difficulties.

Please give her enclosed letter ... perhaps it will be diplomatic to seal the envelope first!

Yours sincerely, Neill

To Paulus and Edith Geheeb

Dear Paulus and Edith   *28 September 1959*

I waited before writing to see how Zoë would settle in here again. She seems to have done so and has not gone back to her idle gang. Ena was of course very sad when I brought her home, and I was sad too, but I still think she would not have settled with you. Anji[1] is 15 and can adapt herself, but Zoë couldn't. I don't think it was entirely the difference between our systems of education; I think that she felt so far away from home, and all the vacation she kept saying to me: 'Ecole is nice, the people are nice, but why do you send me away when you give other children freedom to decide for themselves?' I found it almost impossible to answer. It may be when she is older that she may want to return to you. (...)

Yours, Neill

[1] Angela Neustatter.

To Helen Neustatter

My dear Helen   *10 December 1959*

(...) Angela is at Paul Geheeb's school in Switzerland. I sent Zoë there at Easter but she didn't like it so I brought her home again. The system is so different, so Deutsch ... *Schweigezeit bein Essen* [silence at mealtimes]; a teacher reads a sentence from Goethe or Nietzsche and the kids have two minutes *Schweigezeit* to contemplate it; as Zoë said: 'All I contemplate is what is coming for grub.' (...)

Love and blessings (pagan ones, of course), Old Beans

To Ilse Ollendorff Reich

Dear Ilse   *17 August 1960*
(...) Zoë is tall and good to look at. She goes to no lessons and Ena worries but I don't. Self-regulation doesn't produce perfect kids ... *Gott sei Dank* [God be thanked]. (...)

Yours as always, Neill

To Constance Butler

Dear Constance   *6 September 1960*
Nice to hear that my daughter didn't disgrace herself. Now my fear is that that girl will return demanding a horse which I can't afford, and have no fencing to keep one in. Too much to hope that her riding will have scunnered her of [put her off] all horse flesh. (...)

All the best, Neill

To Constance Butler

Dear Constance   *25 May 1961*
(...) Zoë plaguing me for a horse which I can ill afford, but she is so mad abt it I must get her one, I fear. (...)

Yours, Neill

To Constance Butler

Dear Constance   *21 June 1961*
(...) Yes, Zoë won and she has got her mare, a dark grey one, quite quiet. Unfortunately she picked up a cheque I'd got from my USA book, and I couldn't tell her the sad tale that I couldn't afford a nag. (...)

Yours, Neill

To Claude Ferrière

Dear Claude   *11 January 1962*
    (...) I find my only daughter, Zoë, now 16, quite enough, demanding horses and radio sets. Not to speak of cigarettes; all the warnings abt lung cancer don't touch her, but no kid can see tomorrow ... luckily in an H bomb era. (...)
    All the best, Neill

To Seishi Shimoda

My dear Shimoda   *30 December 1962*
    (...) Zoë is 16 but doesn't yet know what she is to do in life. No hurry; she will find her place. Her art work is very good and so is her imaginative writing. (...)
    Yours warmly and sincerely, A. S. Neill

To Constance Butler

Dear Constance   *9 January 1963*
    (...) Zoë is in love with an ex-Catholic, ex thank the God that never was or is. But I wish she would fall out of love with her horses, who only eat and seldom get ridden. Why do we have kids? (...)
    Love to all, Neill

To Constance Butler

Dear Constance   *11 February 1963*
    (...) I'd let Di leave at 15 myself and choose anything she wanted, that is, if you have good polytechs in Derby. Anyway your kids will go their own way, just as Zoë will. It's their lives and if they have to learn the hard way (as Zoë always does) it's their funeral. (...)
    Love, Neill

To Bryn Purdy

Dear Bryn   *29 December 1963*
(…) Zoë has little interest in schools … Summerhill has been her
enemy in a way – an only child with fifty brothers and sisters who take
up all her parents' time and interest. Moral: never be born in a school.
(…)
The best, Neill

To Antoine Obert

Dear Tony   *16 December 1964*
(…) Zoë is now 18 but hasn't decided on her career yet. I don't
worry. She has character and good brains.
Yours as always, Neill

To Harold Hart

Dear Harold   *15 March 1965*
(…) I am trying to encourage Zoë to write and illustrate a children's
book, for she seems to have some talent for writing and drawing, but like
her father she is damned lazy. (…)
Yours ever, Neill

To Willa Muir

Willa, me dear   *17 May 1966*
(…) Zoë returns this week. Been out in Oslo for four months getting
to know her own psychology … she wants to run S'hill after me, and I
told her she had to get to know herself a bit. Her therapist, one of Reich's
best men, told me he had never had a patient so free in body and mind.
Nice. (…)
Love and blessings, Allie

To James Stern

Dear Jimmy   *20 June 1966*
(...) Zoë is mad about horses and takes lessons twice weekly. She says she is going to write you. I hate the bloody animals, and it is just my perverse luck to have a daughter who meets the huntin' shootin' bastards. But she is a sound kid and won't get corrupted, I fancy. (...)
Love to you both, Neill

To Lois Wyvell

Dear Lois   *17 November 1967*
(...) I'd never experiment with any drug myself and Zoë is too sensible to do so also. She was 21 this month, tall, nice, intelligent but not intellectual. She had six months with Ola Raknes, and Ola said that of all his patients in years she was the most relaxed in body and mind. Her interest is horses. She has qualified as a riding mistress. I hoped that her interest would be kids, but I am content that she has an interest at all. (...)
Warm wishes, Neill

To Ben Morris

Dear Ben   *23 January 1969*
(...) Good news of your family. Luckily seldom does a kid follow in father's footsteps; when they do they are inferior as a rule. Wagner's son, Marie Lloyd's daughter, Randolph Churchill. My Zoë, now 22, took the horse line and teaches our kids with a stable of six and, alas, I haven't an ounce of interest in the animals. Still you and I shd be thankful, for we might have produced a Cabinet Minister or a Billy Graham. (...)
Love, Neill

To Erna Gal

My dear Erna   *21 November 1971*
(...) Zoë married a young local farmer and seems content to enter a fraternity of Tory people who never heard of Freud or maybe even Shakespeare, but she has chosen that milieu and seems content, and it is her life, bless her. She is two months pregnant. (...)
Love as of old, Neill

To Greta Sergeant

Dear old Greta   *3 January 1973*
   (...) Zoë married a farmer and they live in that farm along the road.
Her baby Amy is six months old and I get a hell of a lot of joy with her;
she is nearly always smiling, thanks maybe to Zoë's sane way of dealing
with her. But it pains me to know I'll never see her grow up, and, not
believing in any after-life, I can't comfort myself by thinking I'll look
down, or more probably up, to see her grow up. Too many things come
too late. (...)
   Love, old pal, Neill

10

Fame and Recognition

Mr Neill, I have not the slightest doubt, is a genius. He is doing experimental work of the greatest social value, and he ought to be provided with an endowment by the Board of Education, which he would probably accept, and a peerage or at least a knighthood, which he would probably refuse.

C. E. M. Joad in the *New Statesman*, May 1937

To Lilian Morgans

Ffestiniog, North Wales
Dear Lilian   *22 January 1944*
     Tut, tut! Giving me a bad conscience. But do realise that my post is enormous and my letter-writing consists almost entirely of replies that mean nothing to me. ... What'll I do with my son who steals? Where can I be psycho-analysed? What books shd I read on child psychology? What are yr fees?
     I can't say I have any real correspondence with anyone, but as I write books I expect I make them an *ersatz* for letters (getting paid for them too). (...)
     Other day when I lectured in London and hundreds couldn't get in, I felt life in Wales was just existence.
     Yours, Neill

To Angus Murray

Dear old Angus   *26 November 1944*
     Thanks for letter. No, *Picture Post* had an article on a Lancs village school run by E. F. O'Neill. They photoed us a few months ago, but I hear they decided not to include us. And I don't care a damn either. We don't need that kind of publicity, in fact with over 200 waiting to get into the school, propaganda is useless. (...)
     All the best, Neill

To Constance Butler

Dear Constance   *5 April 1961*
    (...) I never hear from Henry[1] now, but if I go to USA in autumn I'll try to meet him. Lots want me to go but I funk it, too strenuous flying all over a continent and talking to strangers. Besides I might not get a visa. I spent a night in Hull giving two lectures, also two in Cheltenham. They bring in a little but not much.
    My USA fan mail still keeps up but now I answer the same day, which makes it easier. End of term on Saturday. I have no play this time, but will cook up something half an hour before the plays start. And next term is the influx of visitors and I dread it more and more each year. I wanna be ALONE. (...)
    Cheerio, Neill

[1] Henry Miller

To Constance Butler

Dear Constance   *25 May 1961*
    (...) Got more pupils but can't get the staff ... a real headache, as is my fan mail from USA; I can hardly cope with it. I tried a woman secretary for a day but I can't dictate letters; they aren't my style. (...)
    Asked to appear on *Lifeline* in the autumn, also may be interviewed by Malcolm Muggeridge on ITV. But I wish I got the £100 fee the singers are said to get.
    Stopping now to get on with that American pile. Alas, none are signed Rockefeller.
    Cheerio, Neill

To Constance Butler

Dear Constance   *1 February 1962*
    (...) Got a job for you ... the only friend I can trust to do it. To write a letter to the *Times Educational Supplement*, EC4, on these lines: 'Now that royalty has broken the Public School tradition by sending Prince Charles to Kurt Hahn's Gordonstoun, can it go a step further and enrol Princess Anne in A. S. Neill's Summerhill?' It might raise a smile in some quarters.[1] (...)
    Henry Miller sent me 1000 dollars as a gift to the school. What a man!

Money apart I loved him when we met, but Perlès didn't impress me much.

Love to the family, Neill

[1] A few years later Princess Margaret and Lord Snowdon sent their son and daughter to Bedales.

To Elna Lucas

Dear Elna   *14 December 1962*

Shoot me; I shd have answered you long ago. I do so now cos it is end of term and I am free to tackle the pile of letters on my desk ... appalling lot, mostly American fan mail. Costs me 6d a time to answer ... title for a short story: The Scot who Renounced Fame as being too Expensive. (...)

I was very tired after my five days' lecturing and won't do it again. In fact I feel like giving lecturing up, partly because holding an audience, as I can do, doesn't give me the old kick of exhibitionism.

Hoping to see you both when and if I come to Cambridge, Neill

To Ishbel McWhirter

Tishy, me dear   *7 May 1963*

(...) I had a lovely five days in hospital in a private ward at 30 gns a week, free of course as Wally's stepfather.[1] Not too much pain and delightful nurses and good food and a private phone. How nice to be completely unknown; doctors and staff had never heard of the great ASN ... Good morning, Mr McNeill, or next morning O'Neill. (...)

Love to both, Neill

[1] Wally Neustatter.

To Eva Leff

Dear Eva   *22 December 1963*

(...) My USA fan mail is just a nightmare to answer, and I am becoming more and more of a TV personality. I'm on ITV Sunday January 12th at seven in a discussion on religion. And next week I record a discussion with Robert Morley for the BBC. But if it were cancelled I wouldn't care a damn, whereas if I'd been 40 or less I'd have been thrilled to have my beautiful face seen by millions. Most things in life come too late. Barrie put it: They give you nuts to chew when your teeth have gone.

Love to the family, Neill

To Bill MacKinnon

Dear Bill   *14 January 1964*
Luckily I got £35 for it. Mistake no chairman; we couldn't get a word in edgeways with the other guys, but it comforts me to think that they got rope enough to hang themselves. I am handicapped because I hate arguing with people. Oh for half an hour to say what I want to! Now Robert Morley tells me he is putting himself and me on *Juke Box Jury*. That shd be funny. I recorded a programme with him last week. A nice guy, Robert; says he'll make me a TV star ... at my time o' life ... impossible. (...)
Love to you both, bless you ... if a pagan can bless. Neill

To Bill and Käte MacKinnon

Dear Bill and Käte   *2 May 1965*
(...) I didn't know abt John's honour.[1] No one has ever offered me one. I'd refuse any common Sir or Lord and might even reject an O.M. ... easy to say seeing as how I'll never be offered even a university LLD. (...)
We reopen next week and then hell for the term with hundreds of USA rubbernecks. But to be cheerful, Johnson might start the world war, and so rescue me from the USA.
Love from us all, Neill

[1] John Aitkenhead.

To Gordon Leff

Dear Bunny   *24 January 1966*
I have a queer feeling of shame at being taken into the Establishment.[1] Does it mean that I am out of date, or that the universities are coming up to date? I never heard of a degree Master of Educn in my life. I

never use my degree on paper, not even on the prospectus, and I won't use any hon one; I am just curious to know what it wd be, possibly M. Educ. M.E. cd mean Middle English or Mining Engineer. (...)

I am now getting a kind of fame and also making money from USA royalties ... and more when my new book[2] comes out in the Fall (my 60% American pupils are corrupting my English). And I am too old to buy anything barring baccy, and my name in print does not give the old thrill. You as a young writer will have a similar experience. (...)

Love to you and Käte, Neill

[1] Newcastle University had announced their intention of awarding Neill an honorary degree.
[2] *Freedom not License!*

To Willa Muir

27 January 1966

Tut, tut, dear old Willa, I have sunk into the Establishment at last. Comic too. The local council sent me a letter of congrats and the paper headlines my honour. Write about 20 books and no one notices you, but get a university to honour you, and you are accepted as someone of moment. *Warum*? [Why?] Cos in their hearts people look on a university as a criterion of success. Barrie's auntie ... What are you going to be, James? An author. What, and you an MA! (...)

Love and blessings, Allie

To Gordon Leff

Dear Bunny   *2 February 1966*

(...) An academic friend says that universities follow each other like sheep and that I shd expect a plethora of hon degrees. Almost makes me pray for a nuclear war first.

Good to hear you say lots in universities are progressing. But I don't expect my own Varsity of Edinburgh ever heard of me. My phobia is that they will want to make me Lord Summerhill; that honour I could not accept, but it is not likely to be offered anyway. (...)

Thine, Neill

To Willa Muir

Willa, me dear   *17 May 1966*
    I had a glorious time in Newcastle, sort of Christ with scores of students being received by me, only my halo didn't fit very well. University lent us all gowns and trenchers, and, anxious about yr saying there will be a plethora of degrees offered me now, did Edwin have to buy a gown or hire one each time? Cos if so I'm no gaein'. (...)
    Willa, how dead university teachers are. God, I met scores of em in both York and Newcastle and they were dead, humourless, narrow, dead but no to be buried for thirty years or so. But you ken a' that ... think of that walking corpse Blyth Webster or the decayed one Saintsbury. Aye, the dead hand on all education is the university. (...)
    Love, Neill

To Willa Muir

My dear Willa   *October 1966*
    (...) Sorry for Ritchie Calder getting that nasty letter about his socialism in the *New Statesman*. But he shdn't have taken that title; maybe he felt that his own name wasna good enough. Fancy the horror of a Sir H. G. Wells or a Sir Bernard Shaw. Yet the same criticism cd be made about my M.Ed. of course. I doubt if Edwin ever signed himself Dr. When you are Dame Willa ... ah, weel. (...)
    Love, old dear, Allie

To Ben Morris

Dear Ben   *28 May 1968*
    (...) At 84½ I have had to cut out most of my lecturing, but promised Robin Pedley to talk to his lot when I get my LLD from Exeter next month. Now that I am a member of the Establishment I tremble lest old Harold Wilson will offer me a knighthood. Luckily I guess he never heard of me. (...)
    Thine, Neill

To Ben Morris

Dear Ben   *4 June 1968*
    No, I couldn't take a title. Found that a friend was trying to wangle
getting me made Lord Neill of Summerhill. I stopped him at once. Feel
kinda ashamed taking hon degrees, so joining the Establishment. Good
thing that my Edinburgh University never heard of me. Funny that when
I go north and am introduced to anyone it is as the author of *A Dominie's
Log* ... 53 years ago. (...)
    Peety, man, that Bristol is so far awa. I get oceans of visitors, but they
all want to be given to; I miss so much meeting loons like you who have
much to give.
    I am sending on a few copies of that article. It is, alas, adding to my
USA fan mail, which already piles my desk. Good thing about English
fowk ... they don't write fan letters ... to the Beatles yes, but to dominies,
nay.
    Love to the family, Neill

To James Stern

Dear Jimmy   *29 June 1968*
    I saw a sign to Tisbury as I was driven to Exeter on Thursday, and
sighed cos I cdn't look in to see you both. Weekend previous I flew to
Dublin to a live TV show with 250 guests, all RC I guess. I had some
nice battles with the priests and their hated religion. One said a child is
born in sin and they beat a kid to make it good. I asked him if he saw
any sin in a new-born babe, and to my astonishment the audience
applauded me. Christ, what a country ... *verboten* [forbidden] are divorce
and contraceptives; sequel more drunkenness than I have seen since 1895
in Calvinist Scotland. I think I threw a spanner or two in their bloody
hateful machinery. (...)
    Love to both, Neill

To R. F. Mackenzie

Dear Bob   *8 October 1968*
    Chap who approached me was from the Labour group.[1] My refusal
was in part dislike of being mixed up with any political party. I wouldn't
mind being a candidate as an independent, with no necessity to do any
electioneering. I don't think I'd stand a chance in a university largely of

medicals who never read anything. The opposition seems minor ... Kenneth Allsop and some local councillor. Anyway it is too late. Eighty-five in ten days, it wd be a trauchle [trouble] even to journey north for the Rectorial speech, but I could manage it. I wouldn't get much support from the Senatus, which possibly never heard of me and certainly would hate my guts, for I'd be with the students all the way for freedom and the Pill.

Thanks anyway for offering to speak for me. (...)

Neill

[1] Neill was asked to stand for election as Rector of Edinburgh University.

To Kenneth Allsop

Dear Kenneth Allsop   *21 December 1968*

In case you did not see my 'Rectorial', I enclose it.[1] My candidature was comic. A student, Bob Cuddihy, wrote asking me to stand. I replied with a No, saying that 95½ of the students never heard of me. He said they had and I consented, partly to prove my point. I did so at the bottom. It wd have been a tragedy had I been elected, for at 85 I could not have kept trekking to Edinburgh, yet I have just returned from New York after being on an Orson Bean show NBC. But I guess that Edinburgh Senatus wouldn't stand me a first-class air fare with unlimited champagne and room to stretch out.

What a Lord Rector does I simply don't know. All I can guess is that you'll be on the side of youth all the way.

I'd say Bless you in your task if I weren't a bloody pagan.

Yours, A. S. Neill

[1] Neill wrote an article for the *Times Educational Supplement* in Scotland, headed 'My Unrectorial Address', after Kenneth Allsop had been elected rector.

To Gordon Leff

Dear Bunny   *25 February 1969*

Ain't one prof (Barton) enough to damn an education system that doesn't believe in education.[1] Letting the side down, you are. So I won't congratulate you cos I know it can't mean anything to you, just as my Exeter LLD meant bugger all to me. The only value lies in the realisation

that you have done a hell of a lot of good work to be recognised. (...)
Our love, Neill

[1] Gordon Leff had just been made Professor of History at York University.

To Constance Butler

Dear Constance 17 *April 1969*
    Yes, it was a lousy show, with an RC man who never heard of me,[1] but I felt that if I made two in a few millions think abt kids it was worth it ... plus the meagre fee of £75. I didn't talk to Wilfred Hyde White or Barbara Murray; only Henry Cooper came to the bar, but didn't drink. I liked his unspoiled personality and had a long talk abt boxing. It was the wrong programme for me, I know, but neither TV lot wants me in a serious programme. The audience in New York was all on my side. (...)
    I dread the flow of visitors this term. Dunno what time Whitsun is, but I'll allow you to come along on condition that there is no 'Mr Neill, how do the children fit into after life?' Now to spend two hours answering USA letters ... God, how wearisome.
    Love to you both, Neill

[1] Neill had appeared on the Eamonn Andrews Show.

To Kenneth Allsop

Dear Kenneth Allsop 18 *April 1969*
    J. W. M. Thompson had a para in the *Spectator* saying that Edinburgh University had turned down 'starchily' a proposal that I get an honorary degree. I wrote asking him about it and he said all he knew was that the SRC almost unanimously had suggested it, but advised me to get in touch with you. Now I am not asking for any secret sessions and their like; I don't want ever to take it to the Press, mainly because at my age an hon degree doesn't mean all that much, even one from Edinburgh. But if you have any gen on the subject I'll be glad to have it, keeping it private of course. (...)
    A. S. Neill

Kenneth Allsop to Neill

Fellows' Quad, Merton College, Oxford

Dear Mr Neill   *26 April 1969*

Your letter has just reached me here. The *Spectator* paragraph was the outcome of a talk my wife and I had with John Thompson: we both felt this decision by the Senate at Edinburgh deserved to be more widely known. The history of it is this. After the Rectorial election was known I had a telegram from one of your campaign committee, saying he 'hoped I was happy' at defeating a man of your stature, or some such phrase. I replied suggesting that he had no right to assume that I felt any such emotion, and that my knowledge of your writings and admiration of your pioneering in education might well be double his in years. Later we met – amicably – and he asked if I would be willing to put forward a recommendation, as Rector, that the university should confer an honorary degree upon you. I was (a) amazed that your own university had not already done so, and (b) delighted to have the opportunity of dong so, and this I did via the Principal in person. I had by that time found that there was general enthusiasm among the student body that this should be done. As you know, the proposal was turned down. No reasons were given. By word of mouth, I'm fairly sure that it was suggested that you would, if offered it, turn it down (my reaction to that was that, even should that happen, Edinburgh was presumably stable enough to withstand such a snub) and also that your article in the *Times Ed Supp* was thought too derisive and disrespectful of the academic structure. My personal view is that the decision was mean-spirited and paltry. It can be put forward again when the next Honours List is in preparation, and this I intended to do. I know you will understand that all the above is passed on to you openly as far as I'm concerned, but confidentially vis-à-vis my situation in the Rector's office. (...)

I had a personal reason for wanting, if I could, to do this small service: because I know the schooling system in this country, where it is at its best, is so because of your influence and teaching, which has permeated into even the crustier quarters; and it would have been an anonymous appreciation. I'm only sorry it didn't work.

Yours, Kenneth Allsop

To Kenneth Allsop

Dear Kenneth   *28 April 1969*

If you don't mind I'd rather you didn't put my name forward again. I'd hate to have a degree from a Senatus that had to have a name suggested to them. I think that Newcastle and Exeter were genuinely in favour.

Scottish universities, like Scots education, are behind England. (...) I appreciate your kind generosity all the same.

I'd like to meet you one day; you sound somehow more sophisticated than the other guys on *24 Hours*, and that ain't no flattery.

Yrs, A. S. Neill

To Elsworth Baker

My dear Baker   *1 May 1969*

Yesterday the gown arrived; today your letter. What a gorgeous gown! The sad thing is that there are so very few occasions a gown like that can be seen by others. With it and the cap and hood I got from Exeter I almost look like a gentleman. Proud to have it. I think the customs might have let it in free as an honour, but no, they charged £13 ... about 32 bucks I think. Most grateful to the College for paying this duty.[1] (...)

Every day I seem to feel that I know bugger all about anything. It isn't that I doubt ... e.g. never could I accept the Skinner rat trend in USA and over here. It may be my large fan mail that tells me I am a wonderful guy when I know that there aren't any wonderful guys, not that wonderful anyway. Feel kinda guilty too, for the greater guy Reich is unknown to most. Maybe a man's importance is in inverse proportion to his prominence. Where ten know Reich ten millions know the Beatles. Of course the Billy Grahams and pop stars are popular because they have nothing to say. I guess that Jonny Carson has a hell of a big income from TV and a guy like you, with something to offer a sick world, has little chance of reaching millions as a TV star has. And you have to work harder to earn a living. To go back to that fan|mail, its only brightness|is in its showing that some people are seeking freedom for kids. (...)

With warm feelings, Neill

[1] Neill had been made the first honorary member of the newly established American College of Orgonomy.

To Constance Butler

My dear Constance   *20 October 1969*

Many tas for yr wishes. Wish I cd write at length but my mail was 29 this morning and I'll have to spend the day replying. You can see my beautiful face on BBC 2 *Late Night Line Up* on Thursday this week. (...)

Just refused an offer of £1000 to do ten lectures in Australia. Only money. It wd kill me.

Love and blessings, Neill

To Helen Neustatter

My dear Helen   *11 August 1970*

(...) Now that *Summerhill* is the best seller in Germany letters and students come in crowds and I am so old and tired and weary now. Fame doesn't compensate for old age aches and pains. Fame is really quite *unbedeutend* [unimportant] after you have left the conceit of youth behind you. Of course it is pleasing to know that countless folks have been influenced by my books. (...)

Damn ... four Deutsch students have arrived and I am on vacation and don't want them, but can't be impolite, so I'll have to say: Good morning *und aufwiedersehen*.

Love and memories, Old Beans

To Roger Anscombe

Lieber Roger   *7 December 1971*

(...) Tragedy of age is the going of thrills. *Last Man* titled *Die grüne Wolke* is a best seller in Germany. (...) Some town had a general meeting to give first prize to the writer of the best kids' yarn of the year. So in January a deputation of 8, including the mayor, is coming to present me with a miniature golden bull ... and I can't get a thrill about it. Wilde's: 'There are two tragedies in life: not to get what you want, and the second is to get it. The latter is the greater tragedy.' Good old Oscar.[1] So I got some fame of a minority brand and when it came it was worthless. (...)

Love and blessings, Neill

[1] The sentiment was in fact Shaw's.

11

The American
Connection

To many of the parents I have counselled, the
reading of *Summerhill* produced almost a cathar-
sis. The shock was first negative, but the after-
reaction was thoughtful contemplation and
sometimes dynamic action in their own efforts
to work with, live with, and grow with their
children.

Barbara Leonard, New York Association for
Counselling and Therapy, May 1961

To Harold Hart

Dear Harold   *14 June 1961*
   (...) Been thinking of that school.[1] Why build one? It wd be so fine
no kid wd dare throw a spud at the dining-room window. Much better
to acquire an old country house with all its wear and tear. You simply
cannot have a S'hill in a posh house. (...)
   I asked the American Embassy here if I were still on the black list for
a visa. No reply, so I went to see them. My case has been sent to
Washington for a verdict. Important guy is Neill. (...)
   And what is this rumour about all the Reich adherents walking out of
the Society? Has there been a clash of theories about the school? One of
them visiting here said they thought the elaborate organisation wd kill
the idea. God, I wish I cd talk it all over with you. I am so much at sea.
   All the best, Neill

[1] The recently formed Summerhill Society had decided to raise funds in order
to build an American version of Summerhill.

To Dan Doran

Dear Dan   *5 August 1961*

Yr letter disturbs, all the more cos various visitors from USA have said things similar.[1] I can't do anything about it, and anyway, what the hell! My job is here and according to my fan mail and the many USA callers, the book has stirred folks up, so that, whatever Hart's motives, something practical has been done. But I confess to a feeling of envy when I think of the money the Society is to raise for their school, when Summerhill as usual is in the red and can't get staff cos it can't pay decent salaries. I get fan mail, yes, good, but I'd rather see fan cheques. (...)

I think most knowers of Reich have walked out of Hart's society. I had great difficulty in getting him to allow references to Reich in the book. Rumour that he is being analysed by a Freudian who hates Reich.

All good things, Dan, Neill

[1] Doran told Neill of conflict within the Summerhill Society.

To Dan Doran

Dear Dan   *31 December 1961*

(...) I don't know what to do about Hart, whom an American parent calls my St Paul. If I did come out I'd find myself in a most difficult position, either to back Hart or oppose him. At the moment I don't contemplate coming out. (...) I haven't heard from Hart for weeks now. I wish I knew what is going on in the Society. Wish I knew in what way Hart is alienating the real freedom fans. I hear of broadcasts on TV by Hart and others, but never hear what they say. (...) Is the situation really one of Freud v Reich? Most of the critics of the Society belong to the Reich camp. (...)

All the best, Neill

To Harold Hart

Dear Harold   *6 July 1962*

(...) I can understand your pessimism. You yourself said months ago that interest would soon die. Even if your plan fails I am told of several schools that are claiming to go the Summerhill way, one in Calif. (...)

If there is another Bulletin don't print my article. On rereading it I think it a bit too critical of American parents, and, depending on them for a living now, I shouldn't offend them! (...)

I have been a bit worried at quite a few letters critical of the American S. Socy set-up. I think there is a fear of any organisation among some of the correspondents, a fear that a crowd or a board of management will lose the personal touch that S'hill had from me. I see their point. If a guy called Hart had announced that he would sell his publishing business and run a school, I fancy the support wd have been better. Individualist America wants individuals ... hence their hate of Communism, even socialism. Millionaire Reiner's school Midtown School in California may be a success because he personally runs it. He was in London a month ago and was to come to see us, but got ill and didn't come. Just my luck; only the poor Americans come!

Dunno what to do about American debts. One man owes £72, another, a woman, something like £300. Now we are demanding banker's references with new American pupils. I should have an American lawyer, but can't even afford a British one here.

Warm affection to you and Beatrice, Neill

To Harold Hart

Dear Harold   *22 July 1962*

So you have resigned the presidency, meaning that the USA Summerhill falls flat, for no one else can do the job. Never mind. Be content that you have been the means of making a few thousand Americans think about child rearing and education. Bloody hero, you are! (...)

What is to happen to the funds raised by your organisation? If you see no chance whatsoever of a school's being started, why not propose they give something to us? I'd hate to think they might divide up any cash collected among American schools that they think are free. (...)

Affection to Bea and yourself, Neill

To Harold Hart

Dear Harold   *25 September 1962*

What is the position now as regards the US Summerhill Society? Dead I guess, with the starter out of it. But, if you feel you have failed, you have made Summerhill, for it is now crammed full, almost half Americans. I am having to refuse new applications from USA. (...)

I have just reread your circular about resigning. You couldn't have done anything else. I feared at the time there were too many people involved. Since Summerhill is a minority movement it would be impossible to have an organisation of real believers in freedom. But the impact of the book on America is something perhaps more valuable than an American Summerhill.

Tell me what is happening, what Beatrice and you are doing.

Greetings from house to house, Neill

To Harold Hart

Dear Harold   *30 October 1962*

American visitor here got a letter from the Summerhill Society with a list of committee. Every name was unknown to me. What is happening? I am concerned, for I don't want the name S'hill to be attached to something I know nothing of. They might in courtesy have sent me notice of their society.

Oh, have any funds you raised gone to the new Society?

Love to self and Beatrice from us, Neill

To George von Hilsheimer

Dear von H.   *8 November 1963*

My handicap is that I am almost completely in the dark. I have to depend on letters from all and sundry in USA. Tales of your school, Barker School, Battle Creek so conflicting that I have sent a letter to the *Village Voice* disclaiming any affiliation with any school in USA. I know what rumours are; I know what enemies have said about me and my school ... I am a homo, an alcoholic etc. So when I get correspondents telling of your school I simply don't know what the truth is. One said there is only licence, promiscuous fucking amongst the adolescents with the ten-year-olds trying to imitate them. Another tale – yr young pupils using dope. How can I tell if the tales are true, or if the writers are neurotic projectors of guilt? If I hear about Al Bronstein's school how can I judge? I never met him either.

You will see why I am concerned about the schools my book has inspired. Even at home I never liked the name S'hill to be used in ads. One school advertised for years that it was run on the lines of Neill's Summerhill. Lots asked: Why the hell doesn't the man stand on his own feet? I advised him to cut out the S'hill part, which he did.[1]

I know I have no monopoly of the name Summerhill legally, but the bloody thing is that what happens in American Summerhills is attributed to my Summerhill, and I don't want to hold anyone's baby. Nor do I want any disciples ... they always pervert an idea. No, you and the rest should simply acknowledge that my S'hill was an inspiration and leave it at that. (...) My school means old age ... 43 years, but you young ones have to find your ways with growing pains and you are bound to differ from me, otherwise you are standing still. Make your own experiences. (...)

    Yours, Neill

[1] John Aitkenhead.

To Dan Doran

Dear Dan   *11 November 1963*
    I had replied to von H. a few days before your letter arrived. Looks as if USA is growing a sturdy crop of plague merchants, but it is always so; I always knew it would come in one way or another. I don't know what I can do other than that letter I sent to *Village Voice* disclaiming all affiliation with any school in USA. (...)
    I didn't recommend von H's school that I know of. To a few who asked me if there were any similar schools in USA, I gave the list issued by the Society ... Barker, von H, Al Bronstein. Now I must reread Reich's *Listen, Little Man!* He seems to be legion in USA ... as here.
    Keep me informed, Dan.
    Yours, Neill

P.S. On second thoughts I take yr advice, and will send a letter to the Society. Copy to you in case they suppress it.

To members of the USA Summerhill Society

11 November 1963
I have been informed that you have accepted Summerlane as the school to represent the Summerhill idea and system in USA. I hear that your society is broken up into warring factions ... with three presidents resigning. Old and reliable friends tell me that the Society's ideas of freedom really mean licence ... they have seen my school and know what they are talking about.
    I ask you, therefore, if you will publish in your Bulletin this letter. I

do not want any school in America to claim to be run on Summerhill principles, or to be run with my sponsorship. I should like to hear that your Society has been disbanded or renamed. The name Summerhill has for over forty years stood for something untarnished, for an uncompromising belief in freedom for children. I refuse to have the name used by men and women I have never seen, whose notions of freedom are divorced from mine. I was influenced by Homer Lane, Freud, Reich, but I didn't use their names in a school prospectus. Let your school founders stand on their own feet.

Yours sincerely, A. S. Neill

To the Editor, *Village Voice*

Sir   *14 November 1963*

Since the publication of the book *Summerhill*, several schools have sprung up in America claiming to be founded on Summerhill principles. Some may be excellent: I have no means of knowing, nor have I any means of judging reports that come to me from correspondents. One letter says that one school has licence not freedom, that sex is promiscuous and neurotic, that it is taken for granted that freedom means destroying furniture. I cannot judge. My correspondents are as unknown to me as the new schools are. A letter can be subjective and therefore not balanced. So that all I can do is to declare publicly as I can that my school Summerhill has no affiliation with any school in the USA or elsewhere. That the words 'founded on Summerhill principles' do not mean that the school is automatically approved of by my staff and myself. I am proud to have any school acknowledge the inspiration my work has aroused, but each school must stand on its own feet. I don't want any praise for its success, just as I don't want to be blamed by parents who fancy that I had something to do with its failures.

Yours, A. S. Neill

From Paul Goodman to the Editor, *Village Voice*

Institute for Policy Studies, Washington D.C.
Dear Sir   *21 November 1963*

I am saddened by A. S. Neill's letter. He is 'proud to have any school acknowledge the inspiration of his work', but he is squeamish about directions (and 'excesses') that that inspiration might take. Is it happy, or necessary, to have such a proprietary attitude towards one's contribution and influence?

I am reminded of a conversation I had with Reich nearly 20 years ago in which he asked me not to associate his (and Neill's) ideas with community anarchism. 'Neill', he said, 'has enough trouble with his middle-class parents because of the sexual issue, without bringing in anarchism too.' I could not agree to this request. Their ideas were congenial to anarchism, gave it a new and needed dimension. Further, I felt that to the extent that they did not logically lead to a kind of Kropotkin anarchism, Reich and Neill were untrue to themselves, e.g. Reich in his moralism and authoritarianism, and Neill in both his snobbery and his carelessness of the humanities and politics.

We exist in a stream of revolutionary thought that inspires us; maybe we add a force to it; our own addition will hopefully be made clear and perfected by others. Certainly nobody likes to be misunderstood and misused, but I would rather risk that than suffer the illusion that 'my' ideas are my Property. Neill should be saying, 'The future of Summerhill ought not to be that, it ought to be this' – then we can argue about it – not 'Summerhill is what I say it is.' He talks like a headmaster, and Summerhill can do without a headmaster, thank you.

     Yours, Paul Goodman

To the Editor, *Village Voice*

Dear Sir   *19 December 1963*
    Wilhelm Reich invented the Orgone Accumulator. Its use was empirical; Reich claimed nothing from it, but some of his followers claim cures. ... When sick journalists began to describe it as a means to obtain a sexual orgasm, Reich was furious. I make the guess that Paul Goodman, who knew Reich, would think Reich was right to be angry, but friend Paul seems to think that the man who founded Summerhill should not be 'squeamish about directions (and "excesses") that ... schools inspired by Summerhill ... should take'. I know nothing at first hand about what is happening in America. Correspondents write of adults who, they allege, encourage promiscuous sex, dope, homosexuality; one says that girls were jeered at because they were virgins. Other correspondents deny the reports. But, one may ask, what the devil has it got to do with me and my school? Only this, that practically all my correspondents belong to the Summerhill Society of America. One wrote that the name Summerhill was becoming mud in the USA, for its name was being used as a sanction for anything calling itself freedom for children.

    Now, I have no idea how much truth there is in these rumours. One has always to suspect that a writer of rumour may be a neurotic, shoving his sex complexes onto others. I do not want my school to be associated with any system at home or abroad. One or two, after my letter in the *Voice*, accused me of being anti-sex. All I know is that I am anti-promiscuity in sex, as Reich was; to me it means simply fornicating, that is, sex without tenderness, without interest in whether the partner gets any joy out of the act or not. Don Juan is accepted by all schools of psychology as a sick man. I am against drugs and drink because it isn't fair to let young people learn by experience here. I have seen a few alcoholics who were encouraged to drink at 13 or 14.

I regret now that my good friend Harold Hart ever founded the Summerhill Society. From all I hear it has been a battle-ground of warring tribes. It was founded to set up a Summerhill in America. It has not done so, and I see no reason why it should continue. The idea was wrong from the start. It postulated that Summerhill could be the model for a new school, meaning that the new school would tend to be static. Label yourself Summerhillian or Freudian or Steinerite and you stop growing. The headmasters of the Barker and Lewis-Wadhams schools each taught for a year in my school, but if the Society were to label their schools American Summerhills I should be much concerned. They must go their own way, refusing to be imitation schools. Suppose Bob Barker were to introduce military discipline – an impossible supposition – and advertised his school as one run on Summerhill lines, would Paul expect me to be indifferent? (...)

Let us assume that all the gossip is false. Folks talk, all the same. Mud sticks. Brown is charged with homosexuality. He is acquitted, but he remains 'that guy who was in the homo case, you know'. The acquittal is forgotten.

Summerhill isn't the last word in education. If, for instance, the world ever becomes sex-positive, future schools will be free in a way that cannot be now.

I won't take up Paul's calling me a snob. Who isn't? But when he says I am careless about politics I can give him an answer. Up to around 1940 I thought politics plus psychology might be the answer. My *Problem Teacher* is full of politics. I fancy I lost faith when the initial Russian freedom for youth died an early death and was replaced by character-moulding similar to, but less subtle than, the Western variety. No, politics, like psychoanalysis, is not the answer.

Finally, Paul Goodman is in the audience; he isn't a member of the cast. He doesn't know what dangers a school like mine has to meet. A school went a few steps ahead of us in Britain, and closed. Paul might say: what does it matter anyway? Ultimately not a bit; which of us will matter in a hundred years? But today ... well, hark to the London *Daily Telegraph* on the American attempts to start a Summerhill: 'One such school was refused to buy property because local residents feared that such revolutionary methods represented a branch of international communism.' Given a new McCarthyism probable, any American parents seeking a school with freedom may be arraigned before a tribunal as communists. I don't expect America to realise that under communism Summerhill would not last for a day. I hope I am making myself clear. Anything new, anything anti-Establishment can be killed by talk and bigotry and hate in general. I can defend my own school. Let the others stand up and protect their schools.

   Yours, A. S. Neill

To Carlos Kruytbosch

Dear Carlos   *18 May 1964*

   (...) At various times old pupils have played with the idea of making a book written by ex-pupils, to show the world what they think they gained or lost in their education (sic). At present I have to rely on a few stock phrases when one of the million US visitors drawls: Say, Mister Neill, how do the graduates of S'hill fit into after life?

   I say diffidently: Well, well we have a barber, a bricklayer, a bus conductor, some engineers and doctors and lawyers, and (as if an afterthought) four who are university lecturers. I include you, not quite sure if you are lecturing or janitoring in yr university. The others are Bunny Leff, History, David Barton, Maths, Mike Bernal, Physics. Bunny and Barton sent me their books ... far too deep for me to understand ... and I calmly take them from my bookshelf and hand them to the surprised asker.

   Yes, a book wd be good. (...) Now is the time before the S'hill rage subsides in USA. I hear *Summerhill* is now in a paperback edition in US. That book saved us. We were down to 23 pupils, and now are full with a long waiting list, mostly American. Sixty per cent of our pupils are American today, but they are adapting themselves well. In half a term 'I'm going to the beth room' becomes: 'Fuck off, I'm going to the bogs.' (...)

   Love, Neill

To George Dennison

                                          9 December 1969

Damn you, George, you have revived my bad conscience about taking middle-class kids only. No other way, must live on fees, having no grant. You had to go bankrupt.

Your book shd become a classic.[1] It won't among teachers, to whom by the way you are too generous. My many letters from kids in USA abt their schools tell the other side, the anti-life side. I marvel at the success you had agnst bad backgrounds. I get them too. I have a gang of USA little boys who wreck the school furniture and windows, all middle class, all problem kids the parents didn't tell me about, all from broken homes or unloving parents. All the therapy in the world can't cure a neurosis with its root in California homes. Your success with yr kids makes me astonished you got so far. You showed the way as Homer Lane did, but don't look for immediate results among teachers. I guess that most would rather follow the Skinner rat conditioning ... much easier.

I sympathise with you spanking the lad's arse. I've often felt like it, but refrained for the reason you give, that it cuts no ice, that it adds to the hate the kid already has agnst all authority.

Colour. I have had two negresses from USA. Our kids never noticed their colour, but at the same time on TV we saw the hateful faces of white kids stoning black ones in Little Rock. You are right abt kids having no racialism.

It was kind of you to let me off so lightly in your book. Idea ... I'd like to see a book on freedom for kids compiled by Nixon, Goldwater, Reagan.

Go on writing. I get many books sent me from USA but they are so heavy I can't read em. I sat up finishing yours. I'm a bit troubled abt the S. Socy schools. Hear all sorts of rumours abt schools like George von Hilsheimer's. In New York last Dec staying with Orson Bean I thought his school okay, but coffined and confined by being in a city. Here if a kid doesn't go to lessons he has eleven acres to play in, climb trees, cycle, dig caves etc. Plus a workshop always open and the hammering noise away from classes. (...)

Sad that a guy like you is so far away. I am too old now to come to USA ... the December TV trip almost knocked me out. But if you ever come over here do come and see me. You are a born ... not teacher, a born understander of kids and their nature, and there are so few around. (...)

I'd say Bless you, if I weren't a bloody heathen.

Neill

---

[1] *The Lives of Children: the Story of the First Street School.*

12

The Bomb

Neill himself has mellowed a bit perhaps, as
compared with his more militantly rebellious
and hyper-Freudian phases. But he has not
budged one inch on any of his main humanist
points, especially the importance of freedom. If
he worries at all, it is about the Bomb.

New Statesman, June 1961

To Wilhelm Reich

My dear Reich   *28 August 1946*
    (...) I think the international situation depresses us all. Science has
invented the atom bomb, but science of living can't control it, and I have
the nasty fear that the fools who control it may blast us all to hell before
education can control the world.[1] But I want to visit you before that happens. My main hope now is that Russia and China and everyone will discover how to make the bomb, and then each will be scared to use it. A
poor hope indeed, but what is the alternative? (...)
    Neill

[1] The atomic bomb had been dropped on Hiroshima three weeks before.

To Wilhelm Reich

My dear Reich   *20 December 1946*
    (...) Your atomic pessimism is like my own. Humanity isn't evolved
enough to have atom bombs, and the stiff-stomached rulers of all nations
will use it and get the Church to tell them they are waging war for truth.
I have no confidence in USA, which is ignorant, superficial in its education, moral in the wrong way, outside world opinion. The alternative,

a Soviet world, is also unwelcome. How powerless you and I are. A few military or political idiots can destroy our new children and we can do nothing. (…)
Neill

To Wilhelm Reich

My dear Reich   *30 March 1948*
    Both letters from you today. Thanks for the official invitation. And we want to come very much, for we are depressed. We fear that atomic war may be very near … Tito has only to march into Trieste and you have it. The fools in parliament are talking of defence dug-outs etc. USA may get off lightly but this island as an air base for USA would be wiped out with death rays. Zoë's delightful happiness and cleverness and beauty make the picture terrifying for us. (…)
Neill

To Wilhelm Reich

My dear Reich   *20 August 1950*
    (…) I feel I may have dwelt too much on the war danger. My excuse is that while your children over there will have a good chance of survival, ours will not. We are near the danger, and everyone we know here has a similar feeling to the one we have, a terror of what may happen to the young in atomic warfare. It may not come, but something must come, and it is not pleasant to think that half a dozen men in the world can decide whether our children will live or die. (…)
Neill

To Wilhelm Reich

My dear Reich   *13 July 1954*
    Glad to hear from you again. We are all waiting for news of your work and its future, but it seems to be a case of our waiting all the time, waiting to see if Indo-China is to be the starting point of our universal extermination, waiting to see if Ike will show himself a strong man, if Malenkov is any real improvement on Stalin, if McCarthy is finished or

not. The world sure is a melting pot at the moment. The only big quest-ion is: Will we destroy ourselves with H and Cobalt bombs *before* Reich's peaceful orgones are accepted? You ask what has happened to Churchill? I don't know. His position must be most difficult, for he knows that in a war Britain would be wiped out while parts of USA and Russia and much of China would survive. I think that the differences between us and USA arise from the fact that we are much more vulnerable. (…)

    Neill

To Wilhelm Reich

My dear Reich   *5 February 1955*

    (…) To me the matter seems *klein* [small] today when it looks as if the Formosa affair will end us all over here. Bertrand Russell said yester-day that if the Formosa issue is not settled humanity may be destroyed by the end of this year. I see no way out for China or USA; I see no way out at all for us if world war comes. The biggest USA atom bomb air base is seven miles from Summerhill; we'd be the first target, but in any case radiation will destroy life on this island. I think that the fundamental ground is that USA especially will rather see humanity destroyed than have universal communism. I fear your plague is too strong on both sides to save the situation. Long ago you said that World War III would come and I didn't want to believe you. I miserably think you prophesied rightly. (…)

    Neill

To Wilhelm Reich

My dear Reich   *21 February 1955*

    (…) I am very pessimistic these days. I am almost sure that the idiots on both sides will kill us all. The official line now seems to be atomic death to all rather than have communism. But what a choice! I don't have to choose, but I tremble to think that our fate depends on men who must have been made anti-life in their cradles. … Will no great statesman arise and shout: War is universal suicide; no one can win; all must lose. The only chance is to disarm all round, to divide the world and stick to the division. But I fear the plague would not let his voice be heard.

    How there can be peace I can't imagine; too much hate and fear on both sides. Meanwhile we just wait; the common man has no say in his destiny either in East or West. But I wish we did not have to live on the edge of a volcano as we do now. (...)

Neill

To Seishi Shimoda

My good friend Shimoda   *5 May 1958*

(...) I don't know how you feel about the H bomb but sometimes I look at my daughter and her friends and get terrified about their future, for even if war does not come the poisoned air will be a great danger to the coming generations. You and I spend our lives trying to give children love and happiness, and one or two sick men like Eisenhower and Dulles or ambitious men like Khruschev have the power to kill our children and us. Love cannot counter the hate of the world now that the atomic bomb can make the haters all powereful. The London Sunday *Observer* has published last week the first article of two or three about the Japanese fishing boat that met death after the Bikini explosion. It makes sad and painful reading. I'll keep them and post them to you in case the *Observer* does not come to Japan.

With my best wishes, friend.

Yours, Neill

To Constance Butler

Dear Constance   *24 July 1958*

(...) Just beginning to breathe again after the war scare. Luckily the kids never knew anything was happening. Worst of it is that crises will keep coming again. To hell with both their houses, east and west. I dislike the idea of my Zoë being made into cinders because of Lebanon or anywhere else.

All the best, Neill

To the Editor, the *New Statesman*

Sir   *4 August 1961*

Bertrand Russell says that by the end of this year we may all be dead, and who can honestly challenge his guess? He calls on the nation to do something before it is too late. Do what?

Anti-nuclear marches are minority affairs; they don't touch the masses of football fans, TV-watchers; they are not likely to be heard of in America or Russia. The people, whether under democracy or party dictatorship, have no say; they are powerless, vaguely trusting that their wise statesmen will act as our saviours, forgetting Munich, Suez, Hungary, Cuba. Not one statesman seems to have a mind above bomb-rattling and deterrents. As Russell says, we have no idea what the top ones are doing or planning, but none has given any sign of hope. The arms race must end in universal death, and we can only look fearfully at our children and tremble for their future.

Russell is right in saying that time is short. I think he should declare to the nation what it must do to save itself. Personally I cannot see what this nation can do if and when Russia and America do not act also to keep the peace. The fight for humanity is not now one for Communism or Capitalism; it is now simply a fight for life, and a plague on both their houses!

Yours, A. S. Neill

To the Editor, the *Scotsman*

Sir   *19 September 1961*

As a member of the Committee of 100, I decided to make my protest in my own country.[1] I was arrested at 5 o'clock on Saturday night, and we were collected in a hall until 1.30 a.m. and then, all very sleepy, were sent by bus to Glasgow Central Police Court, where we arrived about 4.30.

I was put in a cell with two other people, after our belongings – including toothbrushes – were taken away from us. We slept in our clothes. The cell had nothing at all except a w.c. in one corner – no chairs, no tables. The food was sufficient, but, to me, unpalatable. I think that, seeing we were not criminals in the ordinary sense, we might have had some comfort and even a little freedom. We had no exercise at all from 5 o'clock a.m. Sunday to 1 o'clock midday Monday. (...)

The marchers, on the whole, behaved with dignity and quietness, but I think the leaders should impress more discipline. I personally could not sleep because young enthusiasts kept shouting 'Ban the Bomb' all day and part of the night.

I am not optimistic enough to think that our march will ban the bomb, and I took part mainly because I wanted to try to impress teachers and parents of the dire necessity for action at present.

The limitation of the movement is, I think, that most people are law-abiding and have a fear of the police (I have lost mine after this week-end), and I feel many would do something in a legal way – for example, the National Union of Teachers are to have a one-day strike for salaries: if they had a one-day strike to save the children's lives, the nation would be impressed.

I thought the sentences very severe – why I paid £10 for obstructing a narrow road in Dunoon, while others paid £1 to £3 for obstructing main streets in London, I do not know.

I am etc, A. S. Neill

[1] Neill had joined an anti-nuclear protest at the Holy Loch base in Scotland.

To the Editor, the *Scotsman*

Sir   *22 September 1961*

At Dunoon most of the accused paid a fine. I paid £10 rather than leave my school for 60 days. Others were in the same boat – 'If I go to quod I'll get the sack'; 'I've got a wife and three kids.' And thus the state pulled in four figures of our money.

On the boat coming back I lent my papers to a young lady sitting in front of me in the lounge, saying that I had finished with them and that she could keep them. She smiled, and said, 'I won't need them where I'm going.' She was Pat Arrowsmith, in charge of a wardress in plain clothes.

Since that meeting I have thought a lot: so much so that I have resigned from the Committee of 100. Partly funk, of course, for if I am arrested again it would mean prison; partly shame at evading the issue. I cannot remain a sleeping (or sitting-down) partner while braver souls give up their liberty for the cause. I think now that one should remain on the committee only if prepared to give all. I cannot, not only because of my responsibility to my pupils, but also because I fear that the method of civil disobedience will not bring in enough recruits in the short time we may have.

There is no immediate prospect of banning the bomb while Government and Opposition and the trade unions stand for the deterrent. The slogan, I think, should be World Disarmament or Death, a name that could make the movement an international one or, to begin with, a Western one. And we should demand that Britain shows initiative instead of standing, timidly, between two giants. We have had weeks of alarm, and our political leaders on both sides have said nothing to give us a ray of hope.

Why, oh why, is the Establishment indifferent or passive? The professions, the trade unions, the Churches should all be crying aloud for peace.

They have the passivity of hopelessness ... how can we influence America, Russia? What! ban the bomb and have the Reds march in? The fight for life seems a desperate one, but what is the alternative? To sit, as we do now, frightened to open our newspaper, trembling to read what one of the K's has said, wondering fearfully if any moment might bring unspeakable death.

The answer to our passivity, I think, lies in what a young man at Holy Loch said to me: 'I think I am more afraid of the cops than of the bomb.' He expressed a deep psychological truth. We are conditioned from our cradles to fear parents, teachers, policemen, the law. We cannot rebel because of our unconscious fears. Most of us, therefore, are cowards ... my resignation from the committee proves that I am one.

I am etc, A. S. Neill

To Seishi Shimoda

My dear Shimoda					*5 November 1962*
(...) Maybe in Japan the Cuba crisis was too far away for alarm, but here we really expected sudden death last week. It is an unbearable thought that whatever you and I do for children's happiness one politician can destroy us all at any time. We have no power to stop it. I protested against the Polaris bases in Scotland, spent two nights in prison and was fined £10 next day. Feeling all the time that I had no power to stop the bomb men. (...)

Best wishes, Neill

To R. F. Mackenzie

Dear Bob					*24 December 1966*
I'd wish you a merry Christmas if the damn thing can be merry with your local troubles and with the world ones ... Vietnam, Rhodesia, hate all over the place. 'Unto us a child is born ... sired by the idiots who control the bomb.'

Yours, Neill

13

Old Age, Death and Immortality

Summerhill pupils, tired of being a zoo to 100
visitors weekly, made a law; No More Visitors,
and I am too old and tired to give interviews.
A. S. Neill

Advertisement in *New Statesman*, November
1971

To Ishbel McWhirter

Tishy, dearie   *2 July 1949*
    There is nothing much one can say to you, for, as you say, you lost
her months ago, and the relief in seeing a loved one in pain with no hope
at all, seeing her go out of it all, is real and in a way satisfying. Only,
of course, in the case of a mother the emotion that grieves grieves not
for the exhausted one that dies, but for the mother one knew long, long
ago. Everyone goes through it, and whatever one's age, it is bloody.
    Now for practical things. I think you ought to get away from Prestatyn
as soon as you can. Most of its life went out for you when she died, and
there you won't mix with folks your own age. I'd return to town if I were
you. Or why not come here for a break? End of term is 23rd inst and
about 36 old pupils will be down. Be a coward and run away from it all
for a bit. (...)
    Come on, Tish, luv; come and laze in S'hill a bit.
    Our love and sympathy, Neill

To Constance Butler

Dear Constance   *5 October 1953*
    But what can I say to you? I also have had bitter griefs in my 70 years'
life, and no one could help me bear them. I found that the only way is
to run away from it by working like hell, especially with the young.

231

Some flee from it by taking a voyage (if they can afford it). Much of grief is remorse ... 'If only I had been kinder to her,' much is of course self-pity ... 'I am left alone now,' but of course most is just genuine love with the awful realisation of never more.

So all I can say is: Work. Having no religion I can't pray or Thank the Good Lord for his chastening. With religious belief it is easier ... it is God's will, but with none, one has the whole burden to carry. I like it that way myself. (...)

Yours, A. S. Neill

To Constance Butler

Dear Constance   *5 May 1956*

Tut, tut. I can only guess at your trouble. Of course as you say we make a mess of human relationships because each of us lives ultimately to himself, and we only hang our personal emotions on others *for a time*. The other day in Scotland I passed by the grave of a sister[1] who died 40 years' ago. Her death killed life in me for months. I passed her grave without any emotion at all, and if she had been sitting on the grave waiting for me I should have had nothing to say to her. Love dies as everything must die. Friendship dies ... it is so sad to find that someone you have known for many years has suddenly become a dull bore. Maybe a woman suffers more than a man, for she ages sooner than a man ... girls sometimes glance with interest at me, but what youth will glance at a woman of 72? This isn't boast; it is hard, sad fact. (...)

Yours, Neill

[1] Clunie Neill.

To Constance Butler

Dear Constance   *3 February 1958*

(...) Re my health. I'm okay in the main, just normal I guess at my age in having aches and pains. You'll have to adapt yourself to seeing me at 74 and not 47. Of the classical three – wine, women and song – only the wine part means a thing to me now ... and I daren't have a bottle at supper when the staff look on thirsty.

Be seein yuh, Neill

To Constance Butler

Dear Constance   *19 March 1958*
(...) I have nothing to say that is of any interest, partly cos I've got a touch of the cold going about. Ena is worse but can't go to bed cos the cook is ill and no one can make a dinner. These modern women!

Also my throat is so bad that I have had to renounce all baccy and whisky. How the hell can I be cheerful?

But I don't want you or anyone else to try to cheer me up, see? I'm just on my way to the garden to eat worms.

Yours, Neill

To John Aitkenhead

Dear John   *29 January 1959*
(...) Cold here too, but no cold ever makes me skip my morning cold bath. I feel not so bad at 75 but have to make an effort to teach maths and English daily. (...) My old friends are rapidly falling from their perches, the latest Edwin Muir, who with Willa was with us in Dresden and Austria. A gentle laddie. Makes one feel kinda lonely and makes one sorry one can't believe in the pleasant tale that we'll all meet again on the happy shore. The first guy who propounded the postulate of a future life must have done it in grief. (...)

Love to you all, Neill

To Constance Butler

Dear Constance   *6 July 1959*
Entering my fifth week in bed. I get so depressed and wonder if I'll ever be able to walk again. The pain never gets better. And to miss all this weather is hellish.

So I haven't much to say to you or anyone. They say that pain ennobles. It sure doesn't. It drags one down to a lower level. (...)

The TV set I got from Ena on her birthday helps a bit, tho I can get only BBC. I read a lot too, but have read most books in the school. I can't play my LP records cos there is no one to start and take em off. Pity. But when I'm able to move about the room in 1964 or so then I can play em.

All the best, Neill

To Helen Neustatter

My dear Helen   *6 August 1959*

I couldn't answer yr letter because I have been in bed for almost three months with painful sciatica. I am now up but can only hobble about in pain. Dunno what to do about it. I hate all drugs and injections but am to see an osteopath soon. It is nasty to be helpless with so much young life around. (...)

I try not to live in the Mentone past[1] but it isn't easy, for so many of my friends have died, and having no belief in immortal life I just have to grin and bear it. Lucky those who do believe; it would thrill me if I could believe I'd see Otto again and Lil.[2] *Aber...*

I can't sit up to write more. I'll be 76 in October and guess I am just the usual wreck at the end of life, but I'd dearly love to have another ten years of work and life.

Love, Helen, Old Beans

[1] Refers to the time when Neill and his first wife holidayed in Italy with Helen and Otto Neustatter.
[2] Otto Neustatter and Mrs Lins.

To Willa Muir

My dear Willa   *12 August 1959*

Up at last but can only walk a few steps. Started with an osteopath who may do the trick. In blacker moments I think the sciatica is only a symptom, for I've lost about 20 lbs and conjecture a combination of diabetes, Brights's disease and stomach ulcers and cancer. Unlike Jerome K. Jerome I have already housemaid's knee. I have found that illness shows a gradual dimunition of hold on life. At first it was agony for me seeing others doing my own special jobs ... maths, mending locks etc. Then a stage came of: What the hell anyway? They aren't important. I thought a lot of Edwin and J. B.[1] and Reich, but with a hate of their extinction and a dread of my own some time. I can't see anything in favour of death, which in all cases I fancy means death of the body when the energy and love of life is still strong. Edwin could have gone on enriching for years; Reich's work is *stehenge blieben* [at a halt] cos no one is big enough or mad enough to continue it. For my own part I know that my work has been done for the last few years. I have nothing new to say and as a force I am less in Summerhill now I am old. But I want to live for wee things mostly – seeing Zoë grow, making a brass bowl, laughing with a substitute for J. B. (*Es gibt keine.*) [There is none.] ...

   Lots of love, Allie

[1] J. B. Salmond.

To Seishi Shimoda

My dear Shimoda   *9 October 1963*
   (...) Eighty next week. Sad to grow old. I wish I could live for a thousand years able to work all the time. I find it more difficult now. I get so many visitors, mostly from America, and they tire me out, partly because they all ask the same questions. My work is done. I have no new ideas about children to write about. If I have a main worry it is what is to become of Summerhill. Can it go on without me? If so will it change? Not as long as Ena and Zoë are here, but they can't be here for ever. You see, friend, the Scottish school founded on S'hill by Aitkenhead has changed. It now makes lessons compulsory. We are the only school in Britain where lessons are optional. So what would a new headmaster of Summerhill do? I hasten to say I don't feel like dying now! But I can't have many more years, and each year will find me less able to run the school. But I don't say things like this in print, for too many are saying that Summerhill is Neill and will die without him. That is wrong. I am not the last word in education. (...)
   Well, dear old friend, warm greetings from us all.
      Yours ever, Neill

To Gordon Leff

Dear Bunny   *31 October 1963*
   (...) Now that the years can't be many I worry abt the future of the S'hill idea. I fear that the minister has tolerated it cos I was known, but after I die will it let kids play all day if they want to? If not, S'hill will be truly dead, for compromise on one major point would mean a series of compromises on minor ones ... like washing before meals ... which I never have done in 80 years. Good answer to *Tonight* programme when I am 90 ... Mr Neill, to what do you attribute your longevity?
      Love to both, Neill

To Henry Miller

2 June 1965

But, Henry, you musn't go and get ill again. Guys like us ought to live to 200. I think a lot about death these days for it can't be many years away. I don't think I fear dying; I only fear not living, for life holds so very much, even at 81. (…) It saddens me to think we are controlled by our bodies. Keats, Chopin, Burns and many others could have gone on in spirit for years creating, but their damned bodies let them down. And with atom fall-out, insecticides, artificial manures, contaminated processed food, I guess that many a young potential genius will die off early. Add to that cigarettes and lung cancer. I think mankind is on the road to self-destruction, mainly cos his head has developed while his emotions have remained stagnant. Man isn't big enough to control an H bomb.

On which pessimistic note I stop, with the sincere hope that you will go on living for a long time, bless you.

Warmly yours, Neill

To Pamela Neu

Dear Pam   *8 October 1965*

(…) As an actress did you ever hear of Margot Moser the leading lady in *My Fair Lady* when it was produced in New York? She is a good friend of S'hill and is making her third visit this month. But, why oh why, must a man be 82 when all the bonny lasses come to see him? Too much in life comes too late. I've never had cash to spend until now and there isn't a damn thing I want to buy. (…)

Good luck, Pam, Neill

To Willa Muir

Dear Willa   *27 January 1966*

(…) And hoo are ye the noo? Trauchlin' alang? The book? The aches and pains? My own book is *fertig* [finished] and shd be out here and USA next fall.[1] Yet nothing seems to thrill the old. Barrie again: They give you nuts to chew when yr teeth have gone, but I think someone said it before him. (…)

Life as usual. Teaching maths, answering umpteen Yanks, dodging visitors. I often wonder why I don't want to die, for so much of life is routine and dullness. Maybe about ten highlights in a lifetime … first love, first applause, first book, first anything. Even to relive the joy in learning to drive a car would be a thrill. (...)

Love and blessings, and get on with that book, Allie

[1] *Freedom not License!*

To James Stern

Dear Jimmy   *19 December 1967*

(...) Seen specialist. Prognosis not so rosy, a life of taking care not to worry nor to hurry; not to smoke, but whisky is good for angina. Can't see myself again struggling up Tube stairs, so that any town visit will mean a series of taxis ... but again friends often live flights up. Difficult to be cheerful this Xmas. My dreams are nightmares, so that, unlike Caliban, I don't sigh to dream again. Found too late that life must be 99% fitness if it is to be enjoyed. I guess one gets accustomed to living on broken wing ... young buggers like you have time for the feathers to grow again.

Anyhow, let's pretend that God is in his heaven and that the angels kiss under the mistletoe and shout with all the other self-deceivers ... Merry Xmas to all.

Love to you both, Neill

To James Stern

Dear Jimmy   *17 September 1968*

Sudden impulse to ask *wie es geht bei/mit dir* [how you are]. I have vegetated for weeks; haven't gone away and a necessary trip to town next week-end makes me nervous. Longed to go to warm south with warm seas but couldn't face a hotel with bugger all to do after the bathing. Too old to travel now if half tempted by an invitation to Frankfurt/Main to stay with old friends who speak no English ... tempted to brush up my more than lousy Deutsch, *aber* it would mean evenings with *Gesellschaft*-conversation [business talk] which wd be too boring.

How goes it with the heart? So far I fancy my diagnosis of angina was faulty, but that may be my way of excusing my four ounces a week pipe baccy. Writing nix but answering my fan mail, which seems to grow with my scunner [dislike] at answering it. Bloody vegetable am I. Workmen all over the place spending rapidly the £5000 we raised and will need. Still worried abt what will happen when I baccy-heartedly depart. No one here big enough to follow the guy with the halo. I guess that old Jesus sometimes sighed when he thought of successors ... luckily he couldn't have foreseen Pope Paul.

Kinda depressed ... Czechs, President Nixon looming near, possible Israel war. Plus the rain; luckily we have no rivers near us to flood us. Drop me a line and tell me about self and Tania and her aches and pains.

Love to both, Neill

To James Stern

Dear Jimmy   *3 June 1969*

Wie geht's? [How are you?] Long time no hear. I never seem to get time to write to folks I know, not with a fan mail of 20 by one post sometimes, not with 45 visitors a week. I am just a very tired old man now with little energy, and an old age skin itch that makes going to bed a dread. Tried dieting, no sugar, alcohol, baccy, meat etc. NBG. No cure for age troubles.

Nichts neues. [Nothing new.] The Edinburgh SRC 'students' council put my name to the Senatus for an hon degree. The *Spectator* said it was turned down starchily. My own varsity. It means damn all to me; degrees at 85 are quite *unbedeutend* [unimportant]; most things are now ... ambition, fame, TV appearances have no thrill in them. We when young strive for power or fame or what not, and if it comes it is an empty shell. More and more I like R. L. Stevenson and his: It is better to travel hopefully than to arrive. (...)

Love to both, Neill

To Antoine Obert

Dear Toni   *24 August 1969*

(...) I am a tired old man now. Lost all interest in tools and gave em all to school workshop. But I feel as bright mentally as ever. Michael will find his niche all right. Yes, it isn't easy to get into a university here. Dunno how he will take to a Krishnamurti school. K is too spiritual for me; said he gets more pleasure shaking a friend's hand than another gets out of fucking. I wonder how he knows. Well, that's about all, and now for a pile of fan mail, flattering but oh so wearisome.

Love to you and I hope I'll live to see you in the fall.
Neill

To Erna Gal

My dear Erna   *11 February 1970*
(...) Willi's end didn't bother me.[1] I know I am no genius cos I haven't gone mad like Nietzsche, Ruskin, Swift, Beethoven, dozens of others. Doesn't make any difference to what they did. If I do go mad Summerhill will remain as something I did when sane.

Love, Neill

[1] Wilhelm Reich.

To Josie Caryll

Dear Josie   *17 October 1970*
Once again ta for your *New Statesman* notice.[1] It has had no result so far; hinna seen anybody tak a bannet aff for me yet. Yr annual ad makes me sad for I feel that David shd be there to see it.[2] Most of my old freends are gone and if it werrn't for the kids around me I'd feel lonely.

Sad about F—. I liked her more than I did him; freer with the lassies, I thought. As you say it is all unfair, but it is all just chance; no plan in life. Why should David die and a life hater like Ian Paisley live? All pawns in a game with no one moving the pieces. So when I say I hope to see you on Jany 2nd, mind that I may be a pawn that is high-jacked before then.

Love, auld freend, Neill

[1] An annual birthday wish.
[2] David Caryll was killed in a road accident.

To Harold Hart

Dear Harold   7 June 1971
I get your point. Fact is that with the years I have lost interest in myself and find it difficult to distinguish what is of interest. Example my five years in dreary Wales during the war. The rain, the Welsh sabbath, the miseries of overcrowding and rationing seem dull news today. (...) But I'll try to write more for the Life. Truth is that I don't think I am a very important guy taking the long view. Bertrand Russell is already forgotten just as I shall be. But his books and mine will go on for a few years.

I'll try to hang on until I see the book in print anyway.

Love to both, Neill

To Sheila Chesters

Dear Sheila   *24 July 1971*
    How brave of you, how balanced to take Allan's death so
philosophically. Perfect. No other healthy way.
    As to health, I am just in a maze. Have to take the doctor's pills without
knowing what they are or what they do. Even if I were near Kingston
I have lost much faith. J. C. and Joyce[1] dying of cancer, showing that
food ain't the answer. At my age it doesn't matter what I eat and drink
... my heart specialist prescribed whisky to dilate the arteries.
    No good trying to cheer you up. Grief can't be hived off on to others.
Just a word of advice ... work, work, work; a flight if you like, but what
is wrong with flight?
    My memory is so bad now that I forget even the names of the kids and
your surname escapes me. It will come to me after I have posted this letter.
        Love as of old, Neill

[1] J. C. Thomson, and his daughter Joyce.

To Ethel Mannin

Ethel, me dear   *21 November 1971*
    (...) Wait till you are my 88 and you'll find life a burden with aches
and pains and in my case old age itch that maddens and keeps me awake.
Still I am lucky, Miles Malleson died blind, and Compton Mackenzie tells
me he is almost blind. More than before I often think dying in my sleep
could be a relief, but I still have interests that make me want to carry on.
The ego jibs at going out like a candle to, I take it, nothingness. The worst
of age is that nothing thrills, you anticipate nothing. My little minority
fame is a bubble. Best to have no illusions about one's importance. Russell is now just a name in a library and Gladys Cooper won't have even
a library to store her memory. Damn it ... if a doctor cd cure my itch,
I'd dwell on life and not death. (...)
        Lotten lotten luv, as Zoë used to say, Neill

To Gordon Leff

Dear Bunny   *29 November 1971*
    I'm gey frail now and worry abt the future of Summerhill. Maybe
the Ministry will step in saying we have tolerated this school because of

the outcry if we closed it, but now that the old man is dead we can't allow a school where the kids can play all day and get no education. So, if the attack begins, I hope that a few old pupils will write to *The Times* giving yr jobs and degrees. (...) I'll be a candle blown out, but I want to help Ena to carry on. Pity if S'hill shd die with me. I guess two profs of educn would support you ... Ben Morris, Bristol, Robin Pedley, Exeter, uncommitted Harry Rée might put a word in.

I'm past things now. No energy, aches and pains, the old horse out to grass. I don't fear death and nothingness ... sudden thought: what a shock it wd be to find the devil waiting with a pitchfork, even worse an angel handing me a harp. I have no illusions. Many will talk and write about freedom for kids without mentioning me. (...)

Love, Neill

To Elna Lucas

Dear Elna   *12 December 1971*
(...) I have got my office in the Cottage now and haven't to climb stairs any longer. And visitors have been banned for ever by the kids; suits me, so tired of 100 a week and their questions. So easily tired when old. I used to hate the idea of being blown out like a candle into nothingness, for to me there is no after life, but gradually I have come to accept it, but still hating the idea that I'll never know what happened to S'hill or Zoë or the world. I don't expect that Peter[1] felt otherwise. Death ... the damn thing that keeps one knowing the results of his life work. Disciples will bugger up the S'hill idea as they did with other holy guys like Jesus and Freud and now Reich. Death ... the nice thing that prevents your knowing what a mess others make of your gospel. Cheerful letter. Partly owing to old age itch that keeps me awake at nights. But let the body have its aches and pains so long as the mind is clear. Freud refused pain killers for his throat cancer because he wanted to keep his brain clear ... that was bravery. (...)

Love and pagan blessings, Neill

[1] F. L. Lucas.

To David Wills,

Dear David   *2 January 1972*
I hae ma doots that I can write anything worth while now. Since the press won't publish any article of mine I send you a couple that may or

may not fit into your magazine. I have had returns from *Times*, *Telegraph*, *Guardian*, *New Statesman*, *New Society*... tut, tut, and I fondly imagined I had become a member of the Establishment with my honorary degrees. (...)

Glad to know you are busy. When a man stops being so he dies. In this little town in the last 46 years I have seen many teachers, bankers etc retire, and for two years they wandered aimlessly on the street and then died.

Like you I funk having to die in pain altho I am living in something akin to it, an old age itch that keeps me from sleeping, and there is no cure for it. Not long before he died Compton Mackenzie wrote me that he was nearly blind but (as a good RC) seemed to think it a natural follow-on after a happy and busy life. God seems to punish success as well as sinfulness.

Now I can hear you say: 'If this guy can write a long letter why can't he write us an article?' Fair enough, but I simply feel I have nothing new to say and would only repeat old-hat stuff.

I wish you lived nearer. I get starved for chats with chaps with something to say rather than the usual visitor questioning. Recently I had visits from Colin Wilson and Kenneth Tynan who seem to be writing books on Reich. One man I never could contact was George Lyward, who gave nothing away about his methods ... Shaw,[1] a converted RC, gave too much away.

Tired now, so cheerio, and have as happy a new year as Heath and Nixon and napalm will let you.

Love, Neill

[1] Otto Shaw.

To Nina Kai Nielson

My dear Nina   *6 November 1972*
Thanks for a lovely letter. Mine will be shorter, for I get more tired every day. I do hate to hear you have been ill again. I used to suffer from migraine and it is a terrible pain. Cheer up; with years headaches disappear; haven't had one for years.

Thanks a lot for the Ibsen plays. We saw a new *Hedda Gabler* on TV last week and, tho I know the play almost by heart, I found every minute of it new. I kept wondering if Summerhill could have killed the hate and bitchiness in Hedda. I doubt it.

Pardon me, my dear, for being so short. One of my bad days. Your visit happened to be fortunately on one of my good days, and I enjoyed it with no strain at all. (...)

One of the few joys left is little Amy[1] with whom I have a good relationship. I seem to touch her sense of humour but, oh, I hate not ever seeing her grow up. (...)

Don't get the USA *Neill! Neill! Orange Peel!* Wait for the London edition in spring. If I am still here I'll send you a copy.

Love, dear old Nina, of happy memories of happy days gone by.

Neill

[1] Zoë's first child, Amy Readhead, aged four months.

To Joseph Kirschner

Dear Joseph   *27 March 1973*

I never knew what anarchism meant, but your paper has cleared a lot up.

As for visiting, you should phone me when you come to London. I have my ups and downs, mostly downs, when I can't converse with anyone, all my libido going in aches and pains. At my age even two months are far ahead, and a guy of nearly 90 shdn't make dates. Anyway ring when you come and if I am fit enough we'll meet again.

Meanwhile bugger Father Time.

Yours, Neill

To Gordon Leff

Dear Bunny   *20 July 1973*

Lightning fused our phone. Just as well you didn't come for yesterday was one of my bad days of pain in my guts. I put off going to hospital fearing that if I do I'll come out feet first. Still, I'd like to see my 90th birthday in October. I've been living on borrowed time for some months now. However, if I make some progress, I'll be glad of a visit from you ... the only ex-Summerhillian who makes regular visits.

Love, Neill

To Nell Hutton

Dear Nell   *27 July 1973*
     I have suddenly grown very old, and think more of painkillers than
schools ... Do I sound pessimistic? I often am these days; things often
seem to be going backwards. Today's papers ... Suffolk teachers demand
to keep the cane. My fan mail shows the other side. It grieves me that
I am not fit to answer it now, for I always did, so bugger old age and
its pains and weaknesses, say I. I am now an empty shell with the A. Snail
all dried up. Not self-pity, just raw fact.
     Love, Neill

Glossary of Names

PEOPLE

J. R. ACKERLEY Writer and literary editor of the *Listener*.

JOHN AITKENHEAD One of the founders of Kilquhanity House, later its head. A friend and admirer of Neill. Husband of Morag Aitkenhead.

MORAG AITKENHEAD Co-founder of Kilquhanity House. Wife of John Aitkenhead.

CLIFFORD ALLEN A leading member of the Independent Labour Party, chairman of an association within the New Education Fellowship.

JEAN ALLEN Summerhill pupil.

KENNETH ALLSOP Writer, broadcaster.

SEAN AMES Summerhill pupil.

ROGER ANSCOMBE Summerhill pupil at Lyme Regis.

PAT ARROWSMITH Veteran peace campaigner.

SYLVIA ASHTON-WARNER Pioneering teacher working with Maori children in New Zealand.

LADY HELEN ASQUITH Schools inspector, reported on Summerhill in 1959.

PAT AVERY Summerhill pupil.

J. H. BADLEY Founder and first head of Bedales School, known to his staff and pupils as 'the chief'.

CHRISTINE BAER Head of the Dalcroze International School in Hellerau, Dresden, later helped Neill to start the International School there.

NICHOLAS BAGNALL Editor of the *Teacher*, later education correspondent of the *Sunday Telegraph*.

ELSWORTH BAKER American Reichian therapist.

LADY BETTY BALFOUR Lord Lytton's sister and a supporter of Homer Lane and his work.

BOB BARKER Summerhill teacher, later head of the Barker School in US.

KENNETH BARNES Founder and head of Wennington School.

BRONWEN BARTON Summerhill teacher, mother of David Barton.

DAVID BARTON Summerhill pupil, later a professor of mathematics.

E. T. BAZELEY Matron at the Little Commonwealth.

ORSON BEAN Founder of the Fifteenth Street School, New York, author of *Me and the Orgone*.

LEILA BERG Writer for children, and author of *Risinghill: Death of a Comprehensive School*.

MICHAEL BERNAL Summerhill pupil, later a university lecturer.

JOHN BLACKIE School inspector, reported favourably on Summerhill.

EDWARD BLISHEN Writer, broadcaster, teacher, visitor to Summerhill.

DAVID BOADELLA Student of Reich, author of *Wilhelm Reich: The Evolution of his Work*.

MARGARET BONDFIELD Minister of Labour, first woman member of the Cabinet.

FENNER BROCKWAY Leading member of the Independent Labour Party, editor of their *New Leader*, 'a propaganda sheet for the factory floor'.

AL BRONSTEIN One of the founders of the Lewis–Wadhams School.

GEORGE DOUGLAS BROWN Scots writer, author of *The House with the Green Shutters*, Neill's favourite book.

MAURICE BROWNE Playwright and producer, connected with Dartington Hall.

CYRIL BURT Psychologist, specialised in work on delinquency and intelligence.

BILL BUTLER Teacher, husband of Constance Butler.

CONSTANCE BUTLER Friend of Neill living in Derbyshire.

DIANA BUTLER Daughter of Bill and Constance Butler.

DAPHNE BYNG Summerhill parent, wife of Robert Byng.

ROBERT BYNG Summerhill parent, husband of Daphne Byng. Organized letter to *The Times* to protest against possible closure of Summerhill.

DAVID CARYLL Summerhill parent, killed in a road accident.

JOSIE CARYLL Summerhill parent, secretary of the Summerhill Society.

HOWARD CASE Summerhill parent, founder of Epping House School.

CHARLES CAUSLEY Poet, headteacher, influenced by Neill.

PAXTON CHADWICK Summerhill teacher and secretary. Also artist, and Communist councillor for Leiston.

SHEILA CHESTERS Member of the Thomson family, visitor to Summerhill.

HUBERT CHILD Co-head, with his wife Lois, of Dartington Hall.

ALEC CLEGG Chief education officer of the West Riding of Yorkshire, major influence in the liberalisation of English primary schools.

JOHNNIE COLLIER Summerhill pupil, later a teacher.

CALDWELL COOK Teacher, author of the influential book *The Play Way*.

JONATHAN CROALL Editor at Penguin Books, later author of *Neill of Summerhill: The Permanent Rebel*.

A. J. CRONIN Author of *The Adventures of a Black Bag*, the short stories which inspired the television series *Dr Finlay's Casebook*.

W. B. CURRY Head of Dartington Hall, having taught under Badley at Bedales.

IVOR CUTLER Summerhill teacher, humorist, writer of children's books.

JACQUES DALCROZE Creator of eurythmics, a form of training through dance adopted by many pioneer progressive schools.

A. A. DAVID Bishop of Liverpool, 'pupil' of Homer Lane.

GEORGE DENNISON Radical school reformer and psychotherapist, founder of the First Street School in New York, described in *The Lives of Children*.

HAROLD DENT Editor of the *Times Educational Supplement*.

JOHN DEWEY American educationist, one of the founding fathers of progressive education.

DAN DORAN Member of the Summerhill Society in USA, publisher of some of Neill's books in Israel.

MARGARET DUANE Summerhill housemother, daughter of Michael Duane.

MICHAEL DUANE Head of Risinghill School, friend of Neill, regular visitor to Summerhill.

TOM EAGLE Editor with Neill's publishers Herbert Jenkins Ltd.

GEORGE EARLE Teacher and deputy head to John Russell at King Alfred School.

DEREK EASTMOND Follower of Reich, distributor of some of his books in UK.

DOROTHY ELMHIRST American heiress who, with her husband Leonard Elmhirst, founded Dartington Hall.

LEONARD ELMHIRST Co-founder, with his wife Dorothy Elmhirst, of Dartington Hall.

JACQUIE ELVEY Summerhill pupil.

BEATRICE ENSOR First editor of the *New Era* magazine, employed Neill as co-editor.

CHRISTOPHER EXLEY A schoolboy, later a teacher.

THEODORE FAITHFULL Head of Priory Gate School.

CLAUDE FERRIERE Student visitor to Summerhill.

J. C. FLUGEL Psychologist and friend of Neill.

LUCY FRANCIS Summerhill teacher, left to set up her own school, 'Kingsmuir'.

SALLY FRANCIS Summerhill pupil.

JOHN FREEMAN Editor of the *New Statesman*.

ANNA FREUD Psychoanalyst, Director of the Hampstead Child Therapy Clinic in London. Daughter of Sigmund Freud.

FRIEDRICH FROEBEL Founder of the kindergarten, educational philosopher.

ERICH FROMM Psychoanalyst and sociologist, wrote preface to US edition of *Summerhill*.

RUARC GAHAN Head of Sutton Park School.

ERNA GAL Summerhill teacher, previously friend of Reich.

HAROLD GARDINER Teacher at Bedales.

EDITH GEHEEB Co-founder, with her husband Paulus Geheeb, of the New Odenwald School, and later the Ecole de l'Humanité.

PAULUS GEHEEB Pacifist, co-founder with his wife Edith Geheeb of the New Odenwald School, and later the Ecole de l'Humanité.

PHILIP GOLD Summerhill parent, Reichian therapist.

LIVIA GOLLANCZ Publisher, daughter of Victor Gollancz.

VICTOR GOLLANCZ Publisher, writer, founder of the Left Book Club.

PAUL GOODMAN Writer, anarchist, critic of US school system.

RICHARD GOODMAN Summerhill teacher, poet, editor of *Oxford Outlook* while at university.

BARBARA GRIGOR Summerhill teacher.

ROSE HACKER Summerhill parent, later a school counsellor.

NORMAN HAIRE Gynaecologist and obstetrician, social reformer, started English section of World League for Sexual Reform.

ELEANOR (RANGER) HAMILTON Co-founder, with her husband A. E. Hamilton, of Hamilton School, Massachusetts.

NICHOLAS KING HARRIS Head of St Christopher School.

HAROLD HART American publisher of *Summerhill: A Radical Approach to Child-Rearing* and *Freedom not License!*

BERTRAM HAWKER Member of the Little Commonwealth executive committee.

RAY HEMMINGS Summerhill teacher, author of *Fifty Years of Freedom: A Study of the Development of the Ideas of A. S. Neill*.

HARRY HERRING Summerhill teacher.

MARY HIGGINS Trustee of the Wilhelm Reich Infant Trust Foundation, co-editor of *Wilhelm Reich: Selected Writings*.

TONY HILL Teacher in an English special school.

GRETHE HOFF Patient of Reich, who lived with him for a brief period.

LYDIA HOLLOWELL American schoolgirl.

JOHN HOLT American radical school reformer, author of *How Children Fail, Escape from Childhood*, etc.

WALTER HOPPE German doctor.

CLIVE HORSFIELD Summerhill pupil.

GWEN HORSFIELD Summerhill parent.

KEITH HORSFIELD Summerhill pupil, later a doctor.

DAVID HUME Student teacher.
ROBERT HUTCHISON Editor at Penguin Books.
NELL HUTTON Friend of Neill.
JESSIE IRVING Girl in Gretna Green to whom Neill became engaged.
SUSAN ISAACS Child psychologist, director of The Malting House.
GEORGE IVES Writer, friend of Oscar Wilde.
H. B. JACKS Head of Bedales School.
ROBERT JAMES Actor, played the undertaker in *Dr Finlay's Casebook*.
WALTER JAMES Editor of the *Times Educational Supplement*.
HERBERT JENKINS Publisher of all Neill's 'Dominie' and 'Problem' books.
C. E. M. JOAD Professor of psychology and philosophy.
MARGARET JOHNSON Head of progressive school in Crowborough, Sussex, influenced by Neill.
ALEXANDER KATZ Co-editor, with Paul Goodman, of *Complex* magazine.
W. H. KILPATRICK Disciple of John Dewey, originator of the 'project method' of learning.
JOSEPH KIRSCHNER American university lecturer.
VICTOR KRAVCHENKO Soviet official who defected to the USA. Author of *I Chose Freedom*.
CARLOS KRUYTBOSCH Summerhill pupil.
ROYSTON LAMBERT Head of Dartington Hall.
R. S. LAMBERT Editor of the *Listener* in the 1930s.
SIR ALLEN LANE Founder of Penguin Books.
ALLEN LANE Son of Homer Lane, pupil at King Alfred School while Neill was on the staff.
CORA LANE Daughter of Homer Lane.
HOMER LANE American pioneer worker with problem children, superintendent of the Little Commonwealth. Later lecturer and consultant psychoanalyst.
MABEL LANE Second wife of Homer Lane.
OLIVE LANE Pupil at Little Commonwealth, subsequently Summerhill pupil and housemother. Adopted daughter of Homer Lane; adopted unofficially at his death by Neill and Mrs Lins. Wife of Leslie Thomson.
POLLY LANE Daughter of Homer Lane, pupil at King Alfred School while Neill was on the staff.
RAYMOND LANE Son of Homer Lane.
GEORGE LANSBURY First Commissioner of Works in second Labour Government, later leader of the Labour Party. Wrote article for *New Era* while Neill was co-editor.
JOHN LAYARD Anthropologist, 'pupil' of Homer Lane, visitor to Summerhill.

BERNARD LEACH Potter, taught for a while at Dartington Hall.

EVA LEFF Summerhill parent, wife of Solomon Leff.

GORDON (BUNNY) LEFF Summerhill pupil, later professor of history.

LOUIS LEFF Summerhill pupil, later bookshop owner.

SOLOMON LEFF Summerhill parent, husband of Eva Leff.

BUDDA LEUNBACH Worker with Reich in Oslo.

ELSA LINDENBERG German dancer, lived with Reich in Scandinavia during the 1930s.

BARBARA LONGBROOK American student teacher.

LORD LONGFORD Publisher, politician.

ALEXANDER LOWEN Reichian therapist.

ELNA LUCAS Summerhill housemother, later wife of F. L. Lucas.

F.L. (PETER) LUCAS Writer and university lecturer, author of *Ibsen and Strindberg*, husband of Elna Lucas.

MICHAEL LYNCH Summerhill teacher.

LORD LYTTON Chairman of the Little Commonwealth General Committee, 'pupil' of Homer Lane.

GEORGE LYWARD Founder and head of Finchden Manor.

BERYL MCALHONE Editor of the educational magazine *Where*.

ANNA MACCHERONI Student of Montessori, teacher who helped to make her ideas known in England.

R.F. (BOB) MACKENZIE Head of Braehead School, Fife, and later Summerhill Academy, Aberdeen, from which he was dismissed for trying to put some of Neill's ideas into practice.

BILL MACKINNON Summerhill teacher, also taught at Kilquhanity House and Beltane School. Husband of Käte MacKinnon.

KATE MACKINNON Summerhill teacher, wife of Bill MacKinnon.

NORMAN MACMUNN Head of Tiptree Hall, admired by Neill.

ISHBEL MCWHIRTER Summerhill pupil, later a painter.

BRONISLAW MALINOWSKI Anthropologist, author of influential *The Sexual Life of Savages*.

MILES MALLESON Actor, playwright, Summerhill parent.

ETHEL MANNIN Writer, fervent supporter of Neill and his ideas, of which she wrote in *Confessions and Impressions* and other books. Summerhill parent.

RICHARD MARCUS Summerhill pupil, later a doctor.

DAVID MARKHAM Actor, Summerhill parent.

E. MARTIN Teacher at Dartington Hall.

KINGSLEY MARTIN Editor of the *New Statesman*.

WALTER MARTIN A wealthy cigar merchant, friend of Neill.

MARGARET MEAD Anthropologist, author of *Coming of Age in Samoa*.

CHRISTINE MEEK A state school teacher in Scotland.

KARL MENNINGER American psychoanalyst.

HENRY MILLER American writer, friend of Neill.

WILLIAM MOISE Son-in-law of Reich.

PETER MONK Summerhill pupil.

ASHLEY MONTAGU American anthropologist.

MARIA MONTESSORI Pioneer Italian worker with children, whose ideas influenced English nursery and infant education.

B. H. MONTGOMERY Head of King Alfred School.

LILIAN MORGANS A Scots friend of Neill, living in Saxmundham, Suffolk.

BEN MORRIS Professor of education, friend of Neill.

CHRISTINE MORRIS Daughter of Ben Morris.

FRANK MORTON Head of Beltane School.

LESLIE MORTON Summerhill teacher, husband of Vivien Morton. Later historian, author of *A People's History of England*.

MARGOT MOSER Actress, visitor to Summerhill.

EDWIN MUIR Poet, translator of Kafka, stayed with Neill in Germany and Austria. Husband of Willa Muir.

WILLA MUIR Taught at Neill's International School in both Germany and Austria. Wife of Edwin Muir, translated Kafka with him.

BETTY MULLER Summerhill pupil.

ROBERT MULLER Summerhill pupil.

ANGUS MURRAY Pupil at Neill's International School in Austria. In hospital with sleepy sickness from 1928.

GORDON NAIRN Summerhill pupil.

ENA NEILL (née WOOD) Neill's second wife.

LILIAN NEILL (née RICHARDSON) Neill's first wife, known in Summerhill as 'Mrs Lins'. Sister of Henry Handel Richardson, first wife of Otto Neustatter.

PAM NEU American teenager.

ANGELA NEUSTATTER Summerhill pupil, daughter of Wally Neustatter.

HELEN NEUSTATTER Second wife of Otto Neustatter.

OTTO NEUSTATTER First husband of Lilian Neustatter.

WALLY NEUSTATTER Son of Lilian and Otto Neustatter.

MAURICE NICOLL English psychoanalyst.

NINA KAI NIELSON Visitor to Summerhill.

W. W. NORTON American publisher, rejected *The Problem Parent*.

PERCY NUNN First director of the London Institute of Education.

ANTOINE OBERT Odd-job-man at Summerhill, interned at beginning of Second World War.

ROBERT OLLENDORFF Doctor and psychiatrist, brother of Ilse Ollendorff Reich.

CHARLES OLLER Reichian therapist.

RAYMOND O'MALLEY Teacher at Dartington Hall, acting head for one term.

E. F. O'NEILL State school pioneer, head of Prestolee School, Lancashire.

C. H. C. OSBORNE 'Pupil' of Homer Lane.

ULLA OTTE Summerhill teacher.

PETER OWEN English publisher.

HELEN OXENBURY Illustrator of children's books.

AGNES PARKER Wife of the artist William McCance.

GEORGE PARSONS Summerhill teacher.

ROBIN PEDLEY Professor of education, friend of Neill.

RICHARD PEMBERTON Chief Schools Inspector for Suffolk.

ALFRED PERLES Friend of Henry Miller.

HEINRICH PESTALOZZI Educational philosopher, early advocate of 'learning by doing'.

TAGE PHILIPSON Swedish psychiatrist, student of Reich.

TERRY PHILPOT Journalist.

HARRY POLLITT General secretary of the Communist Party of Great Britain.

JANINA POPENUE Summerhill pupil.

BRYN PURDY Summerhill teacher and student observer, later special school headteacher.

J. D. RADCLYFFE Journalist, 'pupil' of Homer Lane, visitor to Summerhill.

MAX RAFFERTY California State Superintendent of Public Instruction.

OLA RAKNES Norwegian psychotherapist and supporter of Reich.

CHESTER RAPHAEL Editor of some of Reich's books.

HERBERT READ Poet, art and literary critic, author of *Education through Art*.

AMY READHEAD Neill's grand-daughter.

HARRY REE Professor of education, formerly a headteacher, friend of Neill.

EVA REICH Daughter of Wilhelm Reich.

ILSE OLLENDORFF REICH Wife of Wilhelm Reich, author of *Wilhelm Reich: A Personal Biography*.

PETER REICH Son of Wilhelm and Ilse Reich.

WILHELM REICH Psychotherapist and analyst, close friend of Neill.

THEODORE REIK Viennese analyst.

HENRY HANDEL RICHARDSON Pseudonym of Ethel Richardson, sister of Lilian Neustatter.

MAURICE RICHARDSON Journalist, writer, friend of Neill.

MARGARET RITCHIE Girl with whom Neill as a young teacher became infatuated.

PAUL RITTER Founder of the Reichian journal *Orgonomic Functionalism*.

PAUL ROBERTS Head of Frensham Heights School, later organiser of the Co-Educational Schools conferences.

ILSE ROLFE Summerhill housemother.

MICHAEL ROSSMAN American student activist.

ELIZABETH ROTTEN German educationist, member of New Education Fellowship.

HILARY RUBINSTEIN Director of A.P. Watt Ltd, Neill's literary agent.

BERTRAND RUSSELL Philosopher and mathematician, with second wife Dora Russell started Beacon Hill School.

DORA RUSSELL Champion of women's rights and sexual reform, with Bertrand Russell started Beacon Hill School.

JOHN RUSSELL Head of King Alfred School.

PETER RUSSELL Summerhill pupil, later an actor and writer.

GEORGE SAINTSBURY Professor of English literature at Edinburgh University during Neill's time as a student.

J.B. SALMOND Journalist, fellow-student and close friend of Neill's, later editor of the *Scots Magazine*.

LORD SANDWICH Founder of the Little Commonwealth, brought Homer Lane to England to run it.

MERVYN SAUNDERS Summerhill pupil.

GRETA SERGEANT Summerhill housemother at Lyme Regis, later Neill's interpreter in Scandinavia.

STEPHEN SHAPIRO Summerhill pupil.

MYRON SHARAF Worker at Wilhelm Reich Foundation, author of *Fury on Earth: A Biography of Wilhelm Reich*.

OTTO SHAW Head of Red House School.

SEISHI SHIMODA Translator of Neill's books into Japanese.

J.H. SIMPSON Teacher, later first head of Rendcomb College. 'Pupil' of Homer Lane.

MORTIMER STANDING Teacher who worked in collaboration with Maria Montessori.

BRIAN STANLEY Professor of education, friend of Neill.

WILLIAM STEIG American cartoonist, illustrator of Reich's *Listen, Little Man!*

RUDOLPH STEINER Educational pioneer and philosopher.

WILHELM STEKEL Psychoanalyst, member of Freud's circle in Vienna, where Neill underwent analysis with him.

JAMES STERN Writer, friend of Neill.

TANIA STERN Wife of James Stern.

HARRY STACK SULLIVAN American Freudian psychologist.

AMARYLLA STRACEY Summerhill pupil.

H. H. Symonds Head of the Liverpool Institute, 'pupil' of Homer Lane.

Stephen Tallents Editor of the *Listener*.

James Telfer Scots osteopath.

John Thompson A writer for the *Spectator*.

Douglas Neill Thomson Son of Leslie Thomson and Olive Lane.

J. C. Thomson Founder, with his wife Jessie, of the Edinburgh School of Natural Therapeutics, later the Kingston Clinic. Cured Neill of serious illness in 1929.

Leslie Thomson Son of J.C. and Jessie Thomson, took over Kingston Clinic after their deaths. Husband of Olive Lane.

Roger Tilbury Teacher at Dartington Hall, later organiser of Co-educational Schools conferences.

Richard Tolson Summerhill teacher, husband of Rosalind Tolson.

Rosalind Tolson Wife of Richard Tolson.

John Tooke Summerhill pupil.

Philip Townsend Summerhill pupil.

George von Hilsheimer Member of Summerhill Society in US, head of Summerlane School.

Ernst Wangermann Teacher at Kilquhanity House.

Colin Ward Writer, anarchist, editor of *Freedom* magazine.

A. P. Watt Neill's literary agent.

Blyth Webster Lecturer at Edinburgh University while Neill was there.

Evelyn Williams Summerhill pupil, later a painter.

David Wills Pioneer worker with maladjusted children, author of *Homer Lane: A Biography*.

Theodore Wolfe Swiss psychiatrist, translator of Reich's work.

John Wood Head of New Sherwood School.

Peter Wood Neill's stepson by his second wife.

T. C. Worsley Reviewer, author with W. H. Auden of *Education – Today and Tomorrow*.

Lois Wyvell Managing director of the Orgone Institute Press.

James Young University lecturer in Scotland.

SCHOOLS

Barker School, New York Founded by Bob Barker after a spell at Summerhill. Aimed to allow children 'to develop as loving, thinking, acting human beings in an atmosphere of discovery and delight'.

Beacon Hill, Sussex Founded in 1927 by Dora and Bertrand Russell to produce children 'inspired by love and guided by knowledge'. Voluntary lesson attendance, self-government, no corporal punishment.

BEDALES, HAMPSHIRE Founded in 1893 as a boys' school by J. H. Badley, one of the first progressive schools to go co-educational.

BELTANE SCHOOL, HERTFORDSHIRE (LATER GLOUCESTERSHIRE) A progressive school which shared some pupils and teachers with Summerhill.

BURGESS HILL, LONDON Progressive day school, started in 1936 by Kenneth Ottoway. Later run by Jimmy East, a Summerhill teacher. Closed in 1962.

DARTINGTON HALL, DEVON Opened in 1926 by Dorothy and Leonard Elmhirst as one strand of the Dartington Estate. Gradually introduced self-government. Emphasis on arts and crafts, and 'learning by doing'.

ECOLE DE L'HUMANITE, SWITZERLAND Progressive school established in Switzerland in the 1930s by Edith and Paulus Geheeb who, until the rise of Nazism, ran the New Odenwald School in Germany.

EPPING HOUSE, HERTFORDSHIRE Boarding school for emotionally disturbed children, run from 1958 to 1974 on self-governing lines by Howard Case, a Summerhill parent.

FIFTEENTH STREET SCHOOL, NEW YORK Urban school for 'non-problem' children, started in the 1960s by Orson Bean and others, and inspired by Summerhill.

FINCHDEN MANOR, KENT A therapeutic community started in 1930 by George Lyward. Aimed to allow 'intelligent but disturbed older boys' to have back their childhood.

FIRST STREET SCHOOL, NEW YORK The first of the urban 'mini-schools' of the 1960s, founded by George Dennison and others, with inspiration from Neill, Tolstoy and Dewey.

FRENSHAM HEIGHTS, SURREY An offshoot of St Christopher School, opened by Beatrice Ensor in 1925 as a 'demonstration school' for the New Education Fellowship.

HAMILTON SCHOOL, MASSACHUSETTS A farm school for emotionally disturbed children, founded by Eleanor and A.E. Hamilton.

KILQUHANITY HOUSE, SCOTLAND Founded by John and Morag Aitkenhead and others in 1940. Directly inspired by Neill, run on similar lines to Summerhill, except for compulsory lessons. Takes children from local authorities.

KING ALFRED SCHOOL, LONDON Co-educational school started in 1897 by a group of Hampstead parents. Placed emphasis on 'educational value of personal liberty'. Run on self-governing lines.

KINGSMUIR, ESSEX (LATER SUSSEX) A 'branch' school of Summerhill, founded during the Second World War, run by Lucy Francis. Named after Neill's home village in Scotland.

LEWIS-WADHAMS, NEW YORK Country free school 'inspired by Summerhill – dedicated to children and A. S. Neill'. Founded in 1963 by Wilf Blakeley, a Summerhill teacher, Herb Snitzer, a visitor to Summerhill, Al Bronstein and others.

LITTLE COMMONWEALTH, DORSET Community for delinquent children founded in 1914, run by Homer Lane. Organised like a miniature 'state', with 'citizens' governing their own lives. Closed by Home Office in 1917 after inquiry into alleged misconduct by Lane.

MALTING HOUSE, CAMBRIDGE An experimental school for children with high IQs, encouraging freedom of choice, 'discovery learning' etc. Founded by Geoffrey Pike in 1924, directed by Susan Isaacs.

NEW SHERWOOD SCHOOL, SURREY Co-educational progressive school influenced by Neill and Summerhill.

PRIORY GATE, NORFOLK Progressive school run by Theodore Faithfull, influenced both by Freud and the Order of Woodcraft Chivalry.

RED HILL SCHOOL, KENT Founded in 1934 by Otto Shaw, inspired by visits to Summerhill and Neill's books. Self-governing community based on psychotherapy of disturbed children.

RENDCOMB COLLEGE, GLOUCESTERSHIRE Founded in 1920 by Noel Wills, under the headship of J. H. Simpson, who introduced self-government there.

RISINGHILL, LONDON State school in run-down inner-city area, a subject of intense public debate when its head Michael Duane tried to introduce some of Neill's ideas into the school. Closed in 1965.

ST CHRISTOPHER SCHOOL, HERTFORDSHIRE Progressive self-governing co-educational boarding school, founded in 1915 in Letchworth Garden City by the Theosophical Education Trust.

SUMMERLANE, NEW YORK Free school founded in 1960s by George von Hilsheimer and others.

SUTTON PARK, DUBLIN Conventional private school, which became more progressive under the headship of Ruarc Gahan, until his dismissal by the school's governors.

TIPTREE HALL, ESSEX A school for war orphans run by Norman MacMunn, who described himself as the children's 'chief adviser'. Opened in 1919.

WENNINGTON SCHOOL, YORKSHIRE Progressive boarding school started by Kenneth Barnes during the Second World War.

Index

Page numbers in italics indicate letters from Neill to the person named.

257